GOD BLESS AMERICA

Strange and Unusual Religious Beliefs and Practices in the United States

Karen Stollznow, PhD

PITCHSTONE PUBLISHING
DURHAM, NORTH CAROLINA

Pitchstone Publishing
Durham, NC 27705
www.pitchstonepublishing.com

To contact the publisher, please e-mail info@pitchstonepublishing.com

Printed in the United States of America

19 18 17 16 15 14 13   1 2 3 4 5

Library of Congress Cataloging-in-Publication Data

Stollznow, Karen.
 God bless America : strange and unusual religious beliefs and practices in the United
States / Karen Stollznow, PhD.
     pages cm
 Includes bibliographical references and index.
 ISBN 978-1-939578-00-6 (pbk. : alk. paper)
 1. Christianity—United States. 2. United States—Religious life and customs. 3.
United States—Religion. I. Title.
 BR515.S753 2013
 277.3—dc23
                              2013012481

Contents

Acknowledgments

I'm deeply grateful to Matthew Baxter, Bryan Bonner, Rick Duffy, and Nikolas Kovacevic for their unwavering support, advice, and research assistance throughout the writing of this book. My sincere thanks also go to the following friends, family, and informants for their feedback and insight: Michelle Adcock, Banachek, Jere Baxter, Mick Baxter, Mark Bunker, Kernan Coleman, Jamie DeWolf, Tim Farley, Brent Jeffs, Kathy Josey, Reed Esau, Todd Everingham, Stu Hayes, Leon Hostetler, Matthew Kennedy, Rich Orman, Tana Owens, Kelly Nelson, Gaye Stolsnow, John Stolsnow, Paul Turner, and Robert Walker. Finally, I'd like to express gratitude (of the non–New Age kind) to Kurt Volkan of Pitchstone Publishing and to Suzy Lewis of the Richard Dawkins Foundation for Reason and Science for having faith (of the nonreligious kind) in this project. *God Bless America* was made possible because of all of you, and this book is for all of you.

Introduction

_____

Do Satanists really sacrifice babies? Can a Voodoo priest turn a person into a zombie? What happens during an exorcism? Are the Amish allowed to drive cars and use computers? *God Bless America* finds the answers to these questions and many more.

This book explores a range of unique religious beliefs and practices in the United States, including those of the Amish and Mennonites, the Fundamentalist Mormons, and the Quakers, and those found within Charismatic Christianity and Pentecostalism, Voodoo and Santeria, Satanism, Scientology, and New Age Spirituality. These religions encompass beliefs in a God or gods, Satan, Spirit, ghosts, aliens, and UFOs, and draw their theology from doctrines as diverse as the Book of Acts, science fiction, and the Law of Attraction. We look at a wide range of customs and ceremonies, including snake handing, Satanic rituals, Hoodoo spells, shunning technology, polygamy, and healing by gaze.

Few of these religions are all American, as many have origins elsewhere and arrived in the United States only after their followers fled their home countries escaping persecution for their religious beliefs. The United States has traditionally been a haven for people seeking sanctuary and religious freedom. In waves of immigration, Jewish people from across Europe found refuge in America from anti-Semitism, repeated pogroms, and the Holocaust. During the seventeenth century, the Puritans and the Quakers settled in North America to escape persecution in England, whereupon the Puritans began persecuting the Quakers.

Inscribed on a plaque at the base of the Statue of Liberty is "The

New Colossus," the famous poem by Emma Lazarus. The sculpture is a symbol of freedom, and the sonnet a greeting to immigrants. Its final lines are a testimony to acceptance and inclusion. "Give me your tired, your poor, your huddled masses yearning to breathe free. The wretched refuse of your teeming shore. Send these, the homeless, tempest-tost to me, I lift my lamp beside the golden door!" In this welcoming spirit, the United States has cultivated an environment of religious tolerance, while freedom of religion is protected in the First Amendment of the Constitution.

Many Americans defend the right to religious freedom, regardless of whether they agree with the beliefs or not. Part of the American ethos is that it's okay to do whatever you want to do, just as long as you don't hurt other people. Unfortunately, some of these religious practices do hurt other people. Several of these religious groups are closed societies, allowing corruption to flourish. Religious freedom becomes an excuse to commit crimes under guise of God. This freedom has become oppression for some people, and many religious beliefs and practices endanger the physical and psychological health of their followers.

For many people, religious beliefs, and by extension religious practices, are viewed as untouchable, sacred, and inviolable. It has become a taboo to question personal beliefs. Religion is indulged with unquestioning respect, and people shy away from scrutinizing religious practices in fear of being seen as discriminatory or offensive. When abuses occur in these communities, some people simply look the other way, including the authorities. Others argue, what's the harm? This book uncovers the considerable harm enacted in the name of religion, including underage marriage, rape, human trafficking, inbreeding, incest, violent exorcisms, risky rituals, social shunning, animal sacrifice, financial scams, faith healing, and dangerous diets. Fortunately, while the First Amendment protects beliefs, the free exercise of practices is not absolute.

However, there is a paradox. Despite these ideals of tolerance and religious freedom, some religious groups are stigmatized, misunderstood, and mocked for being different. Fair or unfair, right or wrong, they have developed negative reputations. Fundamentalist Mormon groups are denigrated as cults. Satanists continue to be accused of committing

Satanic ritual abuse, decades after such charges have been disproven. In a hate crime known as "claping," Amish people are harassed, their buggies are driven off the road, and their horses attacked with firecrackers or water bombs. Practitioners of Hoodoo and Voodoo are either feared as evil and bloodthirsty, or ridiculed as primitive and superstitious. Scientologists and New Agers are often the butt of jokes, while snake handlers and televangelists are lampooned mercilessly.

God Bless America attempts a sensitive but factual portrayal of these people who believe they have found "the truth." They clearly haven't discovered the meaning of life, but all of these belief systems offer profound insights into the human condition, and we can occasionally see ourselves in them. As different as they appear at first, some aspects of these religions may resonate with you. Like medical students who become convinced that they're afflicted with all of the diseases they study, when I researched the Quaker testimonies, I thought, at times, "I think I'm a Quaker!"—that is, until I found out about the silent worship. In reading *The Satanic Rituals*, I identified with the humor and humanism of Satanism and concluded, "I think I'm a Satanist!"—that is, until I got to the part about the barnyard costumes and the magic spells. The discussion is also critical of religion when it needs to be. Many of these beliefs and practices will seem shocking and dangerous at worst, or absurd and archaic at the very least.

Some of these practices are viewed as old-fashioned or obsolete, but the point of this book is that they are all still found in the United States today. These are groups that wear plain dress, practice arranged marriage, create curses and charms, perform exorcisms, or believe in biblical-style miracles. We find out the reasons why people conserve these often quirky customs, whether they are following a literal interpretation of passages in the Bible, or it's simply a matter of tradition. Disagreements over why or how things are done sometimes spawn breakaway sects or even new religious movements.

These groups uphold their traditions, but their beliefs and practices are often a blend of old and new. Ancient and preorganized religions are practiced in New Age Spirituality, yet they are integrated with modern theories about quantum physics. Some Fundamentalist Mormon women wear prairie dresses, but they might also carry cell phones in their pockets. Exorcists get rid of demons, while psychics cleanse the possessed of negative thought forms. Jesus was believed to raise the dead, but in modern miracles God fills teeth with gold. The flock doesn't even need to attend church nowadays. Instead, people can visit a cyberchurch, listen to podcast worship services and place a prayer request online.

Things never stay the same for these religious groups. Even if they practice segregation, modern society encroaches on their communities. The Amish have an ever-increasing reliance on technology, while the shift away from an agricultural economy affects their employment options. The mass media opens these closed societies. The curious can discover Scientology's hidden sci-fi theology on the Internet, without spending thousands of dollars. Instead of being fed the "milk before meat," would-be Mormons can Google for info about the meat at the same time as the milk.

The facts are often distorted and sensationalized by the mass media. Pop culture influences the way we understand religious groups. Television shows such as *Sister Wives* and *Big Love* shape our perceptions of polygamy. The modern flesh-eating Hollywood zombie is a very different creature from the zombie of Haitian lore. Real claims of demonic possession report far less head-spinning and vomiting than appears in *The Exorcist*. With its touristy voodoo dolls, Louisiana Voodoo barely resembles its origins in West African Vodun, but there is nothing "original" or "authentic" anymore when it comes to religion. Religious beliefs and practices, and our views about them, are changing constantly.

The religious status of these groups is also evolving. Is New Age Spirituality actually a religion? Do members of the Quakers belong to a religious or a social group? Can you be both a Quaker and a Buddhist, or even be a Nontheist Quaker? Is Scientology a religion, a therapy, or a scam? Do Satanists actually worship Satan, or even believe in Satan? Are Fundamentalist Mormons really Mormons? Some of these beliefs and practices are gaining popularity or even becoming mainstream, while others reveal the real-time road from Damascus. These minority groups give us a glimpse into the future of religion in America.

These groups may be small, but their faith is often big. Religion is not only for Sundays, but it is a way of life. For many of these people, religion is heavily intertwined with their very existence, and their beliefs dictate their practices: how they dress, what they eat, whom they marry, and where they live. Some groups are romanticized for their lifestyles, especially the Amish, who are viewed as a piece of old-world America and inseparably associated with handmade quilts, and pies cooling in the windowsill. Similarly, all New Agers are labeled hippies; Satanists are suspected to be serial killers; and Pentecostalists are all believed to be poison-swilling, serpent handlers.

All of these beliefs and practices are stuck with stereotypes. *God Bless America* confirms some of these, but also dispels the myths and misconceptions. We find that fact is often stranger than fiction. This book is about how outsiders see these religions and is colored by my own views, as an immigrant to the United States from Australia. However, we go beyond the stereotypes to discover how these members see themselves. We discover what it's like to be born and socialized into these religions, why some people convert to them, and why in some religions the ex-members consider themselves to be "escapees." To get the inside story I seek out former members as informants, including an ex-member of the Amish, former Fundamentalist Latter-day Saints, and even the great-grandson of L. Ron Hubbard, the founder of Scientology.

This book is also about participation. To gain a better understanding of these beliefs and practices, I experience them. I listen to the sounds of silence at a Quaker meeting, and sit between the beards and the bonnets at a Mennonite service. I'm the sole member of the congregation at a Church of Scientology service, where L. Ron Hubbard's science fiction stories are told as sermons. I witness a Voodoo ritual and watch a deliverance minister as he exorcises the demons from a possessed man. I visit an abandoned Fundamentalist Mormon compound, and find more than I expected. I attend a session of faith healing where participants speak in tongues, and meditate in a cloud of incense at a New Age Church. *God Bless America* lifts the veil on these religious beliefs and practices, and takes a peek behind the closed doors.

Chapter 1

Modern-Day Prophets and Polygamists
Fundamentalist Mormons

"Two girls for every boy."
—The Beach Boys

"Looking Beyond" is the name of the now-abandoned compound in Westcliffe. To explain the numerous bedrooms, the realtor said with a cringe, "This place was used, um . . . a little bit differently than a normal house." She didn't divulge that this had been an FLDS compound. "You could use it as a hunting retreat!" she suggested.

Mainstream vs. Fundamentalist Mormons

When is a Mormon not a Mormon? When the Mormon is a Fundamentalist Mormon—that is, if the Mormons have any say in the matter. Fundamentalist Mormons are the extreme sects of the Church of Jesus Christ of Latter-day Saints (LDS). Former LDS president Gordon B. Hinckley once went so far as to say, "There are actually no Mormon fundamentalists." In fact, there are dozens of breakaway groups who trace their lineage back to the religion founded by Joseph Smith and who call themselves the "true Mormons."

Even without the fundamentalists, the Mormons are controversial, with their sacred underwear, their baptisms for the dead, and their belief

14

that they will all become Gods and Goddesses in the Celestial Kingdom. A Mormon marriage isn't merely "until death us do part." Couples are "sealed" so their union becomes an everlasting covenant known as an "eternal marriage." These sealings are even performed posthumously between a living person and a deceased spouse. In every other regard, their contemporary views about marriage are conservative. Mormons are staunchly against gay marriage, and believe that "the Lord's law of marriage is monogamy, or marriage between one man and one woman." They are also antipolygamy, although it wasn't always this way. At one time, polygamy was doctrine.

Mormon presidents are also believed to be prophets. In the early 1830s, LDS founder Joseph Smith received a revelation from an angel that he must "multiply and replenish the earth." He was to achieve this through plural marriage, just like Abraham, Jacob, and Isaac. If he didn't take on additional wives he would be killed. This was a timely message, because Smith fancied his fourteen-year-old serving girl, Fanny Alger. Now his infidelities could be legitimized as religious creed. However, it wasn't until 1843 that Smith had the guts to introduce polygamy as a doctrine of the Church. By this time he already had about thirty wives, some of whom were already married to other men.

Smith took the angel's advice and became a polygamist, but he was still killed. Actually, he was murdered by an angry mob in 1844, and partly *because* he was a polygamist. Brigham Young became the second President of the Church, and continued the practice. In 1853, he announced that polygamy was a requirement for eternal life, "The only men who become Gods, even the sons of God, are those who enter into polygamy." Following this proclamation, polygamy was openly taught and practiced, although it was still controversial. Many early Mormons were unwilling to enter into plural marriages, but God had told them to do so, so they did. Well, about a quarter of them did.

Even God felt uncomfortable about polygamy. He told Smith and Young that polygamy was a condition of entry into the Celestial Kingdom. God even reaffirmed his decision in a revelation to third Mormon president John Taylor in 1866. He insisted that this was an "everlasting" law that He would never revoke. Despite this apparent conviction, God still couldn't make up His mind and began issuing conflicting revelations to different people. At this time, polygamy was a felony in the United States, and hundreds of polygamist Mormons were imprisoned, while others went underground. Fourth Mormon president Wilford Woodruff received the timely divine revelation that polygamy was illegal and immoral, and so he issued the "1890 Manifesto" to that effect. The Mormon God suddenly concurred with the United States Congress, and Utah was granted statehood.

However, sneaky God told Woodruff to continue allowing polygamy in secret. He also said this to the following presidents, Lorenzo Snow and then Joseph F. Smith. Finally, God stopped His game of polygamy ping-pong with the LDS presidents. God told Joseph F. Smith that He had decided, for once and for all, that the practice was no longer required to enter the Celestial Kingdom. In 1904, the second Smith declared the "Second Manifesto," in which the Church officially renounced polygamy (again) and stopped performing new polygamous marriages—well, at least some people did.

God continued to be two-faced and issued different directions to different people. He told some Mormons that the 1904 decision was His final decision, although he told other Mormons that His 1866 decision was the true decision. These latter people believed that the Church was bowing to political pressure, and that they should form breakaway churches. This led to the creation of numerous splinter groups that have a penchant for lengthy names, such as the True and Living Church of Jesus Christ of Saints of the Last Days, the Church of Jesus Christ of Latter-day Saints and the Kingdom of God, and the infamous Fundamentalist Church of Jesus Christ of Latter-Day Saints. These Mormon sects believe in upholding the customs of the early church—that is, they still practice polygamy.

These groups are not affiliated with mainstream Mormons, who prefer to call these people "Polygamists." However, Mormons just can't shake the polygamy stereotype. Today, polygamy is strictly prohibited by the mainstream Mormon Church. The practice is believed to be in violation of the laws of the land, and the Church. However, the fundamentalists still consider themselves as Mormons who practice plural marriage, not as a new church. They see the mainstream church as "out of order" on polygamy, and hope that it will come back to the fold someday. In the meantime, the mainline Mormons excommunicate those who practice polygamy, while some fundamentalist Mormons excommunicate those who don't.

The Chosen People

The LDS has about 14 million members worldwide. Various sources claim there are some 30,000–60,000 Fundamentalist Mormons, although they are far from global, existing only in parts of North America and Mexico. There is no central authority, as numerous splinter groups sprang up when they spilt from the mainstream church. Since that time, many sects have become defunct. Others are very small, such as the Righteous Branch of the Church of Jesus Christ of Latter-Day Saints, which has only 100 members. Other sects thrive, such as the 10,000-strong Apostolic United Brethren, and the 10,000 members of the Fundamentalist Church of Jesus Christ of Latter-Day Saints (FLDS).

Beyond polygamy, fundamentalist Mormons have many controversial customs. They practice segregation and live in closed communities in remote towns scattered from Canada to Mexico. The largest concentration is the FLDS who live in the twin cities of Colorado City, Arizona, and Hildale, Utah, that straddle the border of the two states. The FLDS has expanded across the continent, establishing compounds in Texas, Missouri, Montana, Colorado, and South Dakota. In order to purchase large parcels of land without arousing suspicion, they often fib to the realtor that they are buying property for a "hunting retreat."

They have a sizeable $110 million treasury called the United Effort Plan, which is funded by tithing. This adheres to another early Mormon doctrine called the United Order, which is meant to create a community coffer, although in reality the leaders control the money. Fundamentalist families live in large do-it-yourself houses, and multiple or interconnected homes or trailers, but they don't own the land on which they are built. All property is owned by the Church, and followers must remain in good standing to keep their homes. Those who are excommunicated are labeled as "Apostates" and are evicted from the property. In particular,

Colorado City and Hildale are totalitarian towns whose administration and police departments are governed entirely by the Church.

The Church owns the schools too. In the more conservative groups, children are homeschooled, or taken out of school by the sixth grade so they can work in construction, farming, or around the home. Child labor is rampant, while these workers are paid little or nothing at all. Escapees from the FLDS reveal that their education is often inadequate, and history was rewritten in their textbooks. They are taught that the church president is also the President of the United States. Science is neglected, and students are told that the Moon landing never happened. There is an emphasis on religious studies, especially learning the proverbs of former president Warren Jeffs, such as the chilling, "When you disobey there must and always will be punishment."

Behind the privacy walls that separate them from the world, fundamentalists are further isolated as television, radio, and the Internet are often prohibited. A few groups are modernizing, such as Winston Blackmore's compound in Bountiful, British Columbia, where the kids attend public schools, carry cell phones, and wear jeans and baseball caps. Others have strict rules about clothing and members must dress for modesty. Girls and women wear long dresses, or long shirts and skirts, while boys and men wear long shirts and pants, which are perfect for those sweltering Arizona and Utah summers. In recent decades, the FLDS has enforced a conservative dress code. Woman and girls wear a uniform of pioneer-style prairie dresses, colored in Easter egg pastels. They are not allowed to wear the modern clothes that we "Gentiles" wear, and cosmetics, tattoos, and piercings are forbidden. Girls wear their hair in intricate braids, while the women wear an elaborate, old-fashioned pompadour style. Women are not allowed to cut their hair, in deference to the Bible passage where Mary Magdalene anoints Jesus with perfume, and wipes his feet with her long hair (John 12:3). Some fundamentalists believe that Jesus was a polygamist, who was married to Mary Magdalene, Mary, and Martha.

Each community has a kind of church government called the Priesthood, which dictates all of these rules. Members of the Priesthood receive revelations from God to guide their decisions. All adult male members of the community are ordained into the Priesthood. Women are not eligible for the Priesthood, nor are black people, who are considered "descendants of Ham" and afflicted by the "curse of Cain" (Genesis 4:11–16). As Warren Jeffs once said, "[Cain was] cursed with a black skin and he is the father of the Negro people. He has great power, can appear and disappear. He is used by the devil, as a mortal man, to do great evils." This fundamentalist policy also excludes black people from participating in ceremonies in temples, not that they want to participate anyway. This racist doctrine originated with the mainstream Mormons, who didn't rescind the policy until 1978.

Like the president of the mainline Mormon Church, fundamentalist leaders claim to be modern-day Prophets. The Prophet talks to God via visions and dreams and is known as the "key holder" or "God's mouthpiece." All Prophets claim to be the "true prophet," resulting in power struggles and the creation of new splinter groups. In some sects, the Prophet wields complete power over the community, and obedience is necessary for salvation. The Prophet is accountable to God only, so he isn't accountable to anyone.

Always the Bride, Never a Bridesmaid

Fundamentalist sects splintered from the mainline church to practice plural or "celestial" marriage, which is also known as "The Principle." However, not all members of these groups are polygamists. Followers of the Apostolic United Brethren aren't obligated to enter into plural marriages, although this is believed to be the only way to reach the Celestial Kingdom, the highest level of Heaven. Mormons believe that there are three degrees of glory in Heaven, as Jesus said, "In my Father's house there are many mansions" (John 14:2). Fundamentalists believe that in the Celestial Kingdom, the husband becomes a God, ruling his own planet that is populated by his wives, who become Goddesses, and his children. Those who don't practice plural marriage can only reach the Terrestrial Kingdom, the middle degree, where Jesus and God visit, although they don't live there. The Telestial Kingdom is a kind of hell for Mormons that is reserved for murderers, thieves, liars, and adulterers.

In the early days, Joseph Smith and Brigham Young took additional wives who were often already married. At least 11 of Smith's wives were already married to other men. Today, fundamentalist Mormons don't practice the general form of polygamy, where women marry multiple husbands, and men take multiple wives. They specifically practice polygyny, where one man marries multiple women. The opposite is polyandry, although a woman with multiple husbands is the much rarer form of polygamy (that is most commonly practiced in Tibet).

Contrary to popular belief, not all fundamentalist Mormon marriages are arranged. More permissive groups allow youths to date and marry for love. Early Mormon plural marriages were for love, or convenience, but most modern marriages are arranged, and the couple is expected to learn to love each other. Joseph Smith had a unique pick-up line for his prospective wives. His proposals were divine revelations. He told the women that he had received a message from God that they were to be married, and that marriage would ensure salvation for her and her family. Like an infomercial, the offer was only valid for the next 24 hours.

Since the 1940s, the FLDS has practiced a similar custom known as Placement Marriage. This is where God plays cupid. The Priesthood or the Prophet receives a revelation from God, who decides who marries whom. When a young man or woman is ready for marriage, they go to the Priesthood or Prophet and ask for a spouse. Men and woman are assigned to each other, but there is no prescreening for compatibility, or preferences for someone who likes piña coladas, and getting caught in the rain. There is no blind date, as this is a blind marriage. There is no engagement period, as the couple is often married that very day. It is considered romantic to not know who one's future husband or wife will be until minutes before the ceremony.

This isn't the end of the job for the divine dating agency. Married men will soon be approached to marry another woman. This isn't for their sexual gratification, but for their spiritual gratification. Three wives is the magical number needed to enter the Celestial Kingdom. The average fundamentalist Mormon husband has three wives, but God certainly assigns a lot of wives to the Prophets. Many church leaders have veritable harems of women. It appears that Joseph Smith had between thirty and forty-eight wives, and possibly more, some of whom were even sealed to him after he died. Brigham Young had fifty-five wives who bore him fifty-seven children. Collecting wives wasn't a trend only of the early Church; Paul Kingston, leader of the Kingston clan, has about forty wives. Warren Jeffs has seventy-nine confirmed wives, although some insiders report he has up to 180 wives. A group photograph of his fifty youngest wives shows an absent Jeffs appearing in a portrait in the background, while there are so many girls they look like they're posing for a school yearbook.

Child Brides

Not all communities wait for the girls to be ready. Some fundamentalist groups force teenage girls, or younger, to marry men who are much older. Girls of the Kingston clan fear that if they're not married by the age of seventeen they are already considered to be "old maids." In the early days of the Church, Joseph Smith married eleven girls under twenty years of age, including fourteen-year-old Nancy Winchester. Brigham Young liked them young too, and he had thirteen wives aged twenty or under. What is considered marriageable age to fundamentalists is viewed as statutory rape by the rest of society. When he was fifty-four years of age, fundamentalist Mormon Tom Green was convicted of child rape for marrying and impregnating a thirteen-year-old. In his late eighties, former FLDS leader Rulon Jeffs is said to have married a woman who was seventy years younger than him. His son Warren Jeffs had twenty-four wives who were under the age of seventeen. There is such a demand for child brides that the FLDS has been suspected of trafficking young girls across the Canadian border into the United States for this sexual slavery, several of whom are thought to have been married to Jeffs.

Taking on additional wives was supposed to be by consent of the wife or wives. However, Joseph Smith's first wife, Emma, was opposed to the practice, so he withheld the "endowment" ceremony that would grant her eternal salvation until she caved in. However, Emma was never happy about Smith's philandering under the guise of marriage, and wasn't aware of most of his marriages because God had instructed him to keep them a secret. Rulon Jeffs' first wife, Zola, the great-granddaughter of Brigham Young, refused to accept a second wife and divorced him, which was a clever move, as he was rumored to have collected as many as seventy-five wives at the time of his death.

In some communities the husband and wife or wives have no choice but to accept another wife. The union has been awarded by God, because additional wives are presented as "blessings." Other men simply wouldn't refuse a pretty young bride, and the more wives a man collects, the greater his social position and prestige. Most importantly, the more wives a man has, the more children he will produce. Having children is very important to fundamentalist Mormons, which explains the choice of polygyny over polyandry. They believe that spirit children are waiting to be born, and through plural marriage they can bring these souls out of preexistence and set them on to the path to eternity. Wives are expected to bear and raise children, and they are encouraged to have children once a year. In the Celestial Kingdom, it is believed that wives will be perpetually pregnant to populate their husband's planet.

Mainstream Mormons already have well above the average 2.4 kids. However, some fundamentalists could rival pharaoh Ramses II's 100-plus children, such as Winston Blackmore, who has over 120 children and counting. Asking a man about the size of his family is tantamount to asking him how much he earns. It is bad manners. However, examples of the size of fundamentalist families can be found in the obituaries. In the death notice for ninety-seven-year-old Alma Adelbert Timpson, the *Deseret News* reported that the polygamist was survived by three wives, sixty-six children, 347 grandchildren, and 151 great-grandchildren.

Father Knows Best

Many people have a fascination with polygamy, as shown by the popularity of the TV drama *Big Love* and the reality show *Sister Wives*. The practice sounds salacious and saucy, and we tend to think their homes must be hotbeds of group sex and lesbian love between sister wives. The truth is far less sexy. Sister wives compete for the affections of their husband. He has sex with his wives on a schedule, and usually in accordance with their ovulation cycles, or those he simply favors sexually. Women are forced to deal with their insecurity, jealousy, and resentment toward their sister wives, and the inevitability of their husband taking on additional wives.

Of course, these negative emotions are sent as tests from God (who only ever seems to test women). On the positive side, some plural wives report that they form bonds with their sister wives and work together as a team to raise their many children and run their enormous households. More frequently, tempers flare, and women fight for the position of "head wife," who dominates the other women.

The husband dominates most of all. He is a member of the Priesthood, and is the "Priesthead" of the household. The father/husband is yet another kind of Prophet, who receives divine revelation over his family. Fundamentalist Mormon communities are patriarchal societies. Women and children are subordinate to their husbands and fathers, who often rule like leaders of a microcult. A man's wives and children are his chattels, and he has complete control over them, that is, after the Prophet. Being viewed as property leaves the women and children vulnerable to abuses. Women are always subservient to men; they are taught to be obedient to their fathers, and then to their husbands. As Rulon Jeffs used to say, "The greatest freedom you can enjoy is in obedience."

Another one of his phrases was "Keep Sweet," which means to stay full of the Holy Spirit to "survive the judgments of God," although it is interpreted differently. "Keep Sweet" has been described variously as a mantra said to keep one's feelings under control, to swallow one's emotions, to suffer in silence, to not make trouble, to not ask questions, to not complain, and to be "immune to gloom." FLDS women are constantly reminded to "Keep Sweet," "Smile," and "Stay Pure." These mottos appear on signs around their towns, and in their newsletters, while women write them down on cards that they carry wherever they go. Like a "Bless This House" for fundamentalist Mormons, "Keep Sweet" appears on wall plaques in people's homes. Rulon Jeffs' compound was decorated with wallpaper that read, "Keep Sweet, No Matter What." Through this constant indoctrination, these women become numb to life.

Gender roles are conservative and strict in these communities. It is the woman's role to bear and raise children, without the support of the father. If a wife has a job, usually in midwifery, teaching, or some other "womanly" profession, she is expected to turn her paycheck in to her husband. Former polygamist wife Carolyn Jessop reports that her prominent ex-husband Merrill Jessop was abusive and selfish. With at least five wives and fifty children he collected his wives' paychecks and went out for expensive meals, leaving his substantial family without money for groceries. Jessop's first wife, Faunita, the mother of fifteen of his children, suffered from mental illness, and he dumped her on the roadside during a family move from Arizona to Texas. A woman achieves status by having children or being sexually preferred, and the men have their favorite wives while they neglect the others. The favorites receive preferential treatment, while the other women and children are ignored and go without decent food or items like shoes.

With so many mouths to feed, many large families suffer immense economic hardships. There are stories of polygamist wives scavenging garbage cans for food to feed their children. Like the Amish and Mennonite families, polygamist communities were better suited to the rural economy of the past. Today, most societies are dependent on wages. Fundamentalist Mormon communities have become welfare societies that rely on financial assistance and food stamps. In what they call "bleeding the beast," FLDS leaders teach that the government is evil and encourage their followers to leech off the system. Technically, the first wife is considered the sole wife, and the celestial wives are therefore portrayed as single parents. They are urged to apply for single-mother welfare, but then expected to hand the cash over to the Priesthood.

Keeping It in the Family

The spouses-to-be aren't always strangers, sometimes they are close relatives. "Kinship marriage" is seen as a divine right, and incest is doctrine in some fundamentalist Mormon communities. Aunts marry nephews, and uncles marry nieces. Marriages among first and second cousins are common, such as the case of fourteen-year-old Elissa Wall, who was forced to marry her first cousin, nineteen-year-old Allen Steed. Sometimes the sister wives really are sisters. Like the practice of pharaohs marrying their sisters in Ancient Egypt, in the Kingston clan marriage between siblings and half-brothers and sisters is common. Sisters are often married to the same man. Joseph Smith was married to four sister pairs of wives. Rulon Jeffs married young sisters Edna and Mary Fischer;

they were a present for his ninetieth birthday. When Rulon died, his son Warren married twenty-nine of his widows. Smith was also married to a mother-daughter pair.

Former FLDS member Debbie Palmer tries to explain her twisted and tangled family tree.

> My father had six wives and I have 47 brothers and sisters. My oldest daughter is my aunt and I am her grandmother. When I was assigned to marry my 1st husband, I became my own step-grandmother since my father was already married to two daughters of my new husband. . . . Several of my stepsons were assigned to marry my sisters, so I also became a sister-in-law to my own stepchildren. After my mother's father was assigned to marry one of my second husband's daughters as a second wife, I became my own great-grandmother. This stepdaughter became my step-grandmother and I her step-mother, so when I gave birth to two sons with her father, my own sons became my great-uncles and I was their great-great-grandmother.

With this intermarriage comes the increased risk of congenital disorders. After decades of inbreeding, Colorado City and Hildale have the world's greatest concentration of a disease called Fumarase Deficiency. The disorder has a range of symptoms, including frequent epileptic seizures, the inability to walk or sit upright, speech impediments, and severe mental retardation. There is no cure. Also known as "Polygamist Down's," this disorder is caused by a recessive gene that has been traced back to the Barlow and Jessop families. Most FLDS followers are descended from these two founding families. They believe their blood is "pure" and they marry to preserve the bloodline. Some sects even teach that they are descended directly from Jesus Christ. To avoid these genetic disorders they have been advised by doctors to outbreed, but unlike the famed missionary work of the mainline Mormons, the fundamentalist Mormons don't recruit new members. They are the chosen few. Outsiders are not welcome, and don't want to join them anyway.

Avoidable illnesses are simply seen as tests from God, and to their credit, these women are usually compassionate mothers to their sick offspring. The community also has a higher prevalence of Tourette's Syndrome, Down Syndrome, autism, blindness, kidney disease, and herpes. Birth defects are common too, and children are born with dwarfism, split organs, and cleft palates. Several children born into the Kingston clan have been born without fingernails. A forty-five-year-old Kingston woman gave birth to a baby with two vaginas and two uteruses, but no vaginal or bowel opening. Ex-FLDS member and activist Flora Jessop reports that her polygamist sister gave birth to a child with no arms or legs. Many women don't seek medical attention for these children because they don't want to explain their complex and illegal marital situations.

A Law unto Themselves

One person's polygamy is another person's bigamy. Polygamy is illegal in the United States, as it was when the mainline Mormons renounced the practice in 1890, and again in 1904. Fundamentalist Mormons argue that antipolygamy laws violate their religious freedom. They may be able to circumvent the laws by claiming their other marriages are merely "spiritual" marriages, if they don't cohabit with these spiritual wives. Joseph Smith never cohabited with his additional wives; he just had sex with them, although modern fundamentalist Mormons usually do live together. Bigamy makes outlaws of these people, but they believe it is worth the glory in the life to come.

However, the authorities tend to overlook polygamy. Individuals are occasionally prosecuted, but the police simply don't have the resources to deal with all cases unless they are underpinned by more serious crimes, such as underage marriage, statutory rape, child trafficking, welfare cheating, or tax evasion. Within their own communities, polygamy and related crimes are completely ignored by the local authorities. This is because in Colorado City and Hildale, the police themselves are polygamists.

In 1953, Arizona governor John Howard Pyle attempted to take action against polygamy. Following allegations of underage marriages, the Arizona State Police stormed the polygamist community in Short Creek. The entire town was taken into custody, and children were taken away from their parents. Known as the Short Creek Raid, some 150 children were held as wards of the state for up to two years, while some kids were never sent back home. The media and public saw this as religious persecution, and were sympathetic toward the polygamists. The Short Creek community eventually rejuvenated, and the town changed its name to Colorado City, while the Utah section was renamed Hildale. These people were the forerunners to the Fundamentalist Church of Jesus Christ of Latter-Day Saints. Ever since this failed raid, which destroyed the governor's reputation and career, the authorities have been reluctant to intervene in cases of polygamy, until recently.

In 2003, Warren Jeffs moved select followers of his congregation to a new "hunting retreat" near Eldorado, Texas. The Yearning for Zion Ranch was founded to shield these favorites from antipolygamy laws. In April 2008, a call to a domestic abuse hotline spurred a police raid of the compound, and 469 children were taken into temporary custody. The initial complaint turned out to be a hoax, but the raid revealed that 60 percent of the girls aged fourteen to seventeen were pregnant, or had already given birth. An investigation soon uncovered other crimes that were happening within the community.

Satan's Prophet

During his leadership, FLDS Prophet Rulon Jeffs created a divine dictatorship when he fired the leadership council known as the Priesthood. He installed the "One Man Rule," giving absolute authority to himself. He died in 2002 at the age of ninety-two, although he had prophesied that he would live to be 350. His son Warren succeeded him to become the "President and Prophet, Seer and Revelator." His followers called him "Uncle Warren," and in the incestral community he *was* an uncle to many of them. During his four-year rule, Jeffs was a depraved tyrant. He wielded Church doctrine to control every aspect of his people's lives, and to satisfy his sexual perversions. Jeffs is well on his way to entering the Telestial Kingdom.

Few Prophets of God manage to get themselves onto the FBI's Most Wanted List. Jeffs had evaded the police for years by living on the run and staying at various "safe houses" across the country. Jeffs was finally captured by Nevada Highway Patrol at a traffic stop near Las Vegas. He was caught with $55,000 in cash, $10,000 in gift cards, fifteen cell phones, four portable radios, four laptops, two GPS systems, a police scanner, and a copy of the Book of Mormon. Jeffs wore the very "Gentile" clothes he had forbidden his followers to wear, and he carried a range of disguises, including twelve pairs of sunglasses, wigs, and fake beards. Jeffs was wanted for forcing teenager Elissa Wall to marry her cousin, and being an accomplice to her rape. However, his subsequent court trials revealed that this was only the tip of the iceberg of his crimes.

From behind bars, Jeffs exercised complete control over his 10,000 followers and issued some bizarre edicts. His people were not allowed to watch television, read newspapers, or use the Internet. All literature was forbidden, except for the Bible and the Book of Mormon. He forced parents to take their children out of school. He banned music, dancing, playing, and children's toys. He forbade the consumption of corn and imposed an all-bean diet. He prohibited the congregation from owning or wearing anything red, as this color was reserved for Jesus. When Jeffs was captured he was riding in a red Cadillac Escalade.

Even during his reign, Jeffs was a micromanaging Prophet. He ordered people how to dress and told them what to eat, where to live, and whom to marry. As the Prophet, Jeffs was the only person with the authority to perform marriages, and he was diligent about this duty. During his leadership, Jeffs arranged over 550 bigamous marriages. Many of these were between underage girls and older men, and often in return for favors. The more young daughters a loyal man would give up, the more young brides he would receive as rewards for his obedience.

Those men that Jeffs saw as disloyal and disobedient were branded "Apostates" and lost their Priesthood. This often meant their excommunication and exile. It always meant "reassignation," where the man's family was torn apart, his wives and children were reassigned to other men, and he became known as a "eunuch." The women and children were then instructed to call the stranger to whom they were reassigned "husband" or "father." All photographs of the Apostate were destroyed, and he was never to be seen or spoken of again by his family. They didn't want him back anyway, because he couldn't get them into the

Celestial Kingdom. During his leadership, Jeffs excommunicated sixty men, and reassigned over three hundred women and children to new families. In his game of marital musical chairs, these women and children were often reassigned more than once. Through reassignment, a man named Fred Jessop amassed eighteen wives and one hundred children, even though he was sterile.

Reassignment was originally practiced upon the death of a husband, but Jeffs turned the custom into a punishment. He destroyed these families for a range of "crimes": badmouthing the Prophet, living like the Gentiles by watching TV, listening to music or violating the dress code, viewing pornography, masturbating, having sex with wives at times other than ovulation, refusing to give up a child for marriage, not having control over wives and kids, associating with Apostates who had been excommunicated or with those who had left the church, including family, committing "immorality in your heart," or any other reason devised by the Prophet on a whim. However, the main reason for reassignment was that Jeffs endeavored to maintain power by ousting men who posed a threat to his leadership.

It seems that Jeffs had another punishment in store for these men. There is evidence that he was attempting to bring back the nineteenth century Mormon doctrine of "Blood atonement." This is the theory that some crimes, such as murder and adultery, are so heinous that the atonement of Jesus wasn't enough and that Apostates who commit serious sins deserve to be ritually sacrificed. During his sermons, Jeffs had been teaching that those who were guilty of adultery must be blood atoned for their own salvation. Former member Robert Richter was working on a "secret project" in which he was asked to design a thermostat that would handle temperatures of up to 2,700 degrees. Richter believes that Jeffs was building a blood atonement room where sinners would have their throats slit, and their bodies would be disposed of in a crematory designed to incinerate DNA.

The Lost Boys

Jeffs wasn't only threatened by men, he was also threatened by the young boys in the community who were competition for the women. With males being born all the time, there simply weren't enough females to go around. Jeffs began expelling boys as young as thirteen from the community for trivial transgressions, such as playing music, watching television, dating, kissing, or simply talking to a girl. Known as the "Lost Boys," these kids were abandoned to fend for themselves without money, support, or a proper education. Not all boys were kicked out of the sect. There are stories of some boys being taken into the desert and shot, while others died mysteriously in car accidents.

Jeffs didn't give away all of the young women; he kept some for himself. The Prophet was a pedophile, as he had at least twenty-four wives under the age of seventeen. During the police investigation a photo surfaced that showed a child bride cradled in Jeffs' arms, kissing him passionately. DNA evidence revealed that Jeffs had fathered a child with this girl when she was fifteen years old. There was an abundance of evidence for his crimes, as Jeffs kept "Priest Records" of everything he did. In one of these diaries he wrote that God had told him to find young girls who can be "worked with and easily taught." As "God's mouthpiece" he also recorded everything he said. In one recording he is heard instructing minors graphically on how to please him sexually. During what he called "heavenly sessions" or "celestial sessions," these girls should "set aside all of your inhibitions." A girl "needs to be excited" to satisfy him, and by pleasing him they were pleasing God. They were also helping to atone for the sins of the community. However, God would reject them if they didn't comply with his every demand. Those who rebuffed Jeffs were exiled to "hunting retreats" across the country for discipline and reeducation.

The evidence included an audio recording of Jeffs sexually assaulting a twelve-year-old girl. A group of his young wives assisted in this crime. The brainwashed girls bound her arms and legs while Jeffs raped her. At the Yearning for Zion Ranch Jeffs built an opulent Mormon-style temple. This was equipped with an altar that was labeled as "the rape bed" by the press. Like the plot of a bad horror movie, ritual sex sessions were performed on the altar and recorded in front of an audience. Prayers were recited both before and after the girls were restrained and molested. During the lengthy trials, the jurors wept openly as they listened to these disturbing recordings.

However, eighty wives were not enough for Jeffs. He was the Principal of Alta Academy, the FLDS-operated school, and he used his position of authority to abuse the students. One day, seven-year-old Jerusha Jeffs was called into Uncle Warren's office. He told her to sit on his lap and flattered her, saying she was a "special" and "beautiful" girl. He promised to help her get to heaven, as long as she didn't tell anyone what he was about to do. Then he raped her. When Brent Jeffs was five years old, his Uncle Warren led him into the bathroom at church one Sunday morning. He was told ominously that what was about to happen was "between you, me, and God." Then Jeffs sodomized his young nephew. The sexual abuse continued for two years, and when Brent was a teenager he became one of the "Lost Boys" along with his brothers, whom he discovered Jeffs had also been molesting. His brothers never recovered from the abuse, and one died of a drug overdose, while another committed suicide.

Jeffs was a tyrannical teacher too. In order to be able to blackmail the community, Jeffs grilled students about their home lives. He cautioned them to not tell their parents, and they received a beating if they disobeyed him. Jeffs punished students harshly for frivolous crimes, such as the young girl who was expelled for writing a note to a boy. He taught that the females should be submissive to males. With an audience of young boys, Jeffs called in one of his wives for a demonstration of this submission. He grabbed his wife's long hair and twisted it, until she dropped to her knees.

During his trial, the raving Prophet warned of a "whirlwind of judgment" from God if His "humble servant" wasn't released. Regardless, Jeffs was given a life sentence. From his jail cell he continued to make false predictions of earthquakes and storms of biblical proportions. He prophesized that the world would end before 2013, but Jeffs was never very good at prophecy. Even before he'd been imprisoned he had named many incorrect dates for the rapture, and built a garden known as the "launching pad" for the ascension to Zion that never transpired.

With their ruler in jail for life, there was confusion over leadership of the Church, but Jeffs continued to issue new bans. He blamed his incarceration on his followers, claiming he was in jail because they were unwilling to repent. He ordered couples to stop having sex, and even to stop touching each other entirely. If a woman desired to have a baby, she must have sex with one of fifteen men handpicked by Jeffs, and the act must be witnessed by two other men from the group. Even behind bars Jeff's bizarre sexual appetite couldn't be quenched. Though he had deemed it to be a sin worthy of reassignment, Jeffs attempted to masturbate up to fifteen times a day. With no shame, he did it in full view of his jailers.

Jeffs suffered mood swings in jail. He tried to commit suicide, and he fasted in protest until authorities put him into a medically induced coma. He wavered back and forth between resigning and claiming he's still the rightful Prophet. In video footage he admitted, "I'm not the Prophet," and asserted that he is the "greatest of all sinners and the wickedest man." In a diary entry he shared his only accurate revelation, "If the world knew what I was doing, they would hang me from the highest tree." However, his followers see him as infallible, and believe he was framed. Like Joseph Smith, he is martyred. Thousands of people still worship the President, Prophet, and convicted felon they call "Uncle Warren", even though they will never see him again.

The Greatest Freedom Is Disobedience
Why do people stay in these fundamentalist Mormon sects? They don't join them to begin with, they are born into them. It is a process of socialization, and the abused often don't even recognize the abuse. Living behind the walls of the compound they are isolated from the rest of society. They experience a lifetime of brainwashing and bullying, and then they repeat the cycle. The leaders discourage and punish freethought and critical thinking. There is no doubt that some fundamentalist Mormon groups are cults, especially the FLDS.

To leave the group is a frightening prospect because it means abandoning everything these people have ever known. Trained from birth to be obedient, they are dependent on their leaders. Women are usually bound with children. If they do escape they will be shunned by their family and friends, and ostracized by the community. They are threatened that the repercussions don't end here on Earth. When they die they'll end up in the Telestial Kingdom for all eternity.

Without money or support, they are not equipped with the education or life skills to leave, and most of them don't want to leave the "safe" and familiar confines of the compound. To further control their people, the leaders cultivate a morbid fear of the outside world, a place where women are raped and their children are stolen. They teach that contact with these heathens will prevent their entry to the Celestial Kingdom.

A few brave followers chose the Telestial Kingdom instead, and decided to leave, at any cost. Like the experiences of Carolyn Jessop, Elissa Wall, and Brent Jeffs, there are a few escape success stories. Sadly, these survivors report personal and eyewitness experiences of physical, psychological, and sexual abuse at the hands of fathers, husbands, and leaders, often in the name of God. They reveal that when people do manage to escape, goons are enlisted to drag them straight back into the fundamentalist fold. Several ex-members are now activists who educate us heathens about these cults, and assist others in getting out, like Flora Jessop, who provides safe houses, support, and counseling to prepare escaped girls to enter the outside world. Former FLDS member Dan Fischer is an entrepreneur who spends his sizeable fortune helping Lost Boys to start new lives.

Perhaps we can help too. As some of these groups slowly venture out of their traditional towns, there is a greater chance we will have contact with these people. Former members of fundamentalist Mormon churches encourage us to use these rare encounters to disprove these peoples' fears about modern society. As Brent Jeffs suggests, "Treat them with dignity and respect and maybe you can plant a seed in their minds: 'Maybe I could leave and have a normal life outside.'"

The Lights Are on but Nobody's Home

In late 2006, a man named Lee Steed purchased a nine-bedroom log home in Westcliffe, Colorado, as a hunting retreat. Neighbors say that a large group of people moved into the home and began constant construction on the house. Bulldozers ran around the clock, ATVs patrolled the property, and gunshots were heard occasionally. Soon the house was surrounded by a maze of metal fences and barred by an iron gate. This wasn't the only house purchased by Steed. He had purchased hundreds of acres of land across Colorado, collectively worth millions of dollars, and he had paid for most of it in cash. It was revealed that Steed was a member of the FLDS and was buying the land on behalf of the Church.

The town of Westcliffe was divided over these newcomers. In the wake of news stories about the FLDS, many were concerned about turning into a town troubled by polygamy, pedophilia, abandoned children, and welfare cheats; or they were worried about their property values. Other townsfolk had a live-and-let-live attitude. In a town of religious diversity they welcomed these people who seemed kind, honest, and hardworking, at least from afar. However, they didn't integrate with the community like the family who runs the Amish bakery. The women wearing pastel prairie dresses could only be spotted through binoculars, and they seemed like prisoners in their own home. When approached, the men were abrupt, or they simply ran away. These people were never seen buying milk in the Country Store, or drinking a cup of coffee in the Have a Nice Day Café. These weren't the kind of neighbors from whom you could borrow a cup of sugar. It's difficult to get past the privacy walls and the "No Trespassing" sign.

It was rumored that up to one hundred people lived in the home. In this single household alone, this figure would have raised the town's population by a quarter. The place was big, but not *that* big. Town Sheriff Fred Jobe went to investigate, but he was only permitted entry with a warrant. His return visit revealed that this wasn't a compound of ill repute. It was the home of Joseph Jessop, his wife Deanna, and their six children. Their extended family included a number of women and their children, and numerous portraits of Warren Jeffs on the walls. It was simply a "safe house" for widows and grandmothers to escape persecution. The family begged the "Gentiles" for privacy and peace. They were happy to be settling in this secluded, picturesque little town.

These people didn't know that they wouldn't be settling in this town. In fact, they have already gone. Some people in Westcliffe never knew they were there anyway, and this is exactly the way the FLDS leaders like it. Leaving a trail of confusion, they buy and sell properties quickly, and change names on property titles. These members live like fugitives and are moved about constantly. You see, these houses in Colorado were intended as safe houses for Warren Jeffs, not for the women. In fact, there is a network of these hideouts across the country. Jeffs' wives and daughters were smuggled to these secret locations at night. They stayed for a few weeks to a few months at a time, before they were sent to another compound. The women were used to being shipped around, and they carried few belongings, but they never knew where they were, or where they were going next.

Like a story out of a spy novel, the women were watched by caretakers who were equipped with GPS systems, numerous phones, and disguises. Even in these tiny, isolated towns the wives were kept under house arrest. They were forbidden to leave the house, or to have contact with their neighbors. Their days were regimented and filled with drudgery. At 6 a.m. they studied sermons, followed by a day of household chores. Their evenings ended in sewing pairs of sacred undergarments. There was no entertainment, television, or newspapers, for fear the women would learn the truth about Jeffs. If anyone heard the news anyway, they were told he was "falsely accused." However, they knew that something was wrong. Every hour they were forced to go to their rooms to pray for Jeffs. Distressed and confused, some of the women hardly ate anything, and they appeared sad and depressed all the time.

Prior to Jeffs' arrest, he would pay furtive visits to his wives at these houses. He had always instructed his followers to shun "Gentile" clothing, although he would appear at the house in jeans and a T-shirt. Often he was wearing a wig or a fake beard. Jeffs would have a meal cooked for him by the women, and then he sat them down for a sermon of his divine revelations. In the months before his arrest he warned that "a test from God" was coming, and the end was near. Sounding like we narrowly averted another Jonestown, Jeffs once told the women to "prepare to meet Rulon in a sacred place." Before he left the house, Jeffs would have sex with a few of his wives. The women were frantic with loneliness and despair and wanted to travel with him, but Jeffs would tell them, "You're not good enough to be with me."

"Looking Beyond" is the name of the now-abandoned compound in Westcliffe. To explain the numerous bedrooms the realtor said with a cringe, "This place was used, um . . . a little bit differently than a normal house." She didn't divulge that this had been an FLDS compound. "You could use it as a hunting retreat!" she suggested.

Two large cabin-style houses with green roofs sit on the 35-acre property in the Bull Domingo Ranch area. The entrance leads you into a kitchen that is big enough for an army unit. The place looked like it had been left hastily, as the cupboard doors were flung open, and the shelves were still full of cleaning products. Each shelf had been neatly marked with labels for "preserves," "relish," and "homemade molasses." The barn was full of empty produce boxes, as the women were often set to work canning and preserving fruit and vegetables.

Branching off the kitchen was a hallway that stretched far enough to hold the long jump for the Olympics. The hall led to 8 bedrooms, making the place look like a school dormitory. Most of these rooms were the size of a prison cell, but they were all interconnected. Upstairs was an enormous room with carpet laid halfway up the walls. This was their makeshift church. There was a stage and podium and a cabinet for storing scriptures, as evidenced by two well-worn copies of *Hymns of the Church of Jesus Christ of Latter-day Saints*. On this floor there were even more bedrooms, but these were clearly for the first-class guests. They were larger, and several even had their own bathrooms. The largest bedroom was clearly for the caretakers. While the other rooms were all laid with drab grey carpet, this room was decorated with a 70s-style shag pile carpet in a gaudy green color.

There was also a basement that had been converted into even more bedrooms for the Hotel FLDS. The realtor had said there were eight bedrooms in the house, but there were easily fifteen to twenty bedrooms, and ten bathrooms. That was in the first house. The second house stored another eight bedrooms, at least. "Was this a camp or something?" I asked the realtor. "Something like that," she lied.

There were some strange things about the house. There were lots of crawl spaces and cabinets, but inside, angry crayon scribble appeared low down. These scratchings looked more emotional than artistic, almost like a child had been locked inside and drawn them out of defiance. In one room a little girl's lemon yellow prairie dress still hung from the closet, left behind in the rush to leave. FLDS mottos were stenciled on the walls and door frames throughout the house as reminders that the women should "Smile" and "Keep Sweet," no matter what.

The rooms and halls were empty, but it was easy to imagine the "ghosts" of the former residents. I could picture the portraits of Jeffs lining the walls, and the women in their prairie dresses as they prepared food in the kitchen. I could visualize a woman with her high hair peering out of the window, hoping she wouldn't be spotted by the nosy neighbors. I could see a woman saying prayers for Jeffs in her tiny bedroom, and sense her feeling of being surrounded by people, but still feeling lonely.

A whiteboard hanging on the wall in the kitchen held a few ghosts too. The mantras "Keep Sweet" and "Smile" had been wiped off the board, but still appeared faintly. I could just make out a few pictures of smiley faces. Even though it had been cleaned, one message was still visible, as the artist had used a permanent red pen that had left an indelible mark. Written in elegant cursive across the board were the words, "We love you Uncle Warren!"

Chapter 2

The Not-So-Simple Life
The Amish and Mennonites

**"It is only when our lives are falling apart
that we have the chance to make our faith real."
—*Amish Grace***

*I stepped out of the car and when I turned around I felt like I had suddenly
stumbled into a BBC period drama. I saw a group of bearded men in black
suits with black hats, accompanied by women wearing long dresses and caps.
Like deer caught in headlights, we were both frozen as we stared at each other.*

The Anabaptists

On January 21, 1525, Swiss Brethren member George Blaurock was
baptized in Zurich, Switzerland. However, he was 34 years old and had
already been baptized as a baby. With this act of adult baptism, Blaurock
became the very first Anabaptist. The movement rejected infant baptism,
instead advocating believer's baptism, when the adult decides to join the
church in a declaration of faith and free will. In the sixteenth century this
was a radical idea. Waiting until adulthood to be baptized was dangerous
as infant mortality rates were high. Dying unbaptized condemned
the baby, child, or youth to a certain Hell. Like many of his brethren,
Blaurock was considered a heretic and he was eventually burned at the
stake.

In the wake of the Protestant Reformation, here was yet another "true Christianity." The Anabaptists also rejected idolatry and the Catholic Mass. They called for the separation of church and state, and insisted on following a more literal interpretation of the Bible. To that end, they believed that the baptisms performed by Paul in Acts 19:1–5 represent true baptism, a ritual that should be carried out *after* the believer has found Jesus Christ. The name "Anabaptist," meaning "re-baptizer," was initially an insult term that critics bestowed on these followers. They adopted the term anyway, and to this day they often have to explain that they are Anabaptists, but not "anti-Baptists."

Like poor George Blaurock, the Anabaptists were persecuted throughout Europe and expelled from Switzerland, Germany, Holland, Poland, and Russia. At the invitation of the famous Quaker William Penn, the founder of Pennsylvania, many Anabaptists migrated to this new territory in the early eighteenth century, where they were granted religious freedom. There were and are many similarities between the Quakers and the Anabaptists. Both groups believe in peace and pacifism, they don't allow weapons, and they refuse to perform military service.

They believe in peace, but they don't always agree with each other, and the Anabaptists suffered many schisms over beliefs and practices in the sixteenth century. The followers of Menno Simon branched off to become known as the Mennonites, while those who supported the ideas of Jakob Hutter became the Hutterites. In the seventeenth century a Mennonite by the name of Jacob Amman criticized the apparent lack of discipline in his church, so he initiated a more draconian clique. These followers became the Amish, who are still known for their strict adherence to the faith.

Anabaptism is the underlying religion of modern Mennonite, Brethren, Hutterite, and Amish churches, and their numerous breakaway sects. Anabaptists can be found in Europe, Asia, Africa, South America, and North America. Today, there are some 40,000 Hutterites, 250,000 Amish, and 300,000 Mennonites in the United States. Anabaptists are found in every state in the country, although they go by many names, and have many different beliefs and practices that usually have their roots in the Bible.

America holds a deep fascination with these people, and especially the Amish. The name conjures up images of green pastures, fresh-baked bread, and smiling children in cute costumes. They symbolize peace, piety, and purity, and are known for their kindness, calmness, and humility. While many Americans demand that immigrants assimilate to the mainstream culture, the Amish are preferred as a time capsule of old-world America (or Switzerland, as the case may be). America has adopted the Amish as their own, and they are deemed as American as (streusel) apple pie.

The Amish have become an industry of wise proverbs, cook books, romance novels, and stories of star-crossed lovers and forbidden love, such as the movie *Witness*, where John the outsider falls for Rachel the Amish woman in a love that can never be. The Amish represent a simpler era that is a welcome relief from the rat race, if only occasionally. There is an abundance of self-help books teaching you how to "go Amish" and simplify your life. Their simple lifestyle that is driven by religious beliefs is conflated with modern concerns of environmentalism, sustainability, and reducing our carbon footprint.

To their admirers, they seem to have achieved Utopia. However, their lives aren't all about handmade quilts and pies cooling on windowsills. Traditionally a closed society, increasing contact with mainstream society has revealed a number of controversies. *Rumspringa* is the rite of passage before joining the church where youths experience the outside world, and often land themselves in serious trouble. If they join the church and break the rules, or leave, they will be shunned by friends and family. Shockingly, many cases of pedophilia, incest, and physical abuse have emerged from these communities. Education is discouraged, and female members are oppressed. Farmers have been accused of illegal health practices, and cruelty to animals for operating "puppy mills." The considerable differences in philosophy between the Anabaptists and mainstream society result in serious cultural clashes.

In what was originally a response to persecution in Europe, conservative Anabaptists live in communities isolated from modern American society. However, there is a paradox. They attempt to resist popular culture although they live in the world's most culturally dominant country. Mainstream society continually encroaches on their world, and in many ways, they willingly draw ever closer to ours.

Hard and Fast Rules

The stereotypical Anabaptists are the Old Order Amish of Lancaster County, Pennsylvania, the oldest settlement in the country. However, they are only one of many different types of orders. As far as their lifestyles are concerned, Anabaptist groups fall somewhere on a continuum of traditional through to modern. Moderate Mennonites are at the modern end of the scale, and are little more than Protestants. They rail at the misconception that female members wear "plain" dress, and that their men have pudding-bowl haircuts. However, the more traditional Anabaptists do wear the beards and bonnets, and these are the groups we will be exploring.

Even among the conservatives there is great variance in their customs. The most traditional groups are described as low, slow, or older orders, while more liberal groups are high, fast, or newer orders. The Swartzentruber Amish are the most conservative Anabaptists and don't permit the use of electricity, gas, or indoor plumbing. Despite their name, the Conservative Mennonites are the most progressive group and allow their members to drive cars and use cell phones and computers.

The church controls these Dos and Don'ts. There isn't a central Amish or Mennonite church; instead there are church districts, and each is its own Vatican. There are thousands of different districts across the United States, comprised of dozens of families. These districts continually splinter, because no single congregation can agree on all possible rules. Agreement is important, because these rules govern almost every detail of their lives. The acceptable length of a man's beard and the style of a woman's underwear become religious decisions. However, there are contradictions and inconsistencies in their rules. Some churches prohibit members from riding bikes, but they may use rollerblades. Some can't own televisions, but they can watch television. Some can't own cars, but they are allowed to ride in them.

These rules are known as the *Ordnung*, meaning "order." These strict regulations determine what is permissible, and what isn't, and are designed to keep the community together, while keeping the modern world away. They are intended to guard against pride, laziness, dishonesty, and envy, which are feared to erode the community. The Ordnung is created by the adult members of the church district. The districts are independent, and with their own rules, they are almost like different religions. The lives of traditional Anabaptists are inextricably interwoven with religion, as they attempt to live the Bible. The Ordnung rules are often supported by scripture.

Obedience to the church's ordinance is a must, as the Ordnung is the church's interpretation of the "Word of God." Infringements are tantamount to sacrilege. A violation receives a reprimand, and any further defiance results in excommunication from the church. Each community believes that God doesn't exist outside of their own order, so excommunication condemns the ex-member to eternal damnation. Sometimes the members decide to leave instead. It's not the pride or envy but the rules that often divide the community. Church districts become polarized over how long a shirt hem should be, or how they should sing hymns in church on Sunday. These disgruntled members may join a new settlement, usually choosing a new one that is less strict. In true Anabaptist style, they may even start their own settlement.

Plain and Simple

Conservative Anabaptists try not to conform to the outside world. Their motto is a paraphrase of Romans (12:2), to be "In this world, but not of this world." In an effort to preserve their culture, they keep separate from mainstream society. To this end they live in enclaves, they don't vote, they shun modern technology, they live close to the land, they wear distinctive clothing, and they speak a modern dialect of German known as Pennsylvanian Dutch. They call Americans who are not part of their commmunity "English," in reference to the English language, although many learn how to speak American English too. As members of the highest order of all, Americans who are not members of their community are also called *Hoch*, meaning "high."

Conservative Anabaptists are known as the "Plain People," but not because they look like the boy or girl next door. They are plain in the sense that they lead simple lives, and they value humility and modesty. They also lead similar lives, to maintain equality among their community. They don't conform to the outside world, but they conform to their community. They live separately from modern society, although their communities are tight-knit. Community support is vital, whether for a barn raising, for quilting, shucking corn, and canning fruit and vegetables, or for helping a fellow member affected by disaster. Whereas modern America values self-reliance and individuality, Anabaptists are more collectivist. They believe in social solidarity, where the needs of the group are prioritized over those of the individual. A core value of the Amish is *gelassenheit*—to give themselves up to God, the church, and to the will of others. To maintain social harmony, the Ordnung forbids lying, stealing, drinking, smoking, swearing, gambling, and the use of illegal drugs.

Their homes are practical and functional, and they don't build "fine and worldly houses." Inside you won't find a Velvet Elvis or a print of *Dogs Playing Poker*, as their furnishings are minimalist. Technology is kept at a minimum too, as it is seen as a distraction from family life. Some orders don't allow radios, television sets, CD players, or musical instruments. Permissible technology is dependent upon the Ordnung, which controls the design of the house right down to the color of the paint. Some orders use candles and lanterns for lighting, and have outhouses instead of indoor toilets. Some disallow indoor and cell phones, but allow outdoor telephone shanties. These little shacks are without comfy seating, so your five daughters don't linger on phone calls asking, "Does he like me?"

More progressive groups accept new technology for business or practical reasons, but not those that are for mere entertainment. They believe that material possessions promote vanity, and by extension, breed discontent that leads to sinning. For a new technology to be accepted it must pass rigorous examination. It needs to have low social impact and to not increase reliance on secular society. It will be rejected if it introduces questionable values. For instance, the Internet can be used to acquire information, but it can also be used to surf for porn. Necessity is the mother of invention, and some get creative with workarounds to defy the Ordnung.

However, some groups are even more powerful than the Ordnung, including the Food and Drug Administration. If a farmer wants to sell milk commercially the milk pail and three-legged stool won't do. Over the years there have been dairy scandals of Amish farmers selling unpasteurized milk to the public. Natural food advocates promote this "raw milk" as healthier, but it is only riskier. Pasteurization kills bacteria such as salmonella, E. coli, and listeria, and has helped to reduce milk-transmitted diseases such as typhoid and diphtheria. No matter how conservative, Anabaptist dairy farmers must have the latest pasteurizing equipment, even if it is powered by gas or diesel generators.

Baby You Can Drive My Car

Like their forebears who traveled by ship to reach the New World, members of conservative orders may travel by boat. They also travel by train, but usually not by plane. Some communities permit the use of bicycles, motorcycles, and rollerblades, others ban them. Cars are often banned, although some orders allow their members to ride in them as passengers. The "English" locals who provide the rides might become known as the "Amish taxi." Conservative Mennonites and a group known as the Beachy Amish are more liberal and most own and drive vehicles. A clear distinction is often made between ownership and usage. In this same way, some orders allow their members to watch television or listen to stereos in a non-Amish home, to rent a car when traveling, or to use a computer at work, but not to own these devices at home.

The preferred mode of transport is the horse-drawn buggy, which is a ubiquitous sight in Amish communities. This choice is intended to keep their lives in the slow lane, to create equality, to place less reliance on mainstream society, and to limit travel so they have more time to spend with family. Buggies have a kind of in-built cruise control, as horses pulling them can't travel more than 5–10 miles per hour. To paraphrase Henry Ford's quote, conservative buggies come in every color, so long as it's black. Newer orders might allow buggies to be painted grey too. Some owners have souped-up buggies outfitted with speedometers, windshields, or solar panels. Displaying lights or orange safety triangle reflectors on the rear of the buggy is the law, although ultraconservative orders ban them because they are considered to be bling. They feel they don't need them anyway, as the ultimate traffic controller is God. Without safety measures in place, buggy accidents are common, and often fatal, but they are always rationalized as God's will.

Old School

Parents avoid sending their children to public schools and prefer Anabaptist schools. In more traditional communities, children attend parochial schools where kids of all ages are taught together in a single classroom. They only attend school until eighth grade, which is the minimum requirement by state law. Higher education is usually banned by the Ordnung. When they leave school at around age 14, most children will begin to learn practical skills on the farm or in an apprenticeship. New female graduates often become the teachers, as no special training is required. Some argue that an eighth-grade Amish education is more advanced than the same level taught at a public school. However, they don't teach arts or science, as they don't see practical value for their communities in these subjects. Instead, they focus on the Three Rs, and add a fourth one, "Religion." They usually teach creationism, that is, the literal interpretation of Genesis. They believe that the world was created in six days, and that God rested on the seventh day.

Conservative parents don't dream that their kids will become doctors or lawyers. The stereotypical image is that of the hardworking farmer, but farming is on the decline today because the cost of real estate has skyrocketed. A lucky few have made unexpected money by selling their farms and moving to cheaper regions, or selling the oil and gas drilling rights on their land. Beyond farming, many men perform construction or factory work, or even take on jobs in offices or restaurants. They like to be cut off from modern society, but they are no longer self-sufficient and often need to trade. They are renowned for their cottage industries. The men make craftsmen furniture or leather goods, while the women make jams, spreads, and bakery items, and quilts that are painstakingly handmade, which is reflected in their prices. They don't like to deal directly with the public, so they often sell their wares through "mom and pop" shops and even online through resellers.

Dog breeding is a popular profession too. There are hundreds of commercial dog-breeding kennels across the country, particularly in Lancaster County, Pennsylvania. Many Amish farmers have been widely criticized for operating inhumane dog-breeding facilities known as "puppy mills," where profit is placed above animal welfare. In these "dog factories" the animals are locked up in overcrowded cages. Rescued dogs are barely able to walk after being chronically confined in wire cages without foot support. The dogs have insufficient food and water, and aren't provided with exercise, grooming, or medical attention. Sometimes the farmers debark the dogs by severing their vocal cords to keep them quiet. Investigations into these kennels have revealed some to be overflowing with feces and urine, and bright green drinking water. The farmers favor boutique breeds, for which they can charge $1,000 or more per puppy. However, in these substandard conditions, many dogs are born with serious health defects, resulting in costly veterinary expenses, or the puppy's premature death. Many Amish farmers have been charged for operating kennels without licenses, breeding unlicensed dogs, and cruelty to animals.

Those who choose to stick with farming might grow cash crops of popular "English" foods, such as hot peppers or tobacco, although they can't smoke it. To earn extra money many Amish open up their communities to the public, offering tours of their farms and homes, complete with buggy rides. Just don't ask them to "say cheese." The Ordnung doesn't permit "graven images," as per Exodus (20:4), and posing for photographs is a form of pride. This rule can sometimes be circumvented if the subject doesn't look at the camera, while unbaptized children and teens are not bound by these regulations.

To end a day with the Amish some families will offer a home cooked meal. Amish fare is generally hearty, and may include dishes such as chicken and dumplings, meatloaf, or butter noodles with sides of mashed potatoes, carrots, and beans. A traditional dish is scrapple, also known as *pon haus*, which is a kind of Amish Spam made from pieces of pig not suitable for anything else. As they say, it contains everything but the oink! An Amish favorite after church on Sunday is a peanut butter spread blended with marshmallow, honey, or molasses, added to pickles, meat, and cheese all lumped together in a sandwich. They are celebrated bakers, and an Amish meal is usually finished with homemade pie, cookies, or cakes. Shoofly pie is a speciality. This molasses pie probably gets its name from the flies it attracts, that must be shooed away.

The Amish are usually thought of as preferring healthy, wholesome food, but they have also developed a fondness for junk food. Their buggies can be seen parked outside McDonald's, and kids are spotted eating Snickers bars and drinking Pepsi outside of Walmart and Family Dollar stores. Whatever they eat, during family meals they say grace both before *and* after eating.

In the Family Way

Family is of central importance to these communities. They typically have large families, and it is not unusual for a couple to have seven or more children. This is assisted by the Ordnung, which bans birth control and abortion. The Amish population doubles every 20 years by way of birth rates, not evangelism, although some call this a kind of "biological evangelism." Marriage is probably the most important milestone in one's life, and members typically marry at a young age, after they have decided to become baptized in the church. Divorce is forbidden, and homosexuality is simply denied, or it is viewed as a sin or a sickness that can be "cured" through confession and prayer.

Most of these groups practice endogamy. The Amish marry the Amish, and only within their own order. As a result, there are lots of common names in every community. In Allen County, Indiana, most people are Grabers, Lengachers, or Schmuckers. Marriage to second cousins is common. Centuries of intermarriage and genetic isolation have led to rare inherited disorders in these communities. These include Crigler-Najjar syndrome, which affects the liver, a type of dwarfism known as Ellis van Crevald syndrome, and Maple Syrup urine disease, a metabolic disorder named for the sweet odor of the sick child's urine. Some diseases are unique to these communities. Troyer Syndrome causes learning disorders and paralysis of the limbs, and is only found in the Old Order populations in Holmes County, Ohio. Infants suffering from Amish lethal microcephaly are born with a small head and underdeveloped brain, and usually only live for six months. This condition only occurs in Old Order groups in Pennsylvania. These communities also have a much higher incidence of muscular dystrophy, cystic fibrosis, and deafness.

One of the few matters not regulated by the Ordnung is health care. They pay their taxes, but they don't accept welfare or Medicare. Many Amish have their own insurance, where members from hundreds of different church districts share large unexpected medical or property expenses. They rarely have health care; it is expensive and is not "trusting in God." An Amish dentist is often the farmer armed with a pair of pliers who isn't squeamish. They often have a distrust of modern medicine. Patients may turn to prayer as a remedy, or simply resign themselves to an illness as God's will. Alternatively, they might visit a veterinarian instead; if the vet is taking a look at the horses he might as well take a look at the child. Livestock are typically vaccinated, but Amish children often aren't.

Instead of conventional medicine, many communities place their faith in alternative therapies, especially chiropractic, homeopathy, herbal medicine, and home remedies. A few people practice as medicine men and women for the community, and they take care of each other, and remember to "visit the sick and afflicted" (James 1:27). Traditional German, Chinese, and Native American folk medicine has become popular. For stubborn sicknesses, some people try powwowing ceremonies and "pain-pulling," where the healthy try to extract the pain from a sick person. If an Amish person will ever travel long distances, it will be for experimental treatments at a clinic in Mexico, or to visit a hot spring. Amish people have also been known to spend a week sitting in old abandoned uranium mines in the belief that it will cure arthritis.

Cut from the Same Cloth

You can't judge a Moderate Mennonite by his or her cover. However, conservative Mennonites and Amish still wear plain dress. This is intended to keep them separate from the "English," and to keep them the same as each other. They must dress modestly. They can't wear wrist watches, belts, or sunglasses, no tattoos, piercings, or jewelry, and they must adhere to a dress code. Typically, men wear a black suit and white shirt to church. On workdays they wear a blue shirt and trousers held up with suspenders. Shirts must be tucked in, T-shirts can only be worn under other clothes, and outside pockets are not allowed. Male members of the really conservative orders "go commando." Their shirts are long and double as a nightie, so they do not need to wear underwear.

These clothes are usually homemade, and every stitch is regulated by the Ordnung. The church dictates the precise design and measurements of seams, cuffs, collars, and colors. Infractions must be corrected, or else the member can be excommunicated. For some groups, even the order of dressing is dictated by the Ordnung, and shirts must be buttoned from top to bottom, although it makes you wonder how they can enforce that rule! The men wear beards, but moustaches are not allowed as historically they were associated with military men who were seen as warmongers, and persecutors of the Anabaptists. Beards also have matrimonial significance. Some stop trimming their beards when they marry, while others must adhere to the Ordnung in matters of length and style. A beard confirms that the man is spoken for in place of a wedding ring, because a ring can be taken off.

The Ordnung doesn't permit the "painting or powdering of face," that is, womenfolk are not allowed to wear makeup. Lipstick, jewelry, and trendy clothes invoke pride and vanity. These bans follow the Bible passage that teaches, "Your beauty should not come from outward adornment, such as elaborate hairstyles and the wearing of gold jewelry or fine clothes" (1 Peter 3:1–7). Instead, they usually wear long, plain dresses and sweaters in solid dark browns, blues, greys, and greens, with decent shoes and stockings. Women in the older orders don't wear bras or underwear as we know it, but that's not as naughty as it sounds. The Ordnung doesn't allow the use of elastic, so dresses are overlaid with an apron or "cape" that covers the bodice for extra modesty. Button, hook, and eye fasteners or straight pins (ouch!) are used instead of zippers or elastic. Instead of the lingerie you'll find at Victoria's Secret, they wear long, loose "unmentionables," lest they be too tight and sexually arousing to the wearer. Yes, there is a case where a young woman was disciplined for that.

As we know, the ultraconservative orders don't have indoor plumbing, so without running water in the home for showering, baths are usually taken once a week. The women in these communities are not allowed to wear perfumes, aftershaves, or deodorants, and women cannot shave their armpits or legs. They don't use tampons or sanitary napkins; instead they use rags that are washed and reused, and often shared among the women within a family.

If you're an Amish women you can leave your hat on, all of the time. The women wear a white prayer cap, while young girls wear a black hood. These head coverings are worn in obedience to Corinthians (11:1–16). "Every woman who prays or prophesies with her head uncovered dishonors her head—it is the same as having her head shaved. For if a woman does not cover her head, she might as well have her hair cut off; but if it is a disgrace for a woman to have her hair cut off or her head shaved, then she should cover her head." For this same reason, women grow their hair long and never cut it. They wind it up into a bun held in place with pins, but "no fancy hair clips," and cover their hair with a cap in public. They are also reminded to "pray at all times" (1 Timothy 2:8) and "always sing spiritual songs" (Ephesians 5:19). This has led to some obsessive theories about wearing prayer coverings. Some women fear that it is a sin to pray or simply think about prayer when they're not wearing their caps. Some are so scared of violating this rule that they wear their caps to bed, and even when they bathe.

Men wear straw hats during work and wide-brimmed black felt hats to church. However, they take off their hats during the service because Corinthians also says that during prayer, "A man ought not to cover his head, since he is the image and glory of God; but woman is the glory of man." Conservative orders are patriarchal. Although they aim for social equality with their plain clothes and simple living, some people are more equal than others. Corinthians teaches that, "the head of every man is Christ, and the head of the woman is man," so the Ordnung states that "the man should be the head of the house," while "the woman should be a help-meet for her husband." They argue that men and women are not unequal, they just have different purposes. Gender roles are distinct, and women are seen as mothers and homemakers. They are solely charged with the domestic tasks of cooking, cleaning, and making clothes, made even more laborious by the lack of modern conveniences. Men are the clear heads of the family, community, and church, while women are taught to be submissive and obedient to men.

Amish Gone Wild

Biologist and atheist Richard Dawkins has criticized the custom of imposing religious labels on children, such as "Catholic child" or "Muslim child," based on the parent's religion. Of course, no five-year-old child has religious beliefs other than those that have been indoctrinated. This is the fundamental concern of Anabaptists, who practice believer's baptism instead of infant baptism. Children may be called "Amish" as an ethnic label, although they are not considered to be members of the religion until they have been baptized. Baptism is only performed upon a person who has reached an age of accountability and has come to the freely made, informed decision to join the church and community. In this sense, it is like the Catholic Confirmation, the rite of initiation that seals the covenant made in baptism.

To enable the decision-making process, liberal Amish groups have the tradition of *Rumspringa*, the infamous "running-around time." Rumspringa is a period where the Amish-in-waiting is in a kind of religious limbo. From the age of 16 until the early 20s, the adolescent must make the choice to become baptized into the church, or not. As they are not yet under the authority of the church, some take this as an opportunity to experiment with the outside world and do the things the Ordnung doesn't allow the baptized to do. They wear "English" clothes and hairstyles, watch television and movies, play sports, listen to music, dance, and avoid church services. Some might get their driver's license and a car, while others might fit out their buggy with a stereo system. Like most other adolescents, they are likely to experiment with sex, drugs, and alcohol. However, Rumspringa isn't a licence to go wild, and this "English" behavior isn't so much allowed as unpunished.

The Amish are the image of wholesomeness and innocence, and so the media adores the irony of the badass Amish boy and the good girl gone bad. They sensationalize rumspringa as a lurid, nonstop partying spring break for Amish youths. The documentary *The Devil's Playground*, an Amish pejorative for the "English" world, shows girls in plain dress smoking cigarettes, and talks about "Amish drug dealers" who've entered the world of organized crime. The "reality" TV show *Breaking Amish* claims that Amish communities are hotbeds of bestiality. These accusations come amid revelations that the show itself is contrived. The actors are lapsed Anabaptists, some of whom have been married and divorced, and already have children. In reality, Rumspringa is more mild than wild and youths simply go on a few dates and play volleyball.

Rumspringa is definitely a time for dating, with the expectation that the youth will find a marriage partner. During their dating they are reminded to "Keep pure," as per Ephesians 5:26–27, Titus 1:15, and Titus 2:14). The Swartzentruber Amish don't have Rumspringa, but they do have a custom that is unexpectedly scandalous. They allow courting couples to go on dates, but a Swartzentruber date is not exactly a movie or school dance. Instead, they practice "bed courtship." The young suitor visits the woman when she's already in bed and asks if he may stay the night. If she accepts, he takes off his hat, jacket, and shoes, and slips into bed with her. They lie side by side in her bed for the night. The temptations are high, and they are allowed to *schmunzle*, that is, to hug and kiss, but they are not supposed to go all the way. Some invariably do, which simply results in a faster marriage. The youths can go on multiple dates, and even see multiple people. Bed courtship is derived from the older European practice of "bundling," where a board is placed between the youths when they share a bed. Another dating practice is the "rocking chair date," where the young couple spend the night together sitting in a rocking chair in the living room or kitchen.

Rumspringa isn't a lost weekend. After they have sown their wild oats for months to years they have to make the decision as to whether they should join the church or not. If they become baptized they must relinquish their driver's licenses, cell phones, jeans, and baseball caps. The girls tend to join earlier than the boys, while the boys often join because they've fallen in love with an Amish girl who has declared her intentions to join the church. Most Amish are prodigal sons and daughters, and between 85–90 percent will become baptized in the church. There are reasons for this high retention rate.

Rumspringa releases these kids into the big bad world, naive and unprepared. In some ways, this shock exposure is designed to drive them back to the safe bosom of the church. It is just too difficult for them to make the transition to the "English" world alone. They are citizens of the United States, but they have no social security number, and more conservative orders do not issue their members with birth certificates. They have no money, support system, or real-world experience. With an eighth grade education and gaps in the curriculum, they are undereducated. An Amish education only qualifies them to be Amish. These youths are coerced to join the church after a lifetime of socialization and religious indoctrination, and their choice is really an ultimatum.

Once they become baptized there is a major deterrent to ever leaving the church. Those who leave face the same fate as those who violate the Ordnung; they are excommunicated and shunned. This social avoidance of erring members is known as *Meidung*, the German word for "avoidance." Those who leave the church are ostracized by their family, friends, and community. As always, there is a biblical model for this, "Now I beseech you, brethren, mark them who cause divisions and offenses contrary to the doctrine which you have learned; and avoid them" (Romans 16:17).

Nothing Is Ever Simple

The Amish attempt to detach themselves from modern society, but the outside world imposes itself nevertheless. In hate crimes known as "claping" or "Amo-bashing," the Amish become victims of verbal and physical assault, property damage, and robberies. Attacks on horses and buggies are common, in which the culprits play college-humor pranks. They scare the horses with firecrackers, squirt drivers and passengers with a mixture of chicken feces and water, and throw rocks, eggs, water balloons, or bags of flour at them. Aggressive drivers swerve at the buggies, cover them in a cloud of dust, or force them off the road. The Amish are easy targets, as they turn the other cheek, and don't fight back. As the Ordnung says, "do not get angry," and "do not seek revenge" (Romans 12:19).

One of the most well-known attacks is the tragedy that occurred at the West Nickel Mines School in Pennsylvania on October 2, 2006. Charles Carl Roberts entered the Old Order Amish classroom armed with a handgun, a shotgun, a rifle, a stun gun, knives, and a tube of K-Y sexual lubricant. He rounded up the female students who were aged six to thirteen, while he freed the teacher and the boys. He phoned his wife from the scene and confessed that he had previously molested two young girls and he was tempted to sexually abuse again. After holding his victims hostage for two hours, he shot ten of the girls, five of whom died. Then he committed suicide.

Sometimes the hate crimes come from within the community. Out of Youngstown, Ohio, came stories of the bizarre exploits of Sam Mullet, an Amish bishop and father of eighteen. Using scissors and battery powered shavers, Mullet and his gang went on a beard-cutting spree of rival community members. They also cut off the long hair of their wives. As we know, beards and women's long hair have spiritual significance to these folks, while facial hair is a sign of manhood. Cutting off a man's beard is like castrating him, but also tantamount to cutting off Sampson's hair. Mullet kidnapped a number of men and imprisoned them in chicken coops, while their wives were forced to live with him in his commune. Some of these women were sexually abused under the guise of "marital counseling." Mullet is one of those who made a fortune out of leasing his land for oil and gas rights.

Amish communities are cloaked in secrecy, but in recent years, these communities are being revealed to be oppressive, abusive environments for women and children. Startling cases of pedophilia, incest, and physical and sexual abuse have emerged from within several Amish communities. One such case is the story of Mary Byler, whose childhood and adolescence were filled with physical attacks and molestation. Her stepfather beat her with shovels, hacksaws, and his fists, in the name of discipline. When she was six-years-old her twelve-year-old brother Johnny began raping her. Soon, her brothers Eli and David started molesting her too. They trapped her in the outhouse, the dairy, or her bedroom, to rape her repeatedly. Amish women aren't provided with a sex education, so Mary couldn't even explain what had happened. The only word she had to describe the events was that her brothers were doing something "bad" to her.

The worst thing about the way these communities deal with crime is that they don't. The Amish often don't report offenders to the authorities. The church ordinances condemn civil lawsuits, and by extension, they prefer not to involve the law but to resolve disputes internally. As the Ordnung says, "Take matters to the church rather than to law enforcement" (1 Corinthians 6:1). This often means they close ranks after a crime has been committed. Amish whistleblower David Yoder admitted a sad crime that was covered up by his community in St. Lawrence County, NY. His sister murdered his niece Amanda Miller within days of her birth, probably as a result of postnatal depression. When she confessed her crime to an Amish bishop, she was told, "This can never leave this room. It has to remain this way for the betterment of the community."

Alternatively, the Amish believe that the perpetrator's confession and repentance is enough. The Ordnung says to "Have a forgiving spirit" (Colossians 3:13). The Amish forgive and forget, the slate is clean, and they act as if the crime never happened. The press and public marveled at the Amish community's forgiveness of the Nickel Mines shooter and compassion for his family, for whom they set up a charitable fund. However, within the community there is no assistance for the victims, and they have no advocates. The Amish ethos protects the abuser instead of the abused. When Mary Byler told her mother about the abuses, she responded with, "You don't fight hard enough and you don't pray hard enough."

Simply, the Amish don't know how to deal with these problems. Mainstream society doesn't know how to deal with these Amish problems either. When the Amish do try to get the authorities involved, they are often reluctant to intervene. The crimes are often misconstrued or dismissed as religious customs, and the involvement of the authorities is therefore viewed as an infringement of religious freedom. Modern society is more often concerned with protecting religious rights than human rights. Amish justice is either too minor, or too severe. Punishments may involve a public confession and apology. At worst an offender may be expelled from church for a few weeks. In this system, someone who drinks to the point of intoxication receives the same punishment as a child molester.

One day Mary's four-year-old sister approached her, admitting that their brother David was doing something "bad" to her. Mary then knew she needed to seek outside help. Her brothers had eventually confessed in church and apologized, but this wasn't enough. When she sought legal recourse, her mother accused her of being "unforgiving." In her eyes, her sons had already been punished. The Amish believe that to err is human but to forgive is divine, but when the community punishes the offender there are no real-world consequences for the criminals. Their unquestioning forgiveness absolves the criminals of restitution and legitimate repentance, and deprives the victims of justice. Fortunately, in Mary's case, her brothers and her stepfather all received time in jail or on probation, and even her mother was placed on probation for failing to protect her daughter.

Mary eventually escaped the Amish, but many emerging stories suggest that her experiences are not uncommon. Women are discouraged from speaking out about abuse. Wives in abusive marriages are trapped, as divorce means excommunication and shunning. Patriarchal societies devalue and even dehumanize women, making abuse easier. The Amish see patriarchy as the natural social order, but in the eyes of modern society, women are treated like second-class citizens in these communities.

The Amish lifestyle is often far from *Utopia* and more like *1984*, with the Ordnung as a kind of Big Brother. By overseeing trivial issues such as the design of underwear, and interpreting violations as sins punishable by excommunication, these communities have uncomfortable parallels to a dictatorship, or a cult. The Ordnung is not the word of God, it is the word of Amish bishops and pastors. The rules are subjective, not divine, as the Bible is strangely silent about cars and computers. Some conservative orders use the Martin Luther version of the Bible in its original sixteenth century German, so the congregation is forced to rely on the clergy's interpretation of the Bible, and rules. Yet followers are unquestioning, and often they don't even understand why some practices are off-limits. The invocation of archaic Bible passages as explanations for the rules is simply confirmation bias for blind faith.

The Amish and these related religions are romanticized by many Americans. No one wants this bubble burst, and they have many apologists. Of course, they are only human, and have problems like everyone else, and there is dysfunction and deviance in every community. Clearly we have unrealistic standards for these people, and we need to take them off the pedestal, and out of the fiction books. In trying to not be discriminatory we are allowing discrimination to occur. In protecting minority values we are defying those of the greater society. If people want to live the Bible they should follow the tenets that teach us to "obey the laws of the land." Despite their desire for segregation, conservative Anabaptist communities still have an unavoidable dependence upon mainstream societies. They must live alongside others in the greater community that is this country, where they are unavoidably influenced by modern morals, values, and culture. They are in this world, and of this world.

The Day of Rest

Outsiders are not openly welcomed to attend worship in Amish and Mennonite churches. Usually the services are conducted in German or Pennsylvania Dutch, so no one would understand what was being said anyway. However, I was an outsider with an inside connection. My father-in-law was formerly the town marshal of a small town in rural Colorado. He spoke warmly of the Mennonite community who never gave him any trouble. He put me in contact with Abram Hershberger, one of the church elders, who kindly invited me to attend a 9:30 a.m. Sunday service.

Amish worship usually takes place in the home of a member, and families take it in turns to hold services. Mennonite services are held in a church that also serves as a schoolhouse and community center. I arrived at the address I'd been given, but the building looked like an old barn house. There was no sign indicating that this was a church. Something was clearly going on, as the car lot was full of large SUVs and trucks, which were all black. I wondered if I had the wrong address. I stepped out of the car and when I turned around I felt like I had suddenly stumbled into a BBC period drama. I saw a group of bearded men in black suits with black hats, accompanied by women wearing long dresses and caps. Like deer caught in headlights, we were both frozen as we stared at each other.

Eventually, I approached them and explained that I had been invited to attend the service. One of the men laughed and replied, "I saw you in your little white car. I thought you were lost!" The "little" car was an SUV. These people are Mennonites but by no means luddites. They had some surprisingly expensive cars, and as we chatted we discussed computers and cell phones. This Mennonite community is somewhat isolated, but they are not completely off the grid. They shop in the local supermarkets along with everyone else, and obviously, they buy their vehicles from car dealerships. Of course they've seen non-Mennonite people before, but just not in *their* church!

The Mennonites were all wearing their Sunday best. The men wore dark suits with suspenders with freshly ironed white shirts. They wore black felt hats, which they took off as soon as they entered the church. They all had beards, indicating they were taken men. These were luxurious, manicured beards that almost looked like they were fake. The young boys were dressed like they were forced to attend a wedding, in white shirts, black trousers, and shiny black shoes. The women were immaculately groomed. They wore ankle-length dresses in dark blue or green, and black stockings with heeled black shoes. Their hair was swept up into neat buns that were covered with white organza caps. These were kept in place with straight pins, and the strings were left untied. The girls wore brightly colored dresses in pastel blue, purple, and even pink. Their smooth hair was long and plaited, and they didn't wear caps. Wearing jeans and a hoodie I stood awkwardly among the taffeta and chiffon, but you would have thought I was wearing haute couture on the runway for the way the young girls stared in admiration of my "English" clothes.

The Mennonites arrive as families, but enter the church as members of the church family. They stood waiting for everyone to arrive, the men to one side, the women to the other. Both brethren and sisters greeted each other with a kiss, but not a demure peck on the check. These were full-blown kisses on the lips, where the men kissed the men, and the women kissed the women. This is not simply a greeting, it is known as the "Holy Kiss," which is symbolic of love and acceptance toward each other, and to God. The act is mentioned in the Bible many times, such as the passage 2 Corinthian 13:12, "Greet one another with an holy kiss." As a punishment, the kiss is often withheld to erring brethren. Some mischievous boys only pretend to kiss, which is known as the "Holy Miss."

As a visitor, I was greeted by everyone with a handshake. I met a woman named Fannie who took me under her wing and introduced me to the other women. "This is Abram's daughter," she said, before introducing me to "another one of Abram's daughters" and yet "another one of Abram's daughters." "What a big family Abram has!" I exclaimed. There were at least fifty people in attendance, but they mostly seemed to be Hershbergers.

"Will this service be similar to a Protestant service?" I asked the ladies. They looked at each other blankly, and then back at me. A woman was brought over as an authority. "I know who we are! We're Amish Mennonites!" she explained. Many Anabaptists don't know the history or even the name of their religion or their specific order. Like "Anabaptist," "Mennonite," and "Amish," these names are often imposed on them.

Everyone began taking their seats. "Where should I sit?" I asked. "Anywhere you like, but we have segregation. The men sit on the left and the women sit on the right." There was generational order to the seating too. As a guest I was invited to sit down the front, but the usual order is that the elder women sit in the front rows while the younger women sit in the back rows. The young, unmarried girls sat at a pew along the wall, while young unmarried boys sat facing them on the opposite side of the room. I sat with Fannie in one of the front rows.

Their plain and simple lifestyle extends to their worship. The inside of the church was sparsely furnished and unadorned. There weren't any crosses or candles, just clocks on the walls and rows of pews. Unlike the Swarzentruber Amish who forbid padded furniture, these Mennonite pews were outfitted with padding. This was fortunate, because the service lasts two hours, although my Amish informant tells me, "Lucky you! Many Amish church services last three hours!"

There is no choir; the entire congregation is the choir. When everyone was seated an elder called out a number. There was a rustling sound as they all opened their hymnbooks. He started singing and they all suddenly chimed in on a German hymn. They sang a cappella style, and sounded like a group of trained opera singers. They even sang in harmony. Fannie sang the melody, while the woman beside me was singing alto notes. The men were singing bass and tenor parts. Whoever chose the hymn would sing the first word of every verse, and then the rest of the congregation joined in with the singing. The sound was so beautiful and overwhelming as it echoed in the large room, and I could feel my eyes welling up with tears.

The clergy are lay members of the community without theological training and they aren't paid for their duties. Pastor Richard gave the first sermon to the congregation, and fortunately it was in English. He spoke about the importance of a woman's role as a wife and mother. "I love holding a baby, but I feel it's so fragile I might drop it. Women have a natural instinct to hold babies and raise them. This is what God intended." In what felt like a speech directed at me, he gently disapproved of those modern women who strive for equality, "Women are different to men and shouldn't try to be like men." He also admitted that he feels sorry for atheists. "When we see a beautiful sunset we can thank God for that sunset. When atheists see beauty they have no one to thank."

Following the sermon it was time for a prayer. Instead of resting on a kneeler in front of the pew, everyone turned to face their seats and knelt down on the cold concrete floor with their hands clasped in prayer. Pastor Richard prayed that the congregation would avoid drunkenness and overcome lust, and that those in courtship would "stay pure." By now my knees were hurting and I realized that my prayer muscles weren't in good shape. The donation basket was then passed around, but only to the men, a few of whom tossed in hundred dollar bills.

Pastor William then took the stand. He also spoke at length about the evils of drunkenness and how hard it is to ignore lust. It was clear that these people are faithful, although they struggle with their faith. It also seemed that they were living their lives for death. "Would I long for Heaven if my life was the way I wanted it to be?" he asked sadly. The simple lifestyle isn't so simple, but they believe that the harder it is on Earth, the sweeter it will be in Heaven.

After the service, the women gathered around me to chat. These friendly people seemed hungry for outside company, and excited to hear about different experiences told in a different accent. I was invited to lunch by four different women. This was their day of rest, and there was no work to be done on Sundays, except for making lunch. I was affected deeply by their kindness and generosity, and I complimented Fannie on this. "Your community has such a wonderful reputation for being hardworking, honest, and peaceful," I said. "Well, that's very sweet," she said shyly, and in the modesty typical of the Mennonites, "but we're only human, and we make mistakes just like everyone else."

Chapter 3
Signs, Wonders, and Miracles
Charismatics and Pentecostals

"These are the days of miracles and wonder."
—Paul Simon

A woman raced over and introduced herself as Cici, the pastor's wife, who would be conducting the ceremony. "What should we expect here tonight?" I asked. "Anything and everything!" Cici said excitedly. "We've witnessed some incredible healings and miracles in the past few weeks. All I know is that God is gonna show up tonight!"

Gifts from God
Charismatic Christianity is not about people with great charisma, although many of its leaders are indeed charismatic. The movement has its roots in the Apostolic Age of the Bible, which is generally taken to be between the years 33–115 AD. Jesus had just been crucified, and it was now left up to the twelve Apostles to preach the Gospel. This was a tough job without the Messiah and his miracles to prove they were under orders from God. So, when Jesus was resurrected he promised to send the Holy Spirit to help the Apostles evangelize. These were the times when the Apostles spoke in tongues, raised the dead, predicted the future, and performed other signs, wonders, and miracles. These were all gifts or "charisms" from the Holy Spirit. The Charismatic movement

and Pentecostals believe that the Holy Spirit is present in our lives today, bringing modern-day signs, wonders, and miracles.

It all began on the first Day of Pentecost after the crucifixion. As it is described in Acts (2:1–41), the Apostles were celebrating this feast day with over 100 pilgrims. Suddenly, a "mighty wind" tore through the room, and "tongues of fire" fell from above. These flaming tongues landed upon everyone at the gathering. They had all been filled with the Holy Spirit, and began speaking about the wonders of God, but something strange had happened. The people were from different parts of the world, including Judea, Egypt, Asia, and Rome, and they all spoke different languages. However, after the Holy Spirit had descended upon them, the people all heard everyone speaking in their native tongue. It was a kind of inverse Tower of Babel. The Bible calls this phenomenon "speaking in tongues."

By now a crowd had gathered, and those who were speaking in tongues were accused of being drunk. The Apostle Peter addressed the crowd, explaining that they weren't drunk; it was only 9 a.m. in the morning! He then preached the story of Jesus, and the members of the crowd felt shamed by their part in the crucifixion. Remorsefully, they asked the Apostles, "Brothers, what shall we do?" Peter replied, "Repent and be baptized, every one of you, in the name of Jesus Christ for the forgiveness of your sins. And you will receive the gift of the Holy Spirit. (Acts 2:38) Some three thousand people were converted to Christianity that day, and Pentecost became known as the "Birthday of the Church." Now filled with the Holy Spirit, the Apostles went on to perform many other signs, wonders and miracles.

To Set Tongues Wagging

The Holy Spirit waited for almost two thousand years before appearing again in Topeka, Kansas (of course). This is where pastor Charles Fox Parham managed his Bethel Bible School. One day he asked his students to ponder the meaning of "Receiving Baptism of the Holy Spirit." After a few days of consideration, the class came to the conclusion that this referred to speaking in tongues, and that one of their fellow students could actually do it! Agnes Ozman had already given them a convincing demonstration. As the story goes, in the first minutes of the year 1901, Parham and his class prayed over Ozman, and performed the laying on of hands. Within minutes, she began speaking in tongues! This time there wasn't a mighty wind, or tongues of fire from the sky. Instead, a halo appeared around Ozman's face, and then she began speaking Chinese. Soon, Parham and the other students began speaking in tongues too. These events are generally believed to have sparked the Pentecostal movement.

Following this discovery, Parham proceeded to open Bible colleges in Houston, Texas, and began baptizing people in the Holy Spirit. One of his students was a young African American man by the name of William Joseph Seymour. He was soon invited to preach at a church in Los Angeles, but he only delivered one sermon before he was locked out of the building for his unorthodox beliefs. He began speaking in private homes instead, and his quirky services quickly gained a following. Seymour found a permanent residence at 312 Azusa Street, a rundown shack that had once been a church, but in recent years had served as a warehouse, a barn, and even a shop that built tombstones. The first meeting was held at this location on April 14, 1906, and it ignited a movement that became known as the Azusa Street Revival.

Within months, the newly named Apostolic Faith Mission was packed with thousands of worshippers on a weekly basis. The meetings would begin in the morning and often last twelve hours or longer. These weren't typical sermons. Instead, there was speaking in tongues, shouting, singing, and shaking, while Seymour kneeled on the ground screaming "Repent!" again and again. The faithful believed these were manifestations of the Holy Spirit, although it seemed more of a manifestation of mass hysteria as they howled, cried, rolled, and jumped. People were slammed against the wall by the spirit, they danced like they were drunk, or they lay still on the floor for hours as if in a coma. They became known as Holy Rollers, Holy Jumpers, Holy Ghosters, and Tangled Tonguers.

The services attracted people from diverse religions, including Methodists, Mennonites, Quakers, Baptists, and mediums from the spiritualism movement. This was during the height of the Jim Crow era, yet the congregation united men, women, and children of all ages, ethnicities, and socioeconomic backgrounds. Not everyone appreciated this at the time. As pastor Parham observed in disgust during a visit, "Men and women, white and blacks, knelt together or fell across one another; a white woman, perhaps of wealth and culture, could be seen thrown back in the arms of a big 'buck nigger,' and held tightly thus as she shivered and shook in freak imitation of Pentecost. Horrible, awful shame!" Parham had hoped to lead this new movement, but it had already evolved beyond him. However, he still had a legacy to fulfill. Parham, married with children, became embroiled in a scandal in 1907. He was arrested on charges of sodomy with two young men, and so, he also established a precedent of hypocritical preachers. The Azusa Street Revival lasted into 1913, but lives on today as the strange origins of the Pentecostal movement.

Pentecostal versus Charismatic versus Christianity

For their crazy antics, these frenzied worshippers were chased out of their churches, so they formed their own, which became known as Pentecostal churches, such as the Assemblies of God, and the Church of God. So, who are the Charismatics? People often get confused between Charismatics and Pentecostals, but they're not the same thing. Like the saying, "All bourbons are whiskeys, but not all whiskeys are bourbons"; all Pentecostals are Charismatic, but not all Charismatics are Pentecostal. The difference is in the origins. Pentecostalism came first, and Charismatic Christianity was inspired by Pentecostalism.

For some people the swinging sixties were also the singing, swooning, and shaking sixties. In 1960 Dennis Bennet took Pentecostalism back into mainline Christianity when he testified to his Episcopal congregation that he had received a baptism of the Holy Spirit. That is, he had spoken in tongues. He was asked to resign from his ministry at the St. Mark's Episcopal Church in Van Nuys, California, but the mighty wind had already begun. Bennett ignited the Charismatic movement in modern Christianity, and it really took hold in the late 1960s.

Charismatics occasionally form their own churches that are known by a confusing array of names, such as Neo-Pentecostal, Neo-Charismatic, Reformed, Empowered, or Renewalist. However, Charismatics typically stay within the mainstream denominations, including the Anglican, Lutheran, Baptist, Orthodox, and Catholic churches. Of course, Catholics are no strangers to mysticism. The infamous Padre Pio claimed to have many ecstatic spiritual experiences, including holy visions and the ability to bilocate, although he is best known for allegedly bearing the stigmata.

With some 500 million adherents worldwide, Charismatics are by no means a minority religion. About 25 percent of Christians are Charismatic, but they are much maligned by other Christians. A divisive debate rages on between the two groups. Mainstream Christians are cessationists, that is, they believe that signs, wonders, and miracles ceased with the death of the early Apostles in the first century. Charismatics are continuationists, that is, they believe that signs, wonders, and miracles continue today.

Mainstream Christians accuse Charismatic beliefs and practices of being unscriptural. In response, Charismatics invoke passages from Romans 12, Corinthians 12, Ephesians 4, and Peter 4 to support their theory that gifts of the Holy Spirit are modern-day experiences. In its usual self-contradictory style, the Bible also speaks of counterfeit miracles and false prophets appearing in the "last days." Therefore, Mainstream Christians believe that the so-called gifts of prophecy, healing, and speaking in tongues are occult practices that are the work of Satan, not of God, and they view the Charismatic movement as a cult. However, Charismatics believe that the Holy Spirit also gives them the gift of "discerning spirits" as either being good or evil. If they encounter Satan they'll stomp on him, or cast him into the fiery pit.

The most famous "gifts" from the Holy Spirit include prophecy, divine healing, speaking in tongues, and the interpretation of tongues. However, the gifts themselves are a matter of interpretation, for example, not all Charismatics practice speaking in tongues. According to the Bible there are additional gifts, including mercy, teaching, serving, and giving, but they aren't supernatural enough, and tend to slip peoples' minds. Some gifts no one seems to want to accept, such as the gift of celibacy. Whatever gifts they believe in or don't believe in, it is all about the personal experience. Some are so desperate to have an experience that they exaggerate their "gifts." Some are so desperate for other people to have an experience that they even fake them.

A Guiding Spirit

A Charismatic service can be like a rock concert. Worship is typically led by a band, or there is a choir, although everybody sings along, and shouts, and claps, and testifies. These services are often large. As they see it, the more the merrier, and they hold sermons and events in mega-churches, amphitheaters, fairgrounds, and football stadiums. Televangelist Joel Osteen of the Lakewood Church in Houston, Texas, has a regular congregation of 38,000 people.

Charismatic services are about expressive worship. When the congregation "comes under the power" of the Holy Spirit, the service becomes a kind of pious possession, or a religious rave. Like the days of the Azusa Street Mission, people enter into a "spiritual drunkenness" where their bodies begin shaking, jerking, twitching, and gyrating. Others lay on the floor frozen in religious ecstasy known as being "slain in the spirit." Some people experience uncontrollable laughter, sobbing, or a burning sensation in their bodies. Often their eyes roll into the back of their heads. The congregation is whipped up into a frenzy by the minister shouting "Fire!" "Lord!" "Jesus!" "Now!" "More!" "Boom!" and "Bam!" like a comic book character. Charismatic Christianity is a religion for extroverts, and a safe outlet for introverts.

This is what happened at the Toronto Airport Vineyard Church in January 1994. In an incident known as the "Toronto Blessing," over one hundred people were spontaneously seized by the Holy Spirit. They fell to the floor in an ecstatic trance, or began rolling, bouncing, crying, and shaking in euphoria. This Woodstock of religion quickly attracted large crowds on a daily basis where people reported divine healings and prophetic visions. Common manifestations included "Holy Laughter," where people "roared like lions" as they fell into hysterical convulsions of laughter, and "crunching," a kind of holy vomiting where people dry heaved as they "cleansed" their bodies of negative experiences.

These events sparked the "Brownsville Blessing" at the Assembly of God church in Pensacola, Florida, in 1995. During a sermon by Reverends

John Kirkpatrick and Steve Hill, a "mighty wind" blew through church, heralding the arrival of the Holy Spirit. Just like the Toronto Blessing, the congregation was struck by religious ecstasy. The good word spread like wildfire and started a revival. People attended services in droves so they too could "get right with God." These Holy Rollers rolled and writhed on the floor as they spoke in tongues, while others "rested in the spirit," laying dead still on the floor for many hours. There were many miracles; drug addicts were delivered, and cancerous tumors disappeared. Between the years 1995 and 2000, millions of people attended these meetings. They waited in the parking lot before dawn to be able to attend a service like they were lining up to get tickets for a rock concert. Their fervor sparked revivals in Atlanta, St. Louis, Anaheim, and many other cities across the United States.

However, it seems the "mighty wind" was just a load of hot air. Revivals are the Holy Grail for ministers. They reinvigorate ministries and attract attendees and donations, and Kirkpatrick wanted one at his church. Months before the service, Kirkpatrick spoke persistently about bringing a revival to his church, and threatened to quit if he didn't have the support of his congregation. Kirkpatrick studied the methods used at the Toronto Blessing, and then coached his congregation by screening videos of the revival. He brought in followers of evangelist Rodney Howard-Browne to demonstrate highly expressive worship, and enlisted evangelist Steve Hill to orchestrate the revival meeting. In reality, the legendary service was a dismal failure. Video footage reveals Kirkpatrick and Hill struggling to coax their congregation to respond. They anoint people and badger them desperately to fall down, with promises that they will witness and experience amazing things. However, most people simply stood around looking confused, while many others left the service in disgust. Kirkpatrick and Hill fabricated the story of an amazing meeting, and spread the news that kick-started the revival. They were obviously better promoters than preachers.

All That Glitters Isn't Gold

In the late 1990s, reports of dental miracles emerged across North and South America. God was apparently transforming people's silver amalgam fillings and crowns or entire teeth to gold during Charismatic services. Dull, old fillings became shiny and new looking. Supernatural fillings and crowns appeared inexplicably where people hadn't even had dental work. It was believed that these "miracles" were the fulfillment of God's promise in Psalm 81:10, "I am the Lord your God, who brought you up out of Egypt. Open wide your mouth and I will fill it." For those who didn't need fillings, they claimed that angels of dentistry cleaned, whitened, or straightened out their teeth. Many patients of this divine dentistry visited their dentists to verify their claims, but the explanations weren't so miraculous. In many cases they were mistaken, and their mortal dentists explained that their amalgam fillings hadn't turned to gold. Those who claimed to have new or shiny fillings had unwittingly polished them by grinding their teeth, or eating something acidic. Others had simply forgotten about dental work that had been done previously.

Claims of supernatural dentistry continue to this day, while modern Charismatics tell of other "creative miracles" they have witnessed. In church services fit for Liberace, people report angel feathers, gemstones, and gold dust raining down "from Heaven." Pastor Bill Johnson of the Bethel Church in Redding, California, says he has seen feathers fall from the skies during church services. At first he thought that birds might be nesting in the air-conditioning ducts. Now he believes that the feathers are from angels, and says he has seen them appear in the homes of congregation members, in restaurants, and even on a plane. He interprets them as a sign from God, and a reference to the biblical passage, "the sun of righteousness will rise with healing in its wings (Malachi 4:2). An investigation by an ornithologist revealed that these feathers were not of heavenly origin, but from an earthly bird. Nevertheless, reports of angel feathers and Holy Ghost feathers have spread across the country.

Another miraculous phenomenon is the appearance of supernatural "gold dust," "diamond dust," or "sapphire dust" falling on parishioners during worship. Brazilian evangelist Silvania Macado sheds gold dust from her hair and oozes holy oil from her skin when she prays for others. Samples of the "gold dust" were tested by the U.S. Geological Survey, which discovered that the substance was a type of plastic film or glitter, with no gold content. Macado responded with the statement, "To me, it doesn't matter what it is as long as it's from God." If it is indeed from God, He must shop at the Hobby Lobby.

Non-Charismatic Christians label all of these phenomena as false signs and counterfeit miracles, while skeptics see them as magic tricks and gimmicks. Evangelist Joshua Mills is the Padre Pio of Charismatic Christianity. He claims that gold dust appears "like a holy explosion" on his clothes, hair, and skin. "Wine-scented" oil oozes from the palms of his hands. These occurrences are about as miraculous as pulling a coin out of someone's ear, and they are simple tricks that any illusionist can replicate easily. A talented piano player, Mills claims that he learned how to play supernaturally, and that the Holy Spirit guides his fingers. However, during an interview he admits that he learned how to play piano as a child.

Patricia King proves that diamonds are an Evangelist's best friend. On her show *Extreme Prophetic TV*, King claims that "gemstones from Heaven" have manifested during her services, and in the homes of her parishioners. Diamonds, rubies, sapphires, and emeralds have appeared in people's shoes, beds, and clothes, and by their feet or under their seats in church. One parishioner says he saw an angel dropping jewels on his front lawn. In photographs these "gems" look like cheap bling from clothing or accessories. Evangelists Todd Bentley and Rick Joyner announce during their meetings that there will be a "supernatural release" of gemstones. However, in several cases, assistants have been caught red-handed planting bird feathers, glitter, and plastic gemstones in churches to fool their congregation into believing they have had a spiritual experience.

Catholic "weeping statues" that cry oil or milk, and those of the Virgin Mary that leak "breast milk," have long been debunked as tricks, but the claims continue. There are also modern miraculous claims of scented oil dripping from church walls and artworks, or seeping out of the pages of Bibles. Other alleged phenomena include visitations of angels, and the appearance of a "heavenly" mist or clouds. Photographs of churches and homes reveal "glory orbs" that are believed to be materializations of the Holy Spirit. These "orbs" were popularized by ghost hunters as "ghosts," although they are a natural phenomenon caused by dust particulates or natural photographic artifacts.

The latest trends in modern miracles include dermatological miracles, where unwanted tattoos, moles, and scars magically "disappear" from people's skin. Money has mysteriously appeared in people's wallets and bank accounts (although typically your money is taken). David Herzog is an Evangelist who claims he can turn metal rods and screws in the body back to bone, and that he can teleport people to a new physical location. He is best known for producing "supernatural hair growth," and "instant weight loss miracles," where parishioners' pounds melt away before their very eyes, although they simply look like they wore baggy clothes to the service. Joshua Mills also performs "supernatural weight loss," although it hasn't worked on his wife Janet.

Prophet or Profit?

A classic charism is the gift of prophecy. This is when someone receives a direct revelation from the Holy Spirit in the form of a vision, dream, or a "word of knowledge." In some Charismatic churches, anyone and everyone receive prophecies. They testify these messages during the service, and a typical revelation may be a text from the Bible, a prayer, a verse from a hymn, a personal experience, advice, or just an idea.

My friend Angie grew up in a Charismatic church in Georgia. When attending church one Sunday she sat down beside her friends. They promptly moved to another pew. Other members of the congregation refused to make eye contact with her. She had no idea what was going on, until her best friend cornered her when she came out of the restroom. The preacher had received a "message from God" that she was doing drugs, and he had advised the congregation that it would be best if they didn't associate with her. Angie was only twelve years old at the time and she wasn't taking drugs. The message was more slanderous than prophetic, especially when she had a real problem in her life. She said, "The worst part of all is that if he was going to get a damn message from 'God,' that he didn't hear the part about my stepdad raping me."

In other churches, only a select few have the gift of prophecy, while the rest of the congregation "discern" the messages, to weed out the false prophecies. There's a fine line between the True Prophet and the fortune-teller. Some believe that messages from God are intended for good, and must comfort, encourage, strengthen, or inspire. If the message creates fear, negativity, or conflict, then it is believed to be from Satan, or someone with an agenda. The Bible has a simple test for determining the legitimacy of a prophet, "When a prophet speaks in the name of the Lord, if the word does not come to pass or come true, that is a word that the Lord has not spoken" (Deuteronomy 18:22). In the Old Testament, the penalty for false prophecy was death, but in the New Testament, false prophets were merely blinded (Acts 13:6–12), cast into a pit of darkness (2 Peter 2:4), or thrown into a lake of fire and brimstone and tormented for all eternity (Revelation 19:20). Fortunately, the Evangelist Bob Jones received a direct revelation from God that modern prophets are required to be accurate only 66 percent of the time.

Evangelists use all of the tricks and techniques of psychics, to give the appearance that they can predict the future. Todd Bentley is known for his horoscope-like prophecies. His parishioners line up and he dispenses ambiguous predictions about their career, health, and relationships. This is a method known as "cold reading," where the person uses generalizations and personal cues to provide a convincing reading. Before anyone can contradict him or ask questions, Bentley strikes them in the name of the Holy Spirit, and they fall backward into the arms of catchers. Many Evangelists also perform "hot readings," otherwise known as cheating. They surreptitiously gather data about their congregation and make "predictions" that are suspiciously accurate.

Many Evangelists stick to vague forecasts about the economy and politics, or safe predictions of common natural disasters, such as earthquakes and hurricanes. If they don't come to pass, they just haven't happened yet and the date is pushed out. When disasters do occur, they are interpreted as God's punishment for our sins. Pat Robertson blamed Hurricane Katrina on America's abortion policy, while John Hagee said it was divine retribution for Southern Decadence, the annual gay pride event in New Orleans. Collectively, these disasters and events are believed to be signs of the end times.

The main problem with specific prophecies is that they can be proven false when they don't eventuate. Nevertheless, Evangelists specialize in failed doomsday predictions. Billy Graham predicted the end of the world in 1952. William Branham, the founder of the modern faith healing movement, preached that Jesus would return to earth in 1977. Pat Robertson prophesized that the world would end in October or November of 1982. When the year came and went he played it safe and said that God had told him the end was nigh, but we could avoid catastrophe if we "prayed real hard." Harold Camping has singlehandedly had almost as many failed end of days predictions as the Jehovah's Witnesses. He predicted the rapture would occur on September 6, 1994. When this didn't happen, Camping revised the date to September 29, and then to October 2 of that year. The boy who cried Armageddon, he tried again for May 21, 2011, and then October 21, 2011.

The Holy Spirit keeps giving bum steers to Benny Hinn too, who predicted the end of the world in 1992, or 1999. Hinn was also given the false lead that Fidel Castro would die in the 1990s. In 1989 Hinn prophesized, "The Lord also tells me to tell you in the mid 90's, about '94–'95, no later than that, God will destroy the homosexual community of America. But He will not destroy it with what many minds have thought Him to be, He will destroy it with fire. And many will turn and be saved, and many will rebel and be destroyed." Hinn fails to even reach the 66 percent mark with that one.

Merchandising God

Many religions teach that money is the root of all evil. Conversely, some Evangelists preach that their ministry is a kind of spiritual savings bank for your money. Many Charismatic churches preach what is known as the prosperity gospel. This is a kind of godly gambling where parishioners are told that if they place a holy bet on their church, they will receive financial "blessings" in return. From late-night televangelists to the minister of the local church, they all solicit donations with a nauseating persistence. With gold and diamonds falling from heaven, surely they don't need the money, although they aren't raising donations for themselves, or for the church steeple. The money you give to them will flow directly from the pulpit to the pews.

Tithing and offerings are mentioned repeatedly in the Bible. In Malachi (3:10) the Lord commands his followers to test him by tithing, "and see if I will not throw open the floodgates of heaven and pour out so much blessing that there will not be room enough to store it." It seems that God wants everyone to be driving a Mercedes-Benz and wearing a Rolex watch. Once known as the "health and wealth gospel," donating to the ministry will not only ensure your wealth, but also your health and happiness.

The prosperity gospel is also known as "seed-faith" theology, where financial donations are "seeds" sown into the ministry that will supposedly yield a return on your investment. Usually, there is some quasi-mathematical formula by which God will repay your donation by tenfold, or a hundredfold. Early Pentecostal minister A. A. Allen promised that God would "turn dollar bills into twenties." Today, Paula White promises you will reap financial abundance if "you sow the seed of your First Fruits" into her ministry—that is, if you give her your first paycheck of the year. To not donate, or to not donate enough, is interpreted as a lack of faith. They also lay on the guilt. If you don't donate, the church will have to close its pearly doors because of you.

From the finger bones of Jesus to splinters from the holy cross, charlatans have been merchandising God for thousands of years. Pentecostalism founder Charles Parham prayed over handkerchiefs and mailed them to the sick. Rex Humbard, the world's first televangelist, pioneered mail-based scams with his Bible Anointing Oil, Prayer Clothes, and Faith Nail. These holy relics were "free," for a donation, and blessed individually, although they're mass-manufactured. Oral Roberts pawned Prayer Candles and paper Prayer Rugs. Today, Peter Popoff offers you his "free" Miracle Spring Water for $27, while Danny Davis wants to give you his "free" No Evil Oil for $20 a bottle; although it *has* been prayed over for seventeen days.

If you don't go to them they'll come to you. St. Matthew's Churches (formerly St. Matthew's Publishing Inc.) is a mail-based ministry that was started by former tent minister James Eugene Ewing. Most of us are familiar with the "Jesus Prayer Rug." This shroud-like paper image of Jesus "opens its eyes" as you pray, like a Messiah magic eye, and then it manifests your desires. When you have finished with the rug, please mail it back (with a donation) because they need to send the good luck on to someone else. Other "churches" mail plastic crosses, blessed medals, and other tacky trinkets, and then ask for donations for these unsolicited items. Some instruct you to send a prayer request (with a donation) and their ministry will pray for you, but they're really preying on you. These requests are often received by staff in offices rather than ministries, where the donations are collected, and the prayer requests are dumped in the trash. Cyberchurches are a recent phenomenon. These Internet churches offer prayer requests, for a donation. Many cyberchurches don't even have physical houses of worship, but they promise that the donor will be prayed for by their virtual congregation of millions.

These scams often target vulnerable people, including the chronically or terminally ill who are desperate for a cure, low-income people who are unable to meet their mortgage payments and bills, and the elderly who may be manipulated by these pseudo-religious tactics. "It is easier for a camel to go through the eye of a needle, than for a rich man to enter the kingdom of God," but Evangelists will try. They often lead extravagant lives, embroiled in financial and sex scandals, living off the back of the false promises they give to their followers. It seems that only ones who prosper from this gospel are the prosperity preachers.

In Bad Faith

Divine healing, also called faith or spiritual healing, is probably the most popular Charismatic practice. This supernatural healing can supposedly cure everything from AIDS to addictions, all with a prayer or a touch. Those with this "gift" heal face-to-face or long distance over television, radio, phone, or even online. Charismatic Christians often perform faith healing in groups. They anoint the "patient" with oil and call for the Holy Spirit's intervention.

Group healing often involves the biblical cure of "laying on of hands." The minister places the left hand on the recipient's shoulder, and right hand on the head, or cups both hands around the patient's head. The minister leads the prayer and petitions the Holy Spirit for healing. Everyone else places a hand on the person as they pray, and they possibly speak in tongues. At the climax of the ritual, the subject falls backward into the arms of the group. They believe this is the power of the Holy

Spirit, but it's usually the power of social pressure, and the minister's fist.

Catholic Charismatics practice faith healing too. Of course, they have a long tradition of miraculous healing phenomena. Saints are petitioned for healing via intercessory prayer, and there is a patron saint for every medical condition from autism to venereal diseases. Healings have been attributed to "weeping" religious statues. Miraculous cures were reported during the alleged Marian apparitions at Guadalupe and Lourdes, or when the Blessed Virgin Mary appeared on a tree and a grilled cheese sandwich. Millions of miracle seekers make the pilgrimage to Lourdes to drink or bathe in its healing spring waters. On display are numerous abandoned crutches (but no prosthetic limbs) as testimonies to the thousands of inexplicable healings that have occurred there. Ironically, many Catholics don't like the fuss of Charismatic faith healing. Instead, they prefer a more subdued healing prayer group, the use of blessed oil, salt, and water to anoint the sick, or the lighting of a candle to petition God for healing. They believe in the healing power of the Eucharist, and take literally the Holy Communion prayer, "Lord, I am not worthy that you should enter under my roof, but only say the word and my soul shall be healed."

Faith healing is most closely associated with televangelists. They promise to heal people in their audience, and viewers at home if they touch their television screens. Individuals in the crowd faint as they are "healed" by the invisible touch of the Holy Spirit, or they line up to receive a physical touch on the forehead from the Evangelist, which catapults them backward into the arms of waiting assistants. They may writhe about in convulsions, requiring disease-causing demons to be cast out in the name of Jesus. Faith healing is practiced by a long list of Evangelists, including Kenneth Copeland, Pat Robertson, Robert Tilton, Benny Hinn, and Peter Popoff. Like the Charismatic prophets, the healers use the cold-reading and hot-reading techniques of psychics to give the appearance that they have supernatural gifts. They have *all* been revealed to be charlatans. In particular, Popoff was debunked in 1986 in a spectacular exposé.

Popoff's divine prophecies are amazingly accurate, but a little too accurate. He knows the exact names of people in his audience and can describe their ailments precisely. He claims to receive this information from God. Working with magicians James Randi and Banachek, crime-scene analyst Alexander Jason attended one of Popoff's healing events and rigged up a surveillance device to detect any covert audio communication. Before long he heard "God" speak to Popoff, and He said, "Hello Petey!" God's frequency sounded strangely like Popoff's wife, Elizabeth. She continued, "Can you hear me? If you can't, you're in trouble!" Throughout the event, Mrs. Popoff provided her husband with names, addresses, personal information, and seat numbers, all collected from the audience prior to the show. Throughout the performance, Mrs. Popoff guided her husband to these unwitting stooges who were astonished at his "revelations." After collecting hours of proof across the United States, magician James Randi exposed Popoff on Johnny Carson's *Tonight Show*. Popoff initially denied the accusations. Then he admitted his deceit, but defended his actions by comparing his ministry to a TV game show. The scandal sent him bankrupt and should have been the end of his career, but Popoff resurrected his ministry, which is now worth more than ever.

According to the Bible, Jesus and the Apostles performed many miraculous healings to prove to unbelievers that they were of God. They allegedly cured people of blindness (John 9:1–41), paralysis (Acts 3:6, Acts 8:7), and birth defects (Luke 6–10). They restored amputated limbs (Luke 22:51–52) and even raised the dead (Luke 7:11–17, John 11:43–44). Modern Evangelists allege that they have replicated these miracles, but these claims have never been authenticated. All that exists are testimonies that can be exaggerated, misrepresented, mistaken, or faked. They don't perform these miracles because they can't. As well as the techniques used by psychics, Evangelists resort to other tricks, such as plants in the audience on crutches who toss them away when they've been "healed." They avoid the real patients with visible conditions, and prefer disabilities or diseases that can't be seen. Evangelist Todd Bentley sticks to New Age claims that he has performed "inner healings" of emotions. Put simply, those who arrive in wheelchairs leave in wheelchairs.

The modern Holy Spirit can cure anything, just as long as it's a headache or hemorrhoids. Some people do experience temporary pain relief induced by euphoria, or they are relieved of psychosomatic conditions. These people are "healed" not by the power of the Holy Spirit, but by the power of the placebo effect. Occasional claims arise of people making spontaneous recoveries from chronic illnesses, such as cancer or multiple sclerosis. These are revealed to be cases of coincidental remission, mistaken diagnoses, or mistaken healings. Sometimes recovery occurs as a result of concurrent medical treatment, although the faithful prefer to give credit to a divine Chief of Staff. Any failure to recover is rationalized as God's will, or blamed on the sick, who are accused of unconfessed sins, or of lacking faith. The Evangelist Jack Coe was known for picking people up out of their wheelchairs and dropping them. If they fell over, he'd scold them with, "You don't have the faith!" In his own display of faith and cockiness, Peter Popoff would steal people's canes and crutches and break them, or toss them away "into the fires of hell."

It is dangerous to place one's faith in faith healing, and unconscionable to have belief on behalf of someone else. Sadly, there are many cases of child abuse where parents withheld medical care in favor of faith healing, resulting in fatalities. One study reviewed 172 cases where children died because their parents relied on religious rituals. The authors concluded that in 140 cases, the deaths were preventable, occurring from treatable conditions such as pneumonia, meningitis, and diabetes. For all but three of the remaining cases, the children would have benefitted from medical care that was denied to them in favor of faith healers.

Dr. William Nolan conducted a study of twenty-three people who believed they had been cured by the Evangelist Kathryn Kuhlman. His long-term follow-ups of these patients revealed that not one of them have actually been cured. For some, their belief is stronger than the "healing," and they stop taking their medication or seeing their doctors, to the detriment of their condition. The faithful shouldn't throw away their crutches too soon. During one of her faith healing services, Kulhman claimed to have healed a woman of spinal cancer. At Kulhman's command, the woman ripped off her back brace, tossed it aside, and ran across the stage. The next day her spine collapsed and she died four months later.

Raising Eyebrows

Unlike the biblical stories of the Apostles, we don't see the faith healers attempting to heal skeptics to prove their abilities. Today's healers preach to the choir. We might wonder why they don't minister to people in hospitals, visit funeral parlors and morgues, and attend accident scenes. Well, One Glance Ministries does just that. To fulfill Jesus' commandment to "raise the dead" (Matthew 10:8), Tyler Johnson founded the Dead Raising Team. Johnson is a former student of the Bethel Supernatural School of Ministry, the ones who find feathers falling from the sky. He has set up teams to raise the dead across the United States. Team members are on call to attend emergency situations to pray over fatalities, and they travel to mortuaries, funeral homes, or family homes to "offer prayers of resurrection on behalf of the deceased." Anyone can undertake a day-long training course to avoid the undertaker, and learn the art of resurrection.

The Dead Raising Team claims to have successfully resurrected nine people, although they don't offer any proof. If they don't succeed in raising the dead, they reframe their purpose as comforting families in the midst of their grief, although it seems more like offering false hope.

Benny Hinn attempted a mass raising of the dead on October 19, 1999. He told viewers of the show *Praise the Lord* to cancel funeral services and place their recently deceased in front of the television set for twenty-four hours. He predicted, "I see rows of caskets lining up in front of this TV set and I see them bringing them closer to the TV set and as people are coming closer I see actual loved ones picking up the hands of the dead and letting them touch the screen and people are getting raised as their hands are touching that screen." Hinn promised that there would be thousands of people raised from the dead around the world, although he didn't achieve a single resurrection.

Prodigy Preacher

Hugh Marjoe Ross Gortner had the worst stage parents ever, but instead of wearing a tiara in a beauty contest, they made him carry a Bible and yell "Glory!" Marjoe was ordained at the age of four, and his Pentecostal parents molded him into the world's youngest evangelist. His name is a blend of "Mary" and "Joseph," and his parents called him a "miracle child" because he almost died at birth. They marveled that the Holy Ghost visited him at age three while he was taking a bath, and that he received sermons from the Lord in his sleep. Marjoe jokes that he was taught how to sing "Hallelujah!" before he could say "Momma" or "Poppa."

During the 1940s, the precocious preacher delivered hellfire and brimstone sermons to packed churches and tents as he led crusades across the Bible Belt. With blue eyes, blond curls, and dressed in a velvet suit like Little Lord Fauntleroy, the mini minister would say cutely, "I'm in town to give the devil two black eyes!" Marjoe was also a faith healer, convincing thousands of people that they had been healed miraculously. He sold holy relics, and gave kisses to the old church ladies in exchange for donations to the collection plate. In reality, his parents coached his performances. If Marjoe didn't memorize his lines correctly they would smother him with a pillow, or pretend to drown him because these methods wouldn't leave any marks. They exploited him for money, but when he was a teenager, his father absconded with the millions Marjoe had earned.

He floundered for a few years before trying his hand at other careers in the public eye. However, his audiences wanted Marjoe the minister, so he retuned to the revivalist circuit. Now a charismatic young man in his twenties with an interest in acting and music, Marjoe turns his meetings into rock concerts, incorporating dance routines by Mick Jagger into his stage moves. It is a world of power and corruption, and Marjoe, who never believed he had a gift from God, soon became disillusioned with the deception of the industry. At the age of twenty-six, he decided to do a final tour, and took along a film crew to reveal what goes on behind church doors. The 1972 documentary *Marjoe* is an exposé of the revivalist racket. Marjoe exposes speaking in tongues and faith healing, and reveals the carny tricks he used, such as making a blood-red cross appear on his forehead using sweat-activated ink.

This story is explored in the 2010 movie *The Last Exorcism*. The Reverend Cotton Marcus is a former child evangelist turned exorcist. When he nearly loses his son at birth, Marcus has more faith in the doctors than in God. He soon admits to himself that exorcisms are dangerous and decides to abandon the practice, but he agrees to perform one last exorcism to ease the fears of a desperate family. Marcus takes along a film crew to expose the fraud of exorcism. He reveals the gimmicks he uses to stage supernatural special effects, including a cross that releases smoke at the press of a button. To demonstrate the power of the evangelist, and that people don't listen to what he says, only how he says it, he deftly weaves into his sermon a recipe for baking banana bread.

Slip of the Tongue

Pentecostal and Charismatic Christians are known for their howling, barking, roaring, and groaning, but they are most popularly known for speaking in tongues. This is believed to be a heavenly or angelic language, which is spoken when one is seized by the Holy Spirit. This is a staple practice for Pentecostals. This gift is held to be the initial evidence of receiving the baptism in the Holy Spirit. This means, you only qualify as a Pentecostal if you've spoken in tongues. However, not all Charismatics practice speaking in tongues.

Speaking in tongues is used in public and private worship, and for healing or prophecy, like the Delphic Oracle. Never mind that these predictions are spoken in unintelligible gibberish, some believe they have the "gift of interpretation" to translate the messages. Mainstream Christians fear these are messages from Satan, not the Holy Spirit.

The practice today is a modern interpretation of the biblical story. In the Book of Acts, the Apostles' "speaking in tongues" was understood by speakers of foreign languages. Therefore, the original speaking in tongues was a form of xenoglossia, the spontaneous speaking of unlearned foreign languages. (When cases of xenoglossia aren't hoaxes, they are usually the result of a brain trauma known as bilingual aphasia. This occurs when a bilingual person suffers a stroke or accident which causes them to temporarily or permanently lose one of their languages.)

As we saw earlier, when Agnes Ozman was speaking in tongues, it was reported that she spoke "Chinese." This would be consistent with the biblical story—that is, if her audience spoke Chinese, but no one did. Ozman also produced some examples of "Chinese writing." Both her written and spoken "Chinese" could not be authenticated by linguists.

Similarly, when Parham began speaking in tongues, he believed he could speak "Swedish." Instead, Ozman's pseudo-Chinese and Parham's pseudo-Swedish are more consistent with a phenomenon known as glossolalia.

Glossolalia is uttering a stream of sounds that mimic foreign language. However, it isn't language because it is without words, grammar, and other structural features that characterize language. Speaking in tongues is ecstatic babbling, and is more similar to jazz scatting than speech. When the act is performed under an MRI scan, it is shown to activate the social parts of the brain, but not those that process language. Speaking in tongues is a social phenomenon rather than a linguistic one. In fact, the congregation is socialized into the practice. They are taught how to speak in tongues, and encouraged to imitate others. There is pious peer pressure to speak in tongues, and worshippers report being made to feel guilty if they don't do it.

Snake Oil

Snake handling is one of the most sensational of all modern religious rituals. It is primarily a Pentecostal practice, but it isn't a spiritual "gift" as such. The tradition arose from a literal interpretation of several biblical passages. In Acts (28:1–6) Paul survives a bite from a vicious viper. Mark (16:17–18) promises impunity from snakes and even poison, "They shall take up serpents; and if they drink any deadly thing, it shall not hurt them; they shall lay hands on the sick, and they shall recover." Luke (10:19) gives us the, "power to tread on serpents and scorpions, and over all the power of the enemy: and nothing shall by any means hurt you." However, we're yet to see a church take up the practice of serpent or scorpion treading.

Snake worship has been practiced in many ancient cultures, and so has the street performance act of snake charming. Snake handling is a more contemporary custom. The practice began around 1909 in the Appalachian Mountains region of Tennessee. George Went Hensley of the Church of God was delivering a sermon involving the Gospel of Mark, when a member of the congregation cheekily dumped a box of rattlesnakes into the pulpit. The fearless Hensley handled a snake and was able to continue the service without harm. News of the miraculous event spread, and snake handling became practiced as a test of faith, and a display of obedience to God.

Nowadays, snake handling as a religious ritual is rare, and is branded as backward and rural. It is only practiced in upwards of one hundred churches in a few states, including Alabama, North Carolina, Georgia, Florida, West Virginia, Ohio, Tennessee, and Kentucky. It is outlawed in many areas, so snake-handling services are held covertly in rented halls or private homes. These services last for three hours or longer, building in emotion and intensity, and snake handling is the culmination of an evening of preaching, faith healing, speaking in tongues, and an occasional drink from a Mason jar filled with strychnine-laced water. If they're not clapping their hands or raising their arms in the air they will pick up one of the snakes slithering at their feet and dance with it.

Snake charmers protect themselves from their cobras and vipers by removing the snake's fangs or venom glands. They may even sew the snake's mouth shut, unlike the fearless religious serpent handlers, who use a number of highly venomous snakes, including rattlesnakes, copperheads, cottonmouths, and water moccasins. The snakes may be raised in captivity and be somewhat used to the fanfare, but there are no tricks involved, only an anointing ceremony that is held beforehand. Snake bites are very common. To some believers, a bite might signify a weakness of faith, as it would be to seek medical attention afterward. They believe in Jesus instead of antivenom, while others will spend days in hospital recuperating from an attack.

The excruciating bites from these snakes contain neurotoxic venom that leads to disfigured hands or missing fingers, if the victim is lucky. These people seek the ultimate proof of faith, and some pay the ultimate price. There are over one hundred documented deaths resulting from snake handling, from old-timers who've handled them for decades, to young children who got in the way. Some children are allowed to handle snakes too. As snake handler Junior Church said, "I'd rather lose a child now and have it go to heaven than keep it 100 years and have it go to hell." After receiving dozens of snakebites over the years, Hensley, the founder of snake handling, died in 1955 when he was bitten by a rattlesnake. For true believers, a bite is God's will, and to die by snakebite is a badge of honor.

Handling snakes isn't compulsory in these churches, unless you're the wife of snake-handling preacher Glenn Summerford. With his conservative beliefs about marriage, murder was easier than divorce for this pastor of the Church of Jesus Christ With Signs Following in Scottsboro, Alabama. During a drunken rage he put a gun to his wife Darlene's head as he forced her to write a suicide note. Then he grabbed her by the hair and shoved her hand into a cage of rattlesnakes until she was bitten repeatedly. In a real world miracle, he fell into a drunken stupor and she survived, while the pastor was convicted of attempted murder and sentenced to prison for ninety-nine years.

Charismatic Karaoke

In Charismatic churches, God's day of rest isn't the only time for worship. My husband Matthew and I attended a Tuesday night service at a Charismatic church in Colorado. This is a weekly healing event called "The Healing Place." When we arrived, the room was already full of people patiently waiting for the service to begin. There was a box of tissues at the end of every pew. A woman raced over and introduced herself as Cici, the pastor's wife, who would be conducting the ceremony. "What should we expect here tonight?" I asked. "Anything and everything!" Cici said excitedly. "We've witnessed some incredible healings and miracles in the past few weeks. All I know is that God is gonna show up tonight!"

A live band began playing New Age meditative music as a background to Cici's sermon. This was a stream-of-consciousness, freeform style of praise and prayer, and she would occasionally burst out into song, like she was starring in a musical. The Charismatic crowd was a motley crew of people who were clearly regular attendees. Only a few minutes into Cici's sermon they quickly assumed their usual roles. An elderly gentleman sitting in front of us began sobbing heavily. A woman fell down on the floor in the middle of the room and lay there motionless. A man paced up and down the stage as he performed a flagging dance, waving three pink flags high in the air. The music was hypnotic, and Cici began urging people to take the microphone if they were "moved by the

Holy Spirit." The service became a Charismatic karaoke. A woman sang a hymn in Spanish. A man spoke a soliloquy about the unknown beauty of God's face. One after another they took the microphone and played Evangelist for a few minutes. Others moaned, mumbled, and murmured to themselves, while everyone else raised their hands to the skies and occasionally yelled out "Amen!"

The lunatics were running the asylum, and we stood out, looking like a couple sitting in a church. Cici was keeping an eye on us, and wanted to involve us in the circus. She approached us with her Bible in hand. "I feel like the Lord's laid a scripture in my heart for you two," she said. Cici then recited the irrelevant passage of Isaiah 43, and finished with, "Thank you God for smiling on their destiny." At this she burst into song again, warbling the word "Destiny" over and over again in an overly enthusiastic gospel voice. We felt like awkward customers being serenaded by a mariachi band in a Mexican restaurant.

It was time for some healing. "Does anybody have a lung condition?" Cici asked. An elderly man stood up. A pack of people suddenly raised their hands and were drawn toward him like he was a magnet. They laid their hands on him and started praying loudly as Cici sang. A woman wielding a flag swung it back and forth wildly over the sick man. She was standing right next to me and I had to keep dodging the flag so I wouldn't get hit. Another woman hobbled around the room in circles, as though she believed that with one of those steps her pain would disappear magically.

Of course, everyone was there for the healing. The Healing Place offers fifteen minutes of "personal, targeted prayer from teams trained in healing, deliverance and in the prophetic." Throughout the service a woman named "Muffie" tapped people on the shoulder and then they were whisked away into healing rooms. We decided to experience a healing session, and in filling out a consent form we asked to be healed of "infertility." After two hours we got the call up, and were ushered into a private room that was decorated with candles and statues of angels. Boxes of tissues were scattered everywhere. We were introduced to our Healing Ministers Barry and Pat. Barry had a debilitating tremor in his left hand that the Holy Spirit hadn't cured, but he hadn't lost his sense of humor.

In his thick Texan accent he said, "This is your first time here, but don't worry, we don't bring out the snakes on the first night!"

Barry and Pat had some "words of knowledge" for us from the Holy Spirit. "We laid hands on your file before opening it, and asked God for a word, picture or message just for you. He knows why you're here. The first word he gave me was 'Help.' This means, 'I hear your cry.' Then he gave me the word 'Beloved,' meaning, 'He's able to do something about it.' In testimony after testimony he has given children to those who thought they were infertile." Pat's message from the Holy Spirit was a vision. "I saw images of green fields full of ripe fruit. I saw pictures of fresh fruit in abundance." I couldn't help but think that these "messages" could be made to fit any prayer request, from sickness to financial problems.

Barry anointed us both with oil, and we held hands in a circle. Barry lead the healing with, "God, we ask you to supernaturally intervene and bless this couple with a child." It became a game of dueling prayers, as Barry and Pat both prayed in turns. God received many compliments, that He is "good," "kind," and "awesome," and He received many thanks in advance of the miracle. The prayers were passionate pleas that were peppered with sexual-sounding moans and sighs. You're not usually supposed to laugh in church, but in a place where "Holy Laughter" is encouraged, Matthew couldn't stop giggling. Barry took this as a sign that Matthew was about to be filled with the Holy Spirit, and he took action.

Barry dashed out of his chair and placed his hand on Matthew's chest; he couldn't reach any higher. The diminutive Pat raced behind Matthew, presumably to catch this 6"4' man, should he fall. Pat began speaking in tongues, "Tuturaramatasuturara," but she muttered these sounds under her breath, so it was more of a whispering in tongues. Meanwhile, Barry goaded the Holy Spirit to fill Matthew with his glory. "Come Holy Spirit. More Lord. Keep coming. More Lord. Fill him up. More Lord. Keep coming Lord. Fill him up. Yes Lord, thank you." His prayers sounded more like an obscene phone call. All the while Barry was pressing his hand harder and harder into Matthew's chest, trying to push over this 240-pound man.

Barry continued to pray, while Matthew began laughing harder still. "Go deep Lord. Stir his heart. Give him a full encounter. Yes Lord. Keep coming. Stir, stir. Your presence is all over him. Bless him. Fill him with that joy of Jesus. Receive, receive. Come Holy Spirit. Come Lord. More Lord. Fill him up. Oh Lord, you're so good." However, Matthew wasn't playing along, so Barry finally gave up. After his saucy-sounding dialogue I was surprised that he didn't light up a cigarette. "In another minute you'd have been down," he warned Matthew. Nevertheless, Barry was confident that I would get pregnant soon. "Thanks to the Lord," he said with a wink. "The supernatural is natural for God. There's nothing He can't do."

Ironically, the morning after the healing, we both woke up with colds.

Chapter 4

Hoodoo, Voodoo, and Juju
Afro-Caribbean Religions

———————

"Got my mojo working, but it just won't work on you."
—Muddy Waters

I entered the tumbledown building with its grey hurricane shutters and found an enormous man sitting regally behind a desk. He eyed me quizzically through thick glasses. "Hello!" he bellowed, with the voice of a horror movie narrator. "Upstairs, I have a most magnificent snake!" "I'm sure you do," I quipped, my eyes darting to the door.

That Old Voodoo
Voodoo is most often associated with Haiti, but the religion has traveled far beyond its birthplace. Voodoo descended from West African Vodun, a belief system that began with the Fon and Ewe people in Dahomey, in what is present-day Benin. When West African people were enslaved and transported to Haiti by French colonists, they took Vodun with them.

The spread of Voodoo also led to its evolution. In 1685, King Louis XIV passed the Code Noir that defined the conditions of slavery in French colonies. The code enforced the conversion of slaves to Roman Catholicism, while newcomers had to be baptized within a week of arrival. African religions were now forbidden. The slaves pretended to be Catholic to protect their lives, and they borrowed elements of Catholicism to

88

preserve their religion. In a process that is called syncretization, Catholic saints, symbols, and rituals blended with Voodoo beliefs and practices to become Haitian Vodou.

Voodoo continued its journey when it entered the Southern United States with the transportation of slaves from West Africa. As these parts of the country were French colonies at the time, the people were also subject to the code, that is, the updated Louisiana Code Noir (1724). Voodoo continued to mix with Catholicism, but it didn't end there. The Haitian Revolution (1791–1804) finally ended slavery and colonialization in Haiti. Many Haitians sought refuge in the nearby United States, bringing Haitian Vodou with them. In more recent decades, Haiti has suffered political unrest and natural disasters, and the United States has continued to welcome refugees, and their religion.

American Voodoo

There are an estimated one million followers of Voodoo in the United States today. Perhaps this figure is because there are over one million Haitian immigrants and refugees in the country. There are also Voodoo enclaves across the country, not only where it began in Louisiana, but also in Mississippi, Massachusetts, Connecticut, Pennsylvania, Georgia, Florida, Texas, and New Jersey. In particular, New York has over 300,000 Haitian immigrants and a large community of Voodoo followers.

Various figures estimate that there are between 30–100 million adherents worldwide. Voodoo was granted official religious status in Benin in 1996, and in Haiti in 2003. However, followers in these countries identify their religion as Catholic or Protestant, but identify culturally as Vodun, or Vodou. There is a saying that Haiti is 90 percent Catholic, but 110 percent Vodou. Similarly, American practitioners often don't identify with Voodoo as their religion as such, although they dabble in Voodoo practices. Voodoo's ability to function as an adjunct belief system is the key to its longevity, and its development.

There are a number of religions with a similar lineage to Voodoo that are represented in the United States. In particular, Santeria, also known as Lukumi, is a newly recognized religion here that is experiencing rapid growth across the country. Even the U.S. Bureau of Prisons allows followers of this religion to practice their faith in jail (although they can't sacrifice chickens in their cells). Like Voodoo, Santeria is of West African origin, coming from the Yoruba people who were enslaved and brought to Cuba. Candomblé is also derived from the same tribe, whose people were transported to Brazil. Spiritual lineages are also practiced in many other countries, including Jamaica, Puerto Rico, Trinidad and Tobago, Venezuela, and the United States.

Vodou has played a crucial role in Haiti, comforting people who have endured oppressive governments, poverty, and natural disasters. It has also been used to repress the Haitians, such as during the dictatorship of François "Papa Doc" Duvalier, who ruled Haiti from 1957 to 1971. The despot invoked Vodou to instill fear in his people, along with his ruthless security force the Tonton Macout (who were named after the Haitian "bogeyman" that kidnaps and eats naughty children). Many people believed that Papa Doc was the incarnation of Baron Samedi, the "loa" of death, and to encourage that reputation he dressed in black suits and dark sunglasses just like the depiction of this spirit.

In the United States followers claim that Voodoo has been stigmatized and vilified, and that Hollywood has stereotyped and misrepresented the religion ever since the release of the 1932 film *White Zombie*. Voodoo is synonymous with evil and black magic, and the name conjures up images of zombies, curses, and voodoo dolls that look like pin cushions. Believers maintain that Voodoo is a peaceful religion that promotes healing and love, and they argue that Voodoo has been confused with the more sinister practices of related religions. However, all of these religions are intermingling with each other in the United States, to the point where they are often indistinguishable. Voodoo's migration to the United States became another catalyst for the flexible religion. Voodoo continues to do what it does best. American Voodoo is integrating with Afro-Caribbean religions, Native American traditions, Freemasonry, Pentecostalism, and a myriad of New Age and spiritual beliefs and practices.

Mambo Jumbo
There is no Voodoo Bible. Voodoo has an oral tradition, and its beliefs and practices have been passed down through the generations. There is

no one Voodoo. It is eclectic by nature, and absorbs elements of other traditions with which it comes into contact. Voodoo has different names and customs, across countries, cultures, and time. Ultimately, Voodoo is a personal religion. However, all versions of Voodoo are united by a few common characteristics. There is a God. God is often known by the Haitian name Bondye, meaning "Good God," although there is no corresponding "Bad God." God is all-seeing and all-knowing, but is incomprehensible to humans. Remote and aloof, God can't be contacted via prayer. The intermediary between God and humans are spirits, called loa, while in Santeria and Candomblé they are known as lwa or orisha. Voodoo is monotheistic, but it has a plethora of spirits. From the sea to the sky, there are spirits that represent everything in nature. The spirits also represent the dead. Voodoo practices ancestor veneration of deceased family members and legendary people. Just as there are thousands of Catholic saints, there are thousands of Voodoo spirits. Like the saints, the spirits were once people who led exceptional lives, and have a special patronage.

Voodoo merges with Catholic iconography. Voodoo statues and pictures of spirits incorporate elements of the saints, and the characteristics of Voodoo spirits are transferred onto Catholic saints. The Seven African Powers are the primary spirits: Legba, Obatala, Yemaya, Oya, Oshun, Chango, and Ogun, with many different regional spellings, and they are all identified with Catholic saints. Papa Legba is the guardian of the spirit world, and is recognized as St. Peter holding the key to heaven. Saint Patrick supposedly drove the snakes out of Ireland, so he is mixed with the serpent spirit Dumballah. Agwé is the patron spirit of fishermen, who is personified as the fish-carrying Saint Ulrich. The evil spirit Kalfu is often represented as a demon, and corresponds to Satan.

Like other religions, there is a battle of good versus evil. Voodoo has many bad spirits, and most were criminals in their former incarnation, such as Baron Kriminel, who was believed to have been a murderer. These evil spirits are called upon for assistance with malevolent spells. Some of these spirits reflect the brutal and sorrowful history of slavery. The spirit Dinclinsin is feared for his cruelty, and is often portrayed as a white slave owner carrying a whip. The spirit Agassou was chosen to bring Vodun to

Haiti to ease the pains and sufferings from slavery. Guinee is a kind of Vodou heaven to which the slaves believed their souls would return after their death.

Unlike the unreachable God, the spirits communicate with humans constantly, and they are believed to affect our day-to-day lives. Good spirits give advice and assistance, offer protection, bring good luck, and perform miracles. Like the patron saints, specific spirits can be called upon to resolve financial problems, find love, or cure disease. However, it's a case of you scratch my back, and I'll scratch yours. The spirits will only perform these requests in exchange for gifts. The spirits are very materialistic, and they haven't lost their taste for earthly pleasures. Each spirit is associated with certain foods and objects, so you know what presents to leave for them at their altars. Erzulie adores jewelry and perfume, while Papa Legba enjoys a bottle of rum and a good cigar. Some of the spirits are more demanding when it comes to offerings. Animal sacrifice is often performed in healing rituals, or to ask spirits for favors. According to folklore, the spirit Marinette was burned alive for initiating the Haitian Revolution. To appease her spirit, she expects a chicken to be burned alive. Meanwhile, American Voodoo spirits are usually content with chicken from KFC.

There are no Voodoo popes or bishops, but there are Voodoo priests, known as Hougan. Voodoo is more progressive than Catholicism, and Voodoo Priestesses, called Mambos, play a central role in the religion. Despite the claims that Voodoo is about good magic, it does indeed have a dark side. Voodoo "white magic" is known as rada, while "black magic" is called petro. Bokor are the sorcerers you go to if you want to turn an enemy into a zombie, or in American Voodoo, to make an ex-lover get fat.

These Voodoo clergy are chosen by the spirits, who usually inform them of their spiritual calling via visions and dreams. Hougans and Mambos perform many different kinds of ceremonies, from divination and spirit possessions, to baptisms and weddings. Voodooists can even marry the spirits. Spirits occasionally propose spiritual marriage in exchange for a favor. The wedding is conducted as a marriage ceremony, but married life is conducted via dreams, visions, and thoughts. In a kind of Voodoo polygamy, people may marry multiple spirits, and also keep an earthly spouse.

How Do You Voodoo?

Magical objects are an important part of Voodoo. Amulets are carried for protection from harm, such as an item of jewelry, an evil eye, or a black cat's tooth. Amulets repel bad luck, while talismans are intended to attract good luck. Gris-gris, mojo, juju, toby, pakets, trick bags, and conjure bags are amulets or talismans. These small, preferably red, fabric bags contain a range of magical items: fetishes, beads, buttons, bones, stones, coins, crystals, handwritten messages, herbs, roots, and powders. These are blessed to attract general good luck, or specific desires, such as winning the lottery or scoring at the bar. They are a prayer in a bag, or a spell you can carry, preferably in the left pocket, while the owner focuses on his or her desires and intentions.

With no doctrine, Voodoo is mostly understood in terms of its ceremonies and rituals. A major purpose of Voodoo is to petition the spirits for favors. These requests are often made via ritual spells. Voodoo spells are used for a variety of purposes: for protection, fertility, and gambling luck; to attract love, sex, marriage, money, health, beauty, and career; to keep a relationship exciting; to prevent a partner from cheating; to recover from heartbreak; to persuade an ex-lover to forget you; to stop divorce proceedings, etc. Alternatively, many Voodoo spells are malicious or retaliatory and are intended to place a curse, to remove a curse, to seek retribution, to control and dominate, to reunite with an ex-lover, to break up a relationship, to injure someone, to cause sickness, or even to kill someone.

There are many different types of Voodoo spells. Most of them follow a recipe format, and involve the use of incantations with ritual objects such as oils, candles, herbs, and spices. Often, it's not the angelica root that protects against the plague, but the blessings and spells said over the herbs by a priest or priestess. Many spells are a juxtaposition of Catholicism with Voodoo. Catholic prayers, novenas, and psalms, such as Hail Mary and the Lord's Prayer, are interwoven into spells. Holy water, holy bread, rosary beads, crosses, and vigil candles are used as ritual objects.

Candles are important tools of Voodoo. They are burned to honor spirits, or to petition spirits or Catholic saints for something specific. A Saint Joseph candle is burned to help buy or sell a home, and to stop foreclosure. Saint Jude candles are burned for all situations that appear hopeless, and Saint Expeditus candles are burned for fast assistance in all matters. Offertory candles are used for casting spells, according to color. Red represents love and passion, and green candles are for money, at least in this culture. Seven-day or fourteen-day candles encased in glass are burned over the course of a spell. There are many commercially produced Voodoo, Hoodoo, and Santeria candles, such as "Come To Me," which is burned to attract a lover, and "Road Opener," which is believed to open paths to good fortune.

Most of these candles have harmful intentions, and are painted with ominous images of snakes, grim reapers, or the skull and crossbones. Some "Controlling" candles feature a woman dragging along a man on a leash. Black wax D.U.M.E. ("Death Unto My Enemies") candles are burned to curse, hex, and cause misfortune. "Law Stay Away" candles are to avert unwanted law enforcement visits to your meth kitchen, while "Breakup" candles are intended to break up a relationship. The candles are often inscribed with the name of the person to be worked on, or their photograph is placed underneath. At the climax of a harmful spell, the photo may be burned or cut into tiny pieces, and the remains scattered at a cemetery or crossroads, or sprinkled into running water.

To appeal to the spirits, the candles are decorated with fabric, ribbons, sequins, and glitter. The candles are usually "fixed," that is, they are dressed with oils and rolled in herbs because this enhances their power. Potion oils are also supposed to make Voodoo spells more effective. There are oils designed to bring good luck to you, and bad luck to your enemies. One special type of oil can be used to anoint paperwork when applying for a loan, or worn as perfume during the bank interview—that is, if the lottery oils and bingo oils didn't work. Burning incense is also supposed to empower Voodoo rituals, whether you're trying to clear away misfortune, or to invite the spirits of the dead to communicate.

Magical herbs, beans, nuts, roots, and flowers are commonly used in Voodoo. These can be added to candles, burned with incense, or sprinkled by bedsides and across doorways. Lemon grass helps break bad habits, while rue is supposedly useful for exorcisms. Voodoo spiritual baths are designed for ritual bathing. Special salts, herbs, and oils can be added to your bath, to have you bathing in money, or so you can wash away those jinxes. There are also special cleansers designed to wash away evil. Like a Voodoo Ajax, Chinese Wash is used to ritually cleanse your feet and shoes, and ritually wash the floors of your house. You can even suck your way to success with magical candy. Again, the red ones attract love and sex, while the green candy attracts money.

Sympathy Pains

Nothing says "Voodoo" like a Voodoo doll, but Voodooists say that the doll stuck full of pins is a myth. This is both true and false. "Real" Voodoo dolls aren't the rough-sewn cloth kind, like the small English dolls known as poppets. They are usually made from wax, sticks, clay, metal, wood, rope, and other materials. These are spirit dolls used to attract luck and cure illness, but they are also used in magic with the intention of harming others. They aren't typically jabbed with pins to cause pain in a corresponding body part, but they are commonly used as effigies. There is a belief in Voodoo that performing magic on a victim's representation will result in a real world effect on that person. Personal possessions are used as an extension of the victim's body, such as jewelry, clothing, a sample of handwriting, or dirt from a footprint. Bodily fluids are especially potent, so spells often call for a piece of the victim's DNA, be it a few strands of hair, a fingernail, urine, feces, menstrual blood, or sperm. These personal items are believed to contain the victim's energy, and supposedly solidify the connection between the person and the intention.

Many Voodoo rituals involve this type of sympathetic magic—that is, the belief that like affects like. Cemetery dirt is believed to be a powerful ingredient in Voodoo and Hoodoo spells. Dirt from the grave of a loved one is used in love spells, while dirt from the burial site of a criminal is used for curses. The belief is that dirt from the grave corresponds with the traits of the person buried beneath. Dirt collected from the grave of a famous artist is hoped to inspire creativity, while dirt from the grave of a soldier, police officer, or firefighter may be used for protection. Collecting cemetery dirt is a ritual, so just be sure to ask the spirit for a sample first. It is also a transaction, so leave a silver dime, bottle of whiskey, or other offering in thanks.

In a cornfield near Denver, police discovered a package wrapped in black plastic and tied with yellow nylon ropes. It contained a cow tongue covered with sutures. Inside they found a photograph, a message written in Spanish, and a sprinkling of herbs. This was a Santeria ritual to make someone stop talking, gossiping, or testifying in court. One of the most famous Voodoo spells is known as honey jar magic. There are many variants but they all involve the use of a candle, a jar, and honey, maple syrup, molasses, or other sweetener in a spell to "sweeten" someone to a desire. Voodoo folk medicine often involves sympathetic magic. In typical Voodoo, there are spells designed to heal, but also spells intended to make people sick. One spell involves placing a photograph of a victim upside down to give them a headache.

A Bitter Pill to Swallow

In Haiti the health-care system is struggling, due to a shortage of workers and a lack of infrastructure. Antibiotics and pain medications are purchased from street vendors, often without dosage information, expiry dates, or even packaging. With limited access to healthcare, many people rely on Voodoo folk medicine, and illness is often believed to be caused by angry spirits. Because there is little Warfarin or Prozac, medicine men and women use the everyday materials to which they have access, and treatments often involve prayers and herbal remedies.

In the United States, any kind of medical quackery may be called "Voodoo Medicine," while "Voodoo Science" refers to junk science, and "voodoo" often means "nonsense." However, in many immigrant communities, Voodoo, Hoodoo, and Santeria folk remedies are often used in tandem with orthodox medicine. Like most folk medicine, some of it has genuine medicinal value, while some of it is spurious. Voodoo practitioners also sell health rituals custom-made for their clients' condition. These may involve a ritual performed privately by the practitioner, or a concoction to be taken by the client as a medicine.

Voodoo medicine is not just about the ingredients, but also about what was put into the cure spiritually. The placebo effect is heavily at play in its success. Much of Voodoo folk medicine is preventative too. There are perfumes, sprays, and even chewing gums to ward off sickness, so you'll never know what you could have contracted if you didn't take it.

Botánicas have become very popular in the United States, and can be found in cities such as Miami, New York, Los Angeles, and Denver, showing the increasing popularity of Afro-Caribbean folk medicine. Botánicas are like Walgreens for Santeria and Voodoo that sell folk remedies, including medicinal herbs, aphrodisiacs, and products to stop hair loss. They also function as religious supplies stores that carry items from a combination of religions, including rosary beads, Catholic statues, and even Buddhist and Hindu statues. Botánicas also sell paraphernalia so people can do rituals at home, such as candles that are burned to win a court case, an antihurricane elixir, and spray cans of "Go Away Evil!"

Hoodoo Gurus

Voodoo is often confused with Hoodoo, and there is much crossover between the two. Those who want to differentiate them will say that Hoodoo is folk magic, while Voodoo is classified as a religion. However, Hoodoo involves a lot of the same rituals as Voodoo. Hoodoo is a homegrown blend of practices that originated in the Southern United States. It integrates African-American beliefs and customs, European witchcraft lore and grimoires, and Native American folk medicine. Hoodoo is also very similar to the folk magic and shamanism of Obeah, which is blended with Santeria and Yoruba derived religions, and is practiced in Jamaica, Trinidad and Tobago, and other Caribbean countries.

Also known as Conjure, Tricking, or Rootwork, Hoodoo involves divination and spell-casting. Hoodoo is called "helping yourself," and features spells for attracting love, or enhancing gambling luck. The charm bags called Mojo are a Hoodoo creation. Hoodoo folk remedies and spells include the use of herbs, roots, animal parts, and bodily fluids. The infamous Hoodoo "goofer dust" is a compound that includes a mixture of cemetery dirt, sulphur powder, spider webs, rattlesnake skin, and other unpleasant substances. In fact, there is an emphasis on malignant magic in Hoodoo. Hoodoo is known for its revenge spells, footprint spells, and hot foot powders designed to be sprinkled on an enemy's path to send them packing. Most of these rituals are performed in cemeteries or at a crossroads, as these are believed to be potent places.

Where Voodoo and Santeria melded with Catholicism, Hoodoo borrowed elements of Judaism. Hoodoo has an interesting framing on the characters of the Old Testament. For their miraculous deeds, Moses, King Solomon, Archangel Michael, and other biblical characters are recast as "Conjurors" or "Hoodoo doctors." As the creator of the world in six days, God is the ultimate conjuror. The Bible is a source for Hoodoo spells, and psalms and prayers are recited as incantations. The Bible is also used as a talisman and amulet, and carried around for protection and good luck.

Altar Ego

A lot of Voodoo is about petitions for favors, but nobody likes that guy who only calls when he wants something. Worship is another important part of Voodoo. Altars are sacred spaces dedicated to a spirit that are created for spells, but also for private devotion. They are built on tables, desks, or mantelpieces, and they display ritual objects, including candles, incense, voodoo dolls, and statues of saints. Altars are decorated in shabby chic style, with lace, velvet, ribbons beads, and painted pots covered in sequins. Like leaving out milk and cookies for Santa, offerings are left out for the saints, such as flowers, alcohol, money, food and flags, cigarettes, and marijuana. A popular Voodoo saying is, "Take care of the spirits and they will take care of you."

These gifts are like an application and payment for favors. Each spirit has his or her sacred weekday, holiday, song, preferred colors, foods, and even a favorite tree, and the altar gifts should be appropriate. Offerings for the spirit Chango should take into consideration that he prefers the colors red and white; he likes turtles and machetes, and enjoys eating apples and peppers. Agwe likes fine champagne, but don't be cheap and try to get away with giving him beer instead. To displease the spirits can result in the request backfiring. The spirit Erzulie Dantor will support small business owners, if they supply her with French pastries. However, if she is presented with offerings she doesn't like, the victim is likely to have problems with the police and the IRS.

Voodoo rituals aren't always done alone; often they are performed in groups. These ceremonies are conducted for healing, to end a bout of misfortune, and at birth, marriage, and death. If a specific spirit is being celebrated or petitioned, they are invoked using prayer, chanting, feasting, fire, and traditional music involving drums and bells. Each spirit has its own symbol called a veve that acts as a beacon to attract them. The appropriate veve will be drawn on the ground with cornmeal, wheat flour, or even gunpowder. Interestingly, veves have borrowed Freemason symbols, including the all-seeing eye, the square and compass, and the skull and crossbones.

Similar to Charismatic worship, Voodoo ceremonies involve frenzied singing, dancing, convulsions, fainting, and speaking in tongues. These ecstatic ceremonies build in intensity until someone goes into a seizure-like state, because they have been possessed by a spirit. Unlike Catholicism, possession is considered a good thing in Voodoo. Spirits don't have bodies anymore, so they must borrow an earthly one. The spirit "mounts" its "horse," and then "rides" it. When someone is possessed, they temporarily *become* that spirit and begin to behave like the spirit that entered them. Those possessed by the evil spirit Marinette will confess hideous crimes, while those overtaken by Papa Guédé drink a mixture of raw rum and habanero peppers. Those taken over by the snake spirit Dumballah slither along the floor and are fed whole eggs. People can be possessed by a spirit of the opposite gender too. Men controlled by Erzuli strut about like a sexy woman, and flirt with other men. After the ceremony, the possessed claim to suffer a kind of spiritual amnesia. They have no memory that they were possessed by Ghede, who forced them do the banda, a suggestive dance that mimics sex.

Like the Pentecostal practices of snake handling and drinking poison, some Voodooists injure themselves during a ceremony as a show of faith. Alternatively, it is the "spirit" forcing them to harm themselves, although they claim to be immune to pain during the possession. There are accounts of people eating broken glass and razor blades, handling red-hot irons, plunging a hand into boiling oil, and rubbing chili-infused alcohol onto their skin and hot peppers into their eyes. Those possessed by the spirit of Lenglensou cut themselves with knives, scissors, or razor blades. These feats occur supposedly without injuries, but, like the Pentecostal snake handlers, Voodoo practitioners sometimes lose fingers or their lives. In the American version of Voodoo, this self-torture usually translates to drinking copious quantities of alcohol, and eating hot peppers.

The hypnotic drumming may cause the revelers to fall into a trance-like state. Similar to Native American shamans or psychic mediums, the possessed becomes an oracle for the spirits, who offer advice, instructions, and warn of curses. Prophecy is another important practice in Voodoo. Any kind of object can be used as a tool of divination. Most often cowrie shells, animal bones, or feathers are used to predict the future—or, in some neighborhoods, animal blood or entrails. The spirits also communicate via visions or dreams. It is believed that certain herbs can facilitate dreams from the spirits. Jasmine, eyebright, and hibiscus encourage psychic dreams that provide answers to relationship problems. Chamomile prevents nightmares, and calendula will make you dream of lottery numbers. Simply drink the herbs as a tea before bedtime, or sprinkle them on your pillow.

Sacrifice Operation

The most controversial aspect of Voodoo and Santeria is the practice of animal sacrifice. This is an integral part of the faith. Chickens, roosters, dogs, lambs, goats, cows, pigeons, and pigs are sacrificed as offerings to honor the spirits, or as gifts to enlist their help. In the Catholic Holy Communion the wafer represents the body of Christ, and the wine represents his blood. In Voodoo and Santeria, the blood of the dead animal is believed to turn into the blood of the spirits, while the spiritual energy from the animal supposedly feeds and energizes the spirits.

Animal sacrifice is an important part of Voodoo and Santeria folk medicine. In a common spell, a chicken or pigeon is rubbed all over the patient's body to absorb their illness or misfortune. The problem is transferred magically from the patient to the animal, which is then killed, and the remains are discarded. Practitioners maintain that the animals are killed humanely. Unfortunately, this is often untrue, and the animals are killed cruelly. The heads of live birds are twisted off, and the throats of goats or pigs are slit, and the animal is allowed to bleed to death. Sometimes the animal's meat is consumed, its blood is drunk for ritualistic purposes, and the bones dried and used for spells. Often the carcass is disposed of, so the "evil" is carried away.

Animal sacrifice is often rendered metaphorical in American rituals. Instead of appeasing the spirits by killing a pigeon, the practitioner may leave fruit, cakes, candy, or honey for them at an altar, to "sweeten" them. Instead of killing a dove to use its blood for writing a spell, a jar of fake Halloween blood is used. In place of sacrificing an animal, the practitioner may present the spirits with cooked meat from a fast food outlet, or fresh meat from a supermarket.

Despite the denials of Voodoo and Santeria practitioners, animal sacrifice does occur in the United States. There are regular news items about the discovery of dumped animal parts that have been traced to religious rituals. The legality of animal sacrifice has been raised in court, where the practice was banned, but ultimately legalized. In the 1993 *Church of Lukumi Babalu Aye vs. City of Hialeah* case, the Supreme Court case ruled that prohibiting animal sacrifice violates the First Amendment's guarantee of the free exercise of religion. The 2009 case of *Jose Merced, President Templo Yoruba Omo Orisha Texas, Inc. vs. City of Euless* upheld the right of Santeria adherents to practice animal sacrifice in the United States.

That Voodoo That She Did So Well

Marie Laveau is the most notorious Voodoo character. Born around 1794, Laveau was a free woman of mixed heritage. She was a hairdresser who catered to the wealthy women of the city, until she decided to learn another trade, Voodoo. She learned the craft from a man known as Doctor John, and that craft was deception. More powerful than the curses, cures, and charms she dispensed was her ability to dig up dirt on the wealthy and to pass this off as psychic knowledge, which she would then use to blackmail them.

Laveau's life is relegated to folklore, and stories about her are often contradictory. She is credited with saving the lives of several condemned men using Voodoo, but they were executed in the end. She is known for her kindness and compassion in freeing slaves and caring for the sick and poor, but she sold curses, blackmailed people, and operated a brothel. It is believed that she lived for over one hundred years, all the while maintaining her youth, but she had a daughter who bore a striking resemblance to her. Laveau was the "Voodoo Queen of New Orleans," but until she died she was a devout Catholic who attended mass regularly. Her tomb is a shrine for visitors, even though there is disagreement over where she is buried. She died sometime around 1881, yet she is still a powerful presence in New Orleans.

To this day, American Voodoo is most popularly associated with New Orleans. This particular brand is often called Louisiana Voodoo. Like the city's culture and cuisine, Louisiana Voodoo is a gumbo of beliefs and practices. There are the Wiccan-influenced Voodooists who are more likely to do a tarot reading than perform a Voodoo ritual. Then there are the cultural Voodooists, who enjoy the drumming circles and dressing up like zombies. There are more traditional practitioners who delight the tourists and annoy the locals with their public ceremonies. Addressing the modern-day concerns in the community, they hold rituals petitioning the spirits to punish the city's drug peddlers, thieves, prostitutes, and other criminals. This has an incidental practical purpose. New Orleans is a superstitious city, and its residents often respond better to voodoo rituals than the authorities.

Adherents argue that Voodoo is a religion, but it is most certainly a business. Louisiana Voodoo is a heavily commercialized cultural voodoo. Over time, it has interwoven with the city's infamous Mardi Gras parade, and the Mexican holiday, the Day of the Dead. Voodoo stores are more souvenir shops that sell traditional ritual objects as tourist trinkets. They stock "authentic" gris-gris and black cat bones, beside Mardi Gras beads and jambalaya mixes. This is a kind of watered-down Disney Voodoo, with overpriced Voodoo dolls, and herbal remedies that can be found in a jar at the supermarket. However, everywhere you go, people will whisper in hushed tones, that they can get you access to "real Voodoo dolls," and "Priests who do real Voodoo rituals."

Voodoo Child (Slight Return)

Beyond the Louisiana version, Voodoo has gone mainstream. It has attracted Wiccans, psychics, mediums, and other practitioners of the metaphysical, and even proponents of alternative medicine. They incorporate elements of Voodoo terminology and tools for their street cred. Advertisements in almanacs and phone books and on the Web sell services that "guarantee" to win back an ex-lover, to remove curses, or to force an enemy to move away. Voodoo's biggest community is online. These practitioners are Voodoo masters, princes, kings, or doctors who all practice "authentic," "real," or "true" Voodoo. These sites sell spells that cater to an American audience. They will help you find love, meet that mortgage payment, lose weight, or change the color of your eyes. They will cast these spells for you from their virtual Voodoo temples; they promise! Instead of gifts of candy and flowers, these "spirits" expect offerings of money. Alternatively, many psychics reject Voodoo and Santeria as the occult.

It is often said that this kind of Voodoo masks the "real Voodoo," and that "serious practitioners" went underground because of the commercial popularity of Voodoo, or because it is stigmatized. However, there is no real Voodoo or fake Voodoo, only different types of Voodoo. In the United States, Voodoo is practiced in many different ways by many different people. There are teenagers who buy books of Voodoo spells and experiment with candle burning, through to the Hougans trained in traditional methods that sacrifice animals.

Practitioners say that true Voodoo is conducted behind closed doors. However, Voodoo is mostly practiced in the home because there is no church or organized structure. Many Voodooists are indeed covert about their practices, but this cautiousness has its roots in the historical necessity of keeping the practice a secret. Alternatively, practitioners are secretive because of the stigma associated with Voodoo, or because their practices are socially reproved, such as sacrificing animals. Conversely, there is a respect for Voodoo's history and classification as religion, while criticisms are often interpreted as discriminatory. There is also a fear of Voodoo in the United States, borne of the stereotypes of Hollywood movies such as *White Zombie*.

A Bone to Pick with Zombies

Zombi is a snake god in Haitian Vodou, but this is not to be confused with the reanimated corpse known as a zombie. The original zombie is the creation of a bokor, an evil sorcerer. Using a poison, the victim is taken to the brink of death, and even buried by the grieving family, but then revived by the bokor to become a slow-moving, submissive slave. The Americanized zombie is a character of popular culture in horror books, movies, television shows, video games, Halloween costumes, and zombie walks. The concept first came to the United States in the early twentieth century via terrifying urban legends told by tourists returning from Haiti that became the subject of pulp fiction magazines and then films. In the 1932 movie *White Zombie*, a wealthy plantation owner falls in love with a woman who is engaged to be married. To win her, he seeks the assistance of a Voodoo master, who turns her into a zombie with a potion, and she obeys his every command.

With the 1968 film *Night of the Living Dead*, the modus operandi of the zombie changed forever. The modern American zombie has evolved into a hungry, diseased monster that feeds on the flesh of the living, with a particular taste for brains. They aren't always slow-moving corpses; nowadays the walking dead are often the running dead. Fast zombies can run and jump, while Michael Jackson's music video for "Thriller" features dancing zombies. The process of zombification has changed from an evil sorcerer using magical powders and poisons into a contagious condition. Hollywood zombies have many different causes: they are infected by a virus; radiation from passing asteroids reanimates dead bodies; rage-infected monkeys spread the disease; or a plague is unleashed by the government. This self-replicating zombie inspired the Centers for Disease Control to use the theme of a Zombie Apocalypse to teach people how to prepare for real-life emergencies, such as pandemics, earthquakes, and hurricanes.

These tropes of violent, flesh-eating zombies gave a name to a series of unrelated cannibalistic assaults in 2012 that were feared to herald a real-life Zombie Apocalypse. In the "Maryland zombie attack," student Kujoe Bonsafo Agyei-Kodie went missing, but his disembodied head and hands were soon found stored in metal tins in his home. His roommate

Alexander Kinyua later admitted to eating the man's heart and parts of his brain before disposing of his other remains in a dumpster. In the "Miami zombie attack," Rudy Eugene brutally attacked homeless man Ronald Poppo. He gouged out his left eye and proceeded to gnaw at his face. When police fired a shot at the naked attacker, he growled and snapped his teeth. The second shot killed him, but by this time he had left his victim blind and had already chewed away at most of his face.

There have been several claims of real-life zombies, but not in the United States. In Haiti, the belief in zombies is widespread, and turning someone into a zombie is considered an act of revenge. Zombification is so feared that it is a common practice to stand guard over a fresh tomb for days to weeks to protect the corpse, and to place poisons or charms with the body, or even to decapitate a body before burial. The belief is taken so seriously that zombification is a criminal offense under the Haitian Penal Code (Article 246). According to Vodou lore, the bokor poisons the victim with a mixture that induces a coma. In a catatonic state the victim is mistaken for dead and entombed. Soon thereafter they are exhumed by the bokor, and another potion is administered that reanimates them, but renders them robotic. In some stories the person's soul, spirit, or memory is trapped in a bottle and stored, to keep them zombified, or it is sold as a good-luck spell. The zombie is then exploited for slave labor.

The most infamous real-life case is the story of Clairvius Narcisse, who paid a visit to his sister in 1983, although he had been dead since 1962. Narcisse reported that he had had an argument over property with his brother, who then employed a bokor to turn him into a zombie. Soon he was spitting blood and running a fever, so Narcisse checked into the Albert Schweitzer hospital in Deschapelles. Three days later he was declared dead. However, Narcisse claimed to be conscious during his "death" and stated that he remembered being buried alive. Later that night, the bokor exhumed and revived him. Narcisse was forced to work on the bokor's sugar plantation until his master died two years later. Avoiding his brother, Narcisse wandered aimlessly across Haiti for sixteen years. When he returned upon his brother's death, he was verified by family members because he was able to answer questions about his childhood.

This story is documented in the book *The Serpent and the Rainbow* by ethnobiologist Wade Davis, who visited Haiti to research zombification. The intrepid traveler had brushes with bokors who tried to trick the foreigner with fake formulas, but he eventually acquired samples of the spell. The zombie recipe included a small amount of neurotoxin from puffer fish called tetrodotoxin, including folk ingredients such as human bones collected from the grave of a recently deceased baby, and fragments of toads, sea worms, lizards, and tarantulas. The hallucinogenic datura plant, also known as Jimson weed, was allegedly used to control the zombies. A number of scholars have disagreed that these substances could have the apparent effects, yet still enable the zombie to perform labor, but really, in Davis's samples, the doses were too small to have any effect. Moreover, it was never proven that the man who reappeared was really Clairvius Narcisse, or that the man who died in the hospital was Clairvius Narcisse.

One study examined three alleged zombies. The subjects were all believed to be family members who had returned from the dead. However, they all looked younger than their photographs. Medical examinations revealed that one patient was a catatonic schizophrenic, another was diagnosed with organic brain syndrome and epilepsy, while the final subject appeared to have been born with fetal alcohol syndrome. DNA tests didn't support the beliefs that the zombies were related to the families who claimed them. There appears to be no single explanation for zombies, although many cases probably represent undiagnosed mental illness or disability, and mistaken identity, in a culture that believes in zombies and the power of Vodou.

Bad Juju

Voodoo is said to be mostly performed for good, not harm. However, there are many cases where the beliefs and practices of Voodoo have caused physical, psychological, or financial harm for those people involved. In Queens, New York, six-year-old Frantzcia Saintill was forced into a Voodoo ceremony conducted by her mother. In a ritual she called "loa," Marie Lauradin stripped her daughter naked, and poured an accelerant on her head. The little girl caught alight when she was placed in a ring of fire. Frantzcia's mother and grandmother ignored her panicked cries for help and obvious pain for two days, until she was finally hospitalized. The girl suffered second- and third-degree burns on 25 percent of her small body, including her face, legs, and torso.

In Brooklyn, New York, a woman consulted a Voodoo priest who paid a visit to her home. The candles he lit in a spell to bring good luck ended up bringing considerable bad luck. During the ritual, it seems that the couple began having sex, and because they weren't paying attention, the candles ignited the bed sheets. The blaze spread quickly when a window was opened, allowing the wind to fan the flames. Eleven residents and twenty firefighters were injured in the fire, while fifty families were left homeless. Mary Feagin, a sixty-four-year-old resident of the building, was trapped in the blaze and found dead the next morning.

Esnel Jean was a well-known Voodoo priest in the neighborhood of Little Haiti in North Miami, Florida. He was married to Wilda Pierre, and they lived with her seventeen-year-old son, Evans, and five-year-old daughter, Melinda. One day, Pierre learned that Jean was stealing money from her bank account, and this led to a fierce argument. As part of a deadly spell, Jean murdered his wife and her two children. Police discovered the three bodies entombed in a makeshift crypt, with candles, religious figurines, posters of Catholic saints, and a live pigeon.

On her return from Haiti to Fort Lauderdale, Myrlene Severe failed to declare an item at customs, but we're not talking about cigarettes or alcohol. Immigration officials discovered that Severe was carrying a severed human head in her luggage. This was not simply a skull; the head still had teeth, skin, and hair attached. It also contained a lot of dirt, suggesting that it was disinterred from a burial ground. Severe had obtained the head from a Voodoo priest in Haiti, and its purpose was to ward off evil spirits.

Another danger of Voodoo is the potential for manipulation. There are frequent news stories involving Voodoo-related psychics who convince their clients that they are cursed, or that they need protection from curses. Instead of removing curses, these people remove the victim's money. There are dozens of documented cases of schemes where people have lost their entire life savings to these frauds. Janet Adams bilked an eighty-five-year-old woman out of $80,000, convincing her that it would keep her husband from dying. A San Francisco woman answered an advertisement for a $10 psychic, and ended up paying $108,000, plus a deposit on a sports car. The woman was in love but the fellow wasn't returning her affection, so psychic Lisa Marie Miller told her she was cursed and needed to be cleansed of evil spirits. Keeping the scam in the family, Miller's sister-in-law bilked a woman of $36,000 for a "psychic cleansing," while her mother-in-law bilked another victim of $450,000.

Folk medicine is a dangerous alternative to conventional medicine. It is risky to seek medical advice from people who diagnose disease using divination and possession. It is hazardous when the treatment relies on herbal teas, cleansing baths, elixirs, offerings, altar building, and rituals involving animal sacrifice. Folk doctors are ministering to spiritual needs, and their treatments have placebo value only. Many Web sites sell medicinal herbs claiming they will cure everything from infertility to baldness, such as Planet Voodoo. However, they also offer the disclaimer, "The information provided has not been evaluated by the Food and Drug Administration and is not intended to diagnose, treat, or cure any disease. Use at your own risk." Voodoo candles, oils, and powders should be sold as curios only, and carry obvious warnings. Other Web sites offer expensive Voodoo spells that claim to treat serious diseases. Ancient Magic Spells promises to cure all kinds of cancer with custom-made Voodoo spells, with the disclaimer hidden on another page, "this website is for entertainment purposes only."

Voodoo is also criticized for its practice of animal sacrifice. Practitioners have a number of arguments to support this practice. They claim that animal sacrifice is a traditional Judeo-Christian practice that appears in the Bible. They further argue that it is unconstitutional to deprive a religion of the freedom to practice its rituals, as per the previously mentioned landmark Supreme Court ruling and the Jose Merced case. They also defend the practice by pointing out that animal sacrifice is used in folk medicine, and that they take the animal's life to give life to the patient. This is compared to the use of animals in scientific research.

This shouldn't be a matter of upholding tradition or freedom of religion, but an issue of cruelty to animals. Furthermore, the ritual sacrifice of animals, not to mention Voodoo ceremonies that involve self-mutilation and bleeding, pose significant health and hygiene risks. It is also a question of scientific validity. Practitioners should be forced to prove their claims that animal sacrifice is a valid medical treatment, and that there is a transference of energy from the dying animal to the spirits.

We have seen the actual harm caused by Voodoo, but this is not a matter of judging Voodoo on the basis of its corrupt practitioners. There is plenty of intended harm in the general practice of Voodoo. Followers maintain that Voodoo is mostly "white magic," focusing on love and health. However, many popular spells have malicious intentions, such as footprint magic, crossroads magic, and the popular "Death Unto My Enemies" candles that are burned to cause misfortune or exact revenge. Many Voodoo rituals are dedicated to crossing, jinxing, and hexing, or uncrossing, jinx removing, and hex breaking. Some spells even have the intention to kill. Practitioners argue that these more sinister spells have their background in related faiths, but as we have seen, there is an obvious syncretizing of these religions in the United States.

Many Voodoo spells have unethical intentions, such as the use of candles and oils designed to win a court case unfairly, to control a person, or to break up a married couple. Even seemingly harmless love spells are malevolent and selfish, if the intention is to win the love of someone who is otherwise unwilling. Practitioners are not taking responsibility for their health, career, and relationship problems, but are instead using simplistic and ineffective spells. There are more practical and effective ways to cope with life's challenges than to light a candle or wring the head off a live chicken.

Voodoo falls prey to the logical fallacy known as an "appeal to antiquity," the belief that an idea is legitimate because it is ancient and traditional. Voodoo is afforded respect because it is categorized as a religion, and romanticized as an exotic belief system that has survived and thrived, despite attempts at its suppression, and the oppression of its people. There is no doubt that Voodoo had an important historical purpose, and continues to have great cultural significance, although it is also a superstitious faith that perpetuates dangerous beliefs and practices.

The Snake Man and the Bone Lady

All the Voodoo shops in New Orleans claim to be "the original," but the Voodoo Museum is the only one of its kind. I entered the tumbledown building with its grey hurricane shutters and found an enormous man sitting regally behind a desk. He eyed me quizzically through thick glasses. "Hello!" he bellowed, with the voice of a horror movie narrator. "Upstairs, I have a most magnificent snake!" "I'm sure you do," I quipped, my eyes darting to the door.

"Would you like to see my snake, young lady?" he asked. Before I had time to respond, he whisked out some photographs of a plump, white Burmese python. "This is Eugenie, my albino girl. She passed away," he told me with tears in his eyes. "I once had four children. Now I only have three," he sighed. He handed me his business card, which featured a photo of another python draped across his shoulders. This man was John T. Martin, Voodoo priest.

I took a walk around the museum, which looked like a messy living room with a Voodoo motif. On display were fragments of skulls and animal bones, chipped statues of Catholic saints, and dusty Voodoo dolls and crosses. There were cluttered altars with offerings of Mardi Gras beads, coins, candles, cigarettes, and empty bottles of alcohol. When I emerged from the museum sneezing I found a small snake slithering around the wooden floor. John introduced her as Jolie Vert, and she greeted me with a flick of her forked tongue. I explained that I wanted to experience an authentic Voodoo ritual, even though I was sure he thought he could pass off anything as the real deal to an Australian. John provided me with the phone number for Priestess Miriam, the "Bone Lady." On my way out the door he said, "Come back again. You may pet my snake if you promise to be gentle!"

Priestess Miriam Chamani is the Mambo of the New Orleans Voodoo Spiritual Temple. The temple's building is more famous for a gruesome murder that took place in the apartment above. This was once the home of a young couple named Zackary and Adriane. They became New Orleans icons when they defied orders to evacuate the city following Hurricane Katrina. Before "The Storm" they had been bartenders, and to survive they bartered booze for water, while "Addie" flashed her breasts at police patrols to ensure their continued protection. Following an argument one day, their love turned to lunacy, and Zackary strangled his girlfriend to death. He then took his life savings of $1,500 and spent it on food, drugs, alcohol, and strippers before leaping to his death from the roof of a hotel. His suicide note led police to their kitchen, where they found Addie's charred head in a pot on the stove, her limbs in the oven, and her torso in the refrigerator. Of course, some believe that Voodoo was behind it all.

Priestess Miriam performs Voodoo wedding ceremonies, curse removal, and healing rituals, but I was there to see the Bone Lady for a bone reading, a type of divination. She looked the part of a Voodoo priestess, wearing a white lace dress swathed in a colorful scarf, with long seashell earrings dangling out of her bright pink headdress. She led me into a small room full of burning candles with African drumming playing softly in the background. The eerie light bounced around the room, illuminating African masks and portraits of loa on the walls. We sat down at a table covered by a green cloth adorned with Voodoo symbols. The priestess took my hands and folded them around a black velvet bag. She shook the bag and reached inside. I expected her to withdraw the bones of raccoon penises, or at least a few chicken bones, but instead she took out a handful of cowrie shells. The priestess cast the "bones" onto the table and inspected the pattern they formed.

"I am talking to your ancestors now," she said enigmatically as she continued staring at the shells. "I have messages for you from them." However, my ancestors told me things I already knew about myself; that I like to travel, and that I am interested in other cultures and religions. This was a vague horoscope-like reading that could be applicable to many people. When her predictions were more specific, the priestess was wrong. The "spirits" said that my parents were happily married, although they have been divorced for several decades. I was told that I would become both an aunt and a mother within a year, but neither prophecy came true. It had been a real Voodoo experience alright; this was authentic, commercial Louisiana Voodoo. As the priestess ushered me out, she recommended a juju bag that would give me protection on my long trip home to England.

Chapter 5

Full of the Devil
Demonic Possession and Exorcism

"What an excellent day for an exorcism."
—*The Exorcist*

"Do you know anything about me, Ben? Do you know who I am?"
"No!" cried a terrified Ben.
"I am . . . The Real Exorcist!" Larson shouted dramatically, as the room
erupted into applause and cheers.

Demonic Denominations
Exorcism is a ritual for casting out Satan, demons, spirits, and other evil entities from a possessed person, place, or thing. The practice is often labeled as "medieval," or is dismissed as a theme of horror movies. The strange truth is that exorcism is prevalent today, and not only in African countries where a belief in witchcraft is rampant. Exorcism still thrives in countries such as Australia, New Zealand, Canada, England, and the United States.

The belief behind exorcism is that the devil exists and intervenes in people's daily lives, causing bad behavior and misfortune. Surprisingly, a recent Gallup poll found that 70 percent of Americans believe in the devil. This figure has increased from 55 percent in 1990. Furthermore, a nationwide survey reveals that 54 percent of Americans believe that "a

112

human being can be under the control or the influence of spiritual forces such as demons."

Demons are nondenominational and nondiscriminatory. They are just as happy to possess a Muslim body as a Christian one. Exorcism is practiced by followers of many different religions, denominations, cults, and sects. It is widespread, although obscure. From Catholic exorcists, to deliverance ministers and demonologists, there is much disagreement over definitions, contradictions in reports, and great variance in beliefs and practices.

Jesus is popularly believed to be the first exorcist, but exorcism and the belief in demonic possession have a long pre-Christian history. Archaeological evidence for the belief in demons and the practice of exorcism can be found across cultures and time. The Babylonians peeled away the layers of an onion to symbolize the release of power from demons, and created clay demons that were smashed in order to destroy the real demons. In ancient Egypt and Greece, sickness was attributed to evil spirits that were exorcised by physicians. The Dead Sea Scrolls describe the use of music to drive out demons, and the sacred Hindu text the Atharvaveda describes rituals for casting out demons using charms and amulets.

In the time of Jesus Christ, exorcism was a miraculous cure. Demons and the devil caused disease and disability, but Jesus was able to cast them out with an order. Matthew (8:16) describes one of these events: "they brought unto him many that were possessed with devils: and he cast out the spirits with his word, and healed all that were sick." Ironically, in the Old Testament, the demons were not sent by Satan, but by God. As revealed in Samuel (18:10), "and it came to pass on the morrow, that the evil spirit from God came upon Saul."

Across the centuries, exorcism continued to be practiced as a cure for demons, or disease, although the two were often seen as the same thing. Possession and exorcism experienced their heyday in the medieval period, especially during the European witch crazes where many cases were a result of religious hysteria. The belief in possession became common enough to warrant the creation of the Rite of Exorcism, which was written under Pope Paul V in 1614. At this time, mass public exorcisms were held—notably those that occurred in the French towns of Aix-en-Provence (1611), Loudun (1634), and Louviers (1647), where Ursuline nuns displayed the classic symptoms of Satan, including swearing, speaking in tongues, body convulsions, and the appearance of mysterious wounds that vanished suddenly. Medieval exorcisms were like many modern exorcisms. If prayer failed, the exorcist would try insults, whippings, and beatings until the demon left, or the possessed died.

By the Age of Enlightenment, it seemed as if exorcism was to stay in the Middle Ages. But the business of Beelzebub has enjoyed a few booms in modern times. Exorcism experienced a revival with the birth of Pentecostalism in the early twentieth century and then again with the proliferation of deliverance ministries during the 1960s. The general public's interest in demons, possession, and exorcism has been renewed by Hollywood, with movies such as *Rosemary's Baby* (1968), *The Exorcism of Emily Rose* (2005), *The Last Exorcism* (2010), *The Rite* (2011), and *Possession* (2012), but most notably with the 1973 release of *The Exorcist*.

The movie was based on the 1971 book by William Peter Blatty. The book was in turn inspired by a "true story" that began in 1949. The real case was not about a twelve-year-old girl called Regan, but a fourteen-year-old boy known as Roland. As the story goes, "Roland Doe" lived in Mount Rainier, Maryland. He was introduced to the Ouija board by his aunt Tillie. When she died suddenly, he used the device to contact her, but attracted a demon instead. Roland's demon caused some phenomena familiar from the movie, including shaking beds, levitating objects, and other poltergeist activity. The boy developed supernatural strength, and an aversion to anything holy. He began speaking in a guttural voice, which he used to utter curses and phrases in Latin, that is, if he wasn't vomiting. Bloody welts appeared on his skin, forming the words "evil," "hell," and "well." (Either the demon couldn't spell, or it's difficult to carve words into your own flesh.) Roland spent time in hospital, but his condition wasn't physical or psychological, it was spiritual. He finally underwent a series of spectacular and violent exorcisms that cast out his demons, and he lived happily ever after. Today, the book and movie versions of *The Exorcist* provide most of our stereotypes about possession, exorcism, and exorcists.

The Real Thing

In the United States today, exorcism is still practiced to varying extents by Catholic, Protestant, and Pentecostal churches, and in Judaism, indigenous religions, and New Age groups. Exorcism is most popularly associated with the Catholic Church, which is seen as the experts in the topic. This is not necessarily because there are more possessed Catholics, but because of the Church's long-standing tradition with the practice, and its presence in pop culture. Despite this association with Catholicism, there are relatively few Catholic exorcists in the United States. Canon Law requires that all 185 American dioceses have an official bishop-appointed exorcist. This isn't the case in practice, and the exact number isn't known. Various sources estimate that there is anything from ten (or less) to fifty (or more) Catholic exorcists in the United States. It is also difficult to estimate the number of deliverance ministers and New Age practitioners, as there are thousands of these kinds of exorcists across the country who preach that demons and possession are everyday dilemmas.

It is popularly believed that "real exorcists" won't talk about their work. Like secret agents, they operate undercover and can't disclose their identities. Alternatively, it is said they maintain their anonymity to protect the privacy of the possessed. Exorcists themselves suffer an identity crisis. Father Gabriele Amorth, the Chief Exorcist of Rome, is an Uncle Fester lookalike and a hellfire and brimstone exorcist straight out of the Dark Ages. *The Exorcist*'s Father Damien Karras is portrayed as a hero who clashed with the demon Pazuzu in a contest of wills for the soul of the little girl. In the movie *Constantine*, Keanu Reeves is a sex-symbol exorcist, a chain-smoking renegade who wields a shotgun cross.

The Catholic Church purports to be highly selective about performing exorcisms. They say that exorcisms are rare, because possession is rare. They claim to carefully investigate all cases, and screen candidates for underlying physical and psychological conditions. An exorcism is only performed when all other natural possibilities have been exhausted. Conversely, the Catholic Church also claims that exorcisms are on the increase, and that requests for the ritual have doubled over the last fifteen years. As a result, the Catholic diocese of Milan has established an exorcist hotline to deal with the volume of calls. Monsignor Angelo Macheroni, the Chief Exorcist of Milan, says he knows of one exorcist who performs up to 120 exorcisms per day. Father Amorth claims he has performed over 70,000 exorcisms during his lifetime.

The Church claims there is a rising demand for exorcists, especially among immigrant communities. All Catholic priests can perform exorcisms, although not all are trained in the practice. To meet the demand, the Vatican's university *Pontifical Athenaeum Regina Apostolorum* offers a course in exorcism, and holds conferences in the United States. They founded the International Association of Exorcists, an exclusive, restricted-membership country club for Catholic exorcists. There are a number of organizations in the United States that offer membership and training programs, including the International Society of Deliverance Ministers and the American Association of Exorcists. The latter provides free membership to anyone who simply claims to be an exorcist.

Take Possession

According to the Catholic Church, possession has a wide range of causes, but the demons need an invitation to the possession party. The most common cause is exposure to the occult, including participation in séances, psychic readings, Voodoo, black magic, and the use of divination tools, such as dowsing, astrology, tarot cards, and Ouija boards. Obviously, practicing Satanism will attract the Old Boy, but demons can also be acquired by dabbling in false religions (that is, any religion that is not theirs). These include New Age Spirituality, paganism, cults and sects, or anything connected to Eastern religions, even martial arts and yoga. Despite their claims that the occult attracts demons, Father Benedict Groeschel, an expert in demonic possession, reveals that when cases were referred to him he sought the assistance of a laywoman in his archdiocese "who possessed a gift for discerning spirits." Similarly, Father Amorth admits that he uses "seers and sensitives" in his exorcisms who are adept at sensing demons.

Old-school Catholics believe that idolatry, blasphemy, and other sins and broken commandments leave people vulnerable to possession. Rock and roll, punk, and metal are the devil's music, but he also enjoys irreligious movies, magazines, and books. Disease, mental illness, drug and alcohol addictions, violence, crime, abortion, sexual perversion, homosexuality, being a victim of "Satanic ritual abuse," or sexual abuse also render people susceptible to demonic invasion. All of these open a door or portal to demons, which are always on the lookout for a mortal home.

Unlike the devil dressed in his red bodysuit with a pitchfork, indwelling demons don't have a body, other than the one they've possessed. Instead, they manifest as a set of symptoms. In the Bible, very few signs of demonic manifestations are described. These include muteness (Matthew 9:32–33), blindness (Matthew 12:22), self-inflicted wounds (Mark 5:5), superhuman strength (Mark 5:3-4), and poltergeist-like activity—for example, "whenever it seizes him, it throws him to the ground. He foams at the mouth, gnashes his teeth and becomes rigid" (Mark 9:18). Of course, today we'd recognize these as organic disabilities or disorders.

The popular signs of possession expand on the biblical descriptions and include gifts and abilities, such as xenoglossia—that is, speaking in languages previously unknown to the victim—and clairvoyance—knowledge of the future. Alternatively, the demons unleash emotional, physical, and psychological attacks on their victims. Sickness can be a cause of demons, but also a symptom, especially chronic or undiagnosed illnesses and disabilities. Addictions cause possession, and possession causes addiction, especially alcoholism, drug abuse, obsessive gambling, and the compulsive use of pornography.

Unforeseen forces can cause the victim to bite, scratch, hit, or cut themselves, like the biblical reference to possession involving self-mutilation, "he cut himself with sharp stones" (Mark 5:5). Possession can allegedly incite depression and suicidal tendencies, or lead the victim to develop murderous feelings. In fact, demons have been used as a defense in court. In 1981, Arne Johnson murdered his landlord Alan Bono following an argument. In what became known as the "Demon Murder Trial," Johnson claimed that he was possessed by a demon at the time of the crime. Johnson had previously been in attendance at the exorcisms of his girlfriend's brother, where he allegedly cried, "Take me on instead of him!" These exorcisms were conducted by Ed and Lorraine Warren of

Amityville fame, who became involved in Johnson's case and influenced him to plead possession. His defense was unsuccessful and he spent five years in prison. This hasn't stopped other defendants from also alleging that "the devil made me do it."

You know there's a demon in the room when the temperature drops, and the possessed emits a foul odor that smells like sulfur, cabbages, or a musky-scented animal. Sometimes the demons are just plain vulgar and cause the victim to growl, swear, cough, spit, burp, vomit, yawn, or suffer unholy bouts of flatulence. Demons love sex, drugs, and rock and roll, but they are sensitive to religious material, so the possessed becomes unable to touch religious objects, or even look at them.

Demons that cause convulsions, levitation, and shape shifting clearly watch too much television. In the exorcist trade, these dramatic manifestations are known as "fireworks." Victims of these histrionic demons might eat spiders and flies, drink their own urine, mimic voices, animal noises, and sounds in nature, and speak like they are practicing to join a death metal band. A few unlucky people report to have been raped by demons. Male incubi and female succubi descend upon their sleeping victims and have their wicked way with them. These demons either assume an attractive form, or they have horns, fangs, claws, and tails. They typically attack people during sleep, and given this modus operandi, the victims might be experiencing waking dreams or episodes of sleep paralysis. Other cases have been explained as simple wet dreams, or more ominously, attributed to real-life cases of sexual assault, where it's easier to blame the devil than face the awful truth.

Father Malachi Martin's sensational *Hostage to the Devil* is alleged to be an eyewitness account of the possession and exorcisms of five Americans. The demons in these case studies were behind sexual debauchery, attempted murder, psychic powers, and satanic rituals, while one woman is raped by a giant spider. The exorcisms themselves sound like they are straight out of a movie script, as doors bang open and shut, books fly off the shelves, and the heroic priests are physically assaulted. Martin was a former Jesuit priest and when he renounced his vows he became an author who wrote controversial books about the Catholic Church. He claimed that his book did not exaggerate the events of the exorcisms, but he penned many thrillers, and it seems that *Hostage to the Devil* is just another one of his works of fiction.

Unimaginative demons are behind mundane events, such as nightmares, headaches, dizziness, crying, laughter, dancing, fainting, stomach aches, hiccups, a lack of appetite, and sleepiness, or sleeplessness. Other demons are more mundane and manifest as plain old negative feelings. The list of signs includes an exhaustive array of everyday emotions and behaviors, including aggression, anxiety, hate, anger, insecurity, paranoia, lust, or guilt. Demons can also present as misfortune that is reframed as a curse that manifests as financial problems, relationship woes, or a simple run of bad luck. Some exorcists argue that more moderate symptoms are not characteristic of demonic possession but of demonic "affliction," "oppression," or "vexation" and require prayers, not exorcism. Possession is clearly in the eyes of the beholder.

Exorcising Your Rites

The Catholic Church has an official manual for conducting exorcisms. "Of Exorcisms and Certain Supplications" (*De Exorcismis et Supplicationibus Quibusdam*) is the Rite of Exorcism from the Roman Ritual. The current document was revised in 1999, but the editions aren't updated very often. Exorcisms are often perceived as medieval, and the original version *is* medieval, as it was written in 1614.

Despite the existence of the manual, there is no single formula for performing an exorcism. As we saw above, the Bible outlines some symptoms of possession, but doesn't offer any steps for performing an exorcism. Jesus had several different approaches to exorcism, but he often just ordered the demon out of the victim. Once, Jesus simply touched the sufferer (Luke 13:10), which evolved into the practice of "laying on of hands." Occasionally, Jesus even healed from afar (Matthew 8:8; Matthew 15:22–28), giving rise to modern remote exorcisms by phone, or online. The only set of guidelines is the Rite of Exorcism, but it is just a framework, and there are many methods and techniques.

There are several different kinds of exorcism within the Catholic Church. Baptismal Exorcism is the practice of blessing an infant before baptism, to cleanse it of original sin. There are exorcism prayers to bless salt, water, and olive oil before they are used as sacramentals. There are different grades of exorcism for casting out demons too. "Minor" or "simple" exorcisms are informal rituals for demonic afflictions or oppression. This can often be vanquished with the recitation of a prayer, usually the Prayer to Saint Michael the Archangel. The Rite of Exorcism is reserved for formal rituals known as "major," "real," or "solemn" exorcisms. These should only be performed with the permission of a bishop.

Once it is decided that a solemn exorcism is needed, an exorcist is selected for the event. He must be acting under proper authority, and be a truly pious and moral man. It is a dangerous job. The demon will use techniques to confuse, injure, and demoralize the priest. He will be called nasty names, attacked physically, and his innermost embarrassing secrets will be revealed. The devil will debate with him, tempt him, and make him question his faith. Exhausted and spiritually vulnerable, the priest is at great risk of the demons transferring to him.

The chosen exorcist prepares for the ritual with fasting and prayer. He undergoes confession on the big day. He dons a purple stole, because this was the symbol of authority for Roman officials, and the color is associated with penance and healing. The exorcism can be conducted in the victim's home, but it is safer if it is done in God's house. Exorcisms are a kind of spiritual intervention, so the victim's loved ones should be there for support and backup prayer. The possessed is restrained in a chair or bed, although this never stopped a demon, so light fittings, curtains, tables, rugs, and other potentially dangerous objects are removed from the room.

The tools of the exorcism include the holy book, holy water, holy relics, and crucifixes. Blessed wine, oil, and salt may be used in the ritual too. The exorcist begins by tracing the sign of the cross over the victim, himself, and all present, and then sprinkles everyone with holy water. The ceremony that follows features the exorcist's personal selection of prayers, psalms, and scriptural readings. Many of these are from the Rite, including the Litany of the Saints, Psalm 53, and lessons from the Holy Gospel according to St. John, St. Mark, and St. Luke. In response to all of this holy action there is no projectile vomit or spinning heads, but the possessed might growl, groan, or swear in response, because they think that is what they are supposed to be doing.

In Heaven's Name

During the Rite there is a demon quiz where the indwelling demons are asked for their number, names, and nature. Like the story of Rumpelstiltskin, knowing the demon's name gives the exorcist power over it. If the demon is asked in a certain way, he is compelled to surrender his name, but as we know, the devil is the Prince of Lies and liable to tell big fibs, or to mix lies with the truth. In what is known as pretense, the devil tries to disguise its true identity and intentions. The exorcist might be misled by the tricky demon, and accidentally try to exorcise Furfur when he really needs to get rid of Murmur.

Demons all have names that sound like heavy metal bands. The heavyweights are devils like Lucifer, Beelzebub, and Mephistopheles. Some demons have grand names, such as Lucifuge Rofocale and Glasya-Labolas. Others are kings, princes, or nobility, including Duke Zepar, Count Andromalius, and Marquis Marchosias. Some demons have important political roles in hell, such as Thammuz, the Ambassador to Hell, or Asatroth, the Treasurer to Hell. Hell is more progressive than the Church, and females can be demons too, just like President Amy. Often the indwelling demon is one the possessed is familiar with from television, such as the infamous Jezebel, Belial, or Legion, but only once in the Bible does Jesus ask the demon for its name, "My name is Legion, for we are many" (Mark 5:9).

Get the Hell out of Here

Jesus occasionally rebuked the demons, such as, "Be quiet, and come out of him!" (Luke 4:35) Some exorcists rebuke the devil too, but it's usually as innocuous as, "I rebuke you!" The apostles also performed exorcisms, although they had to invoke Christ's name, just as modern exorcists command the demon to leave in the name of Jesus. The Rite suggests the following order: "I cast you out, unclean spirit, along with every Satanic power of the enemy, every specter from hell, and all your fell companions; in the name of our Lord Jesus Christ. Begone and stay far from this creature of God." The exorcist is to use an authoritative voice, filled with confidence, humility, and fervor. Jesus never needed crucifixes or holy water to exorcise a demon. He didn't even need prayer. Using his authority, Jesus simply ordered the demons to leave, and they obeyed. Father Amorth once stated that ritual elements only make the slightest difference to an exorcism's effectiveness, and that many exorcisms are limited to ordering the demon to go.

Deliverance ministers send demons back to hell, but Catholic exorcists don't tell demons where to go. Biblical demons would simply vanish, although sometimes they would be transferred into something else. In Luke (8:28–36) Jesus cast out devils from a man into an unfortunate herd of pigs who immediately committed swine suicide. In *The Exorcist*, Father Karras begs the demon "take me!" and so it exits the little girl and enters the priest, who leaps out of the window to his death.

There is a final prayer to renounce Satan. Once you get him out, you don't want to invite him back in. If all goes well, the demons are evicted from their mortal home. According to legend, this expulsion is heralded by a gunshot sound, a scream, cry, or other disturbing noise, which is followed by sudden peacefulness. The demons are often expelled from the body through the nose or mouth, although traditional Jewish spirits would leave through a fingernail, a toenail, or the vagina or rectum. The possessed may force a trickle of vomit, cough, sneeze, scream, or spit out the demons. Father Amorth reports he has witnessed people expel a number of curious items during exorcism, including glass, nails, wire, rope, knotted string, thread, blood clots, and even small wooden dolls. This sounds a lot like early séances, where ectoplasm oozed from the medium's mouth, which was later exposed to be cheesecloth, or psychic surgery, where the healer removes "tumors" that are revealed to be chicken entrails.

The exorcism can take many hours, yet it still may be unsuccessful. Usually the possessed is left wondering why the entire experience wasn't more spectacular and supernatural. If the demons haven't departed, the exorcism will be repeated, bearing in mind that demons are sneaky and may only pretend to leave. The possessed also needs to attend church regularly, undergo confession, and receive the sacraments. It helps if they pray, fast, abstain from sex, and adopt a modest diet that includes blessed water, salt, and oil. All in all, exorcism is a treatment that should be taken like ongoing medication. The process may take days, weeks, months, or even years. In some cases, the possessed sees no sign of improvement, and simply gives up on the exorcism.

Spirited Away

Exorcism is a tradition in many established religions, but it has also been reinvented as a New Age practice. These followers often reject the idea of a literal Satan, that's just silly, but they still believe in demons, and possibly ghosts, poltergeists, spirits, trolls, djinn, dibbuks, extraterrestrials, astral beings, or other evil entities. Possession is often reframed as "attachment" or "affliction" by any of these beings. Sometimes possession is a good thing, as when followers of Voodoo or Santeria are "mounted" by the spirits known as loa or orisha respectively. Evil influence also comes in the form of curses, psychic, and spiritual attacks, past life interference, karmic and astral ties, dark or negative energies, vibrations, and thought forms.

Similar to Catholic demons, evil entities and energies see occult practices as an invitation to possess the person dabbling in them. Once an entity gains entry into a host, a hole or tear in the aura or energy fabric is created, allowing more entities to follow. Not only can people become possessed, but also animals, places, and inanimate objects. Ghost hunters fear taking home evil spirits from investigations. Hitchhiking spirits are supposedly picked up from homes, hospitals, cemeteries, battlegrounds, and other stereotypically haunted places. Some people believe that residual negative energies from former owners can be transferred into buildings and personal possessions. Possession supposedly starts when people move into a house with a tragic past, and when antiques or second-hand items are brought into the home, and vintage clothes or jewelry are worn. According to this theory, patients of organ transplants and blood transfusions can empathetically take on the emotions and personalities of their former owners.

The symptoms of attachment are the same as for demonic possession, but even more varied and vague. These entities or energies are believed to affect behavior and attitude, causing mood swings, personality changes, or fears and phobias. Alternatively, they are parasitic, and feed off the living host, causing a lack of energy, memory, and concentration problems, and general aches and pains. By these loose definitions, evil is everywhere and most people are possessed, most of the time.

Spiritual or New Age exorcisms are reinterpreted as cleansings, clearings, detachment, depossession, detoxification, banishment, purification, and soul rescue or spirit release therapy. Often, these rituals are as much about saving the poor, trapped spirit as saving the possessed. Like exorcism, these rituals are intended to be curative, although there are many protective rituals designed to ward off spirits and prevent attachment in the first place, especially before conducting a ghost hunt or a psychic reading.

There are thousands of practitioners of New Age exorcisms in the United States, but they rarely call themselves exorcists. Instead, they are pagan priests and priestesses, demonologists, shamans, psychics, mediums, hypnotherapists, spiritual counselors, healers, and paranormal investigators. Their diagnoses are often based on quick impressions, unlike the cautious evaluations of the Catholic Church. Instead of consultations with clergy and medical evaluations, the attachment is diagnosed using pendulums, tarot cards, and devices to communicate with the dead. The New Age cure doesn't take days, weeks, months, or years, but the length of a standard consultation. Of course, the client will be encouraged to attend future appointments for preventive care, or to treat new spiritual issues.

New Age exorcisms are less about holy water and more about sage. There is no Roman Rite for New Age exorcisms, so the ritual is different each time. They are a mix of old and new, of Pagan, Christian, Jewish, and indigenous rituals. If they aren't performed in the home or place of worship, they can be done over the telephone or online. In intercessory exorcism, the person doesn't know they're being exorcised. The ceremonies may include prayers, but there are also affirmations, spells, spiritual or aura healing, relaxation techniques, meditation, music, hypnosis, visualization, and the use of white light, divine light, mystical shields, and protective circles. They may brandish a cross, but also use amulets and burn incense, herbs, and candles. They use salt, oil, garlic, and eggs, but they aren't making an omelet. They might cast the demons to the pits of hell in the name of Jesus Christ, but they also bind or banish the entities, or gently coax them to go to the light, or cross over. Ironically, clergy and deliverance ministers argue that these very methods open doors to invite demonic possession in the first place.

It's Not Unusual

Deliverance ministers also drive away demons and unclean spirits, although they don't call themselves exorcists. Deliverance ministers are usually nondenominational Christians, and for them, this is spiritual warfare. They are charismatic, bombastic bullies of Beelzebub, and their exorcisms are more sensational than sacred. Protestants pray away the devil, while deliverance ministers rebuke the devil. Catholics sprinkle holy water on the possessed, while deliverance ministers dowse them with cold water to make the victim's body an uncomfortable place for the demon. Psychics visualize the entities traveling toward a white light, while deliverance ministers cast the demons to the bowels of hell, or some scene from a Hieronymus Bosch painting. Ironically, the terminology of deliverance is similar to New Age exorcisms, although deliverance ministers consider spirituality, witchcraft, the paranormal, the occult, and Satanic ritual abuse to be the causes of demons and evil spirits. Their exorcisms are often a kind of counseling or therapy, and demons and curses are excuses for addictions, illness, marital problems, and perversions. Deliverance is a relatively modern concept, although there are hundreds of deliverance ministers in the United States.

Most deliverance ministers think that rock music causes demons, but Pastor Jack Stahl believes one rock star can cast out demons. Better known as the Tom Jones Exorcist, Pastor Jack is the minister of the Progressive Universal Life Church, aka the Church of Tom Jones in Sacramento, California. He performs baptisms, marriages, funerals, healing services, and exorcisms to the tune of Tom Jones songs. Pastor Jack doesn't consider the Welsh singer to be a God, but he believes his voice is soulful, spiritual, and supernatural. He says that Tom Jones' music enables him to get in touch with the Holy Spirit to exorcise demons. To perform his exorcisms he dresses and dances like Tom Jones, while "It's Not Unusual," "Delilah," "What's New Pussycat," and even "Sex Bomb" play in the background. He even operates a twenty-four-hour Tom Jones Exorcism hotline.

Deliver Us from Evil

The *Exorcism of Emily Rose* (2005) is loosely based on the true story of Anneliese Michel, a German girl from a deeply religious Catholic family. In 1968, seventeen-year-old Anneliese began to suffer convulsions, and was diagnosed with epilepsy. She soon began experiencing hallucinations while praying and fell into a deep depression. Anneliese began attributing her symptoms to demonic possession, believing she was possessed in turns by Lucifer, Judas Iscariot, Nero, and Hitler. By 1975 her family began searching for a spiritual solution. She gave up on her medical treatment and chose to rely on exorcisms for healing. Anneliese underwent sixty-seven exorcisms in less than a year. In her delusional state, she talked about dying to atone for the sins of the young, and she began to starve herself. In her severe state of malnutrition and dehydration, she died at age twenty-four. At her death she weighed seventy pounds (thirty kilograms). Clearly, Anneliese was seriously ill, and her case was one of gross negligence. Her story led to restrictions on exorcisms in Germany, but like Americans who go to Canada for their prescription medication, Germans now go to Poland or Switzerland for their exorcisms.

Exorcists like Evangelist Bob Larson argue that if psychological and physiological illness has been ruled out, there is no harm in conducting an exorcism. Contrary to the Church's claims of caution, Father Amorth advocates exorcism as the first step in a process of elimination. He once said, "if the exorcism helps, it is the devil, if not, it isn't." This is reminiscent of the ducking stool test used during the witch craze; if the woman floats, she's a witch, if she dies, she was innocent.

Like bloodletting and trepanning, exorcism as a "cure" is more dangerous than the disease. Exorcisms can result in serious psychological abuse, physical injury, and even death. Particularly abhorrent are the exorcisms of children, of people with mental illness or disabilities, and the practice of "gay exorcism," when the demons that supposedly cause homosexuality are exorcised. Father Amorth brands homosexuality as a "particularly stubborn sin." Members of the ministry Manifested Glory Industries attempted to exorcise a sixteen-year-old boy by beating him for twenty minutes until he vomited and passed out, while his assaulters cried, "Pray out the gay!" Here are some shocking examples of the harm caused by a belief in demons and the practice of exorcism.

After she had been released from a Rhode Island hospital, Mario Garcia thought that his mother-in-law was acting strangely. He decided that she was possessed and required an exorcism. To chase away the demons, Garcia burned leaves, and then rammed two eight-inch steel crucifixes down her throat, as relatives watched and prayed. Blood poured out of her mouth because Garcia had punctured her esophagus. When police arrived on the scene, Garcia screamed, "The devil is inside her!" Fortunately, the woman survived the incident. Others aren't so lucky.

Twenty-five-year-old Kyong-A Ha suffered from insomnia. She began associating with a fundamentalist Christian sect near her home in Emeryville, California. The Reverend Jean Park led a ritual that lasted six hours in which the young woman was held down and struck over one hundred times to "cast out her demons." During the ordeal a towel was used to muffle her screams, which ceased when she died of the brutal assault. Park claimed that "the damage to Ha was done by demons" and she was only practicing exorcism "in the name of Jesus Christ," as mandated in the Bible.

Eight-year-old Terrance Cottrell Jr. was autistic, but his mother was convinced that his symptoms were caused by spirits. She even heard these spirits say, "Kill me, take me, kill me." She began attending evening prayer sessions at the Faith Temple Church of the Apostolic Faith in Milwaukee, Wisconsin. Under the guidance of Ray A. Hemphill, the congregation formed a circle around Terrance and performed an exorcism on him for two terrorizing hours. They forced him to lie on the floor, but he struggled to get up, kicking and scratching—further evidence that he was possessed. Instead of a laying on of hands they restrained his feet, arms, and head, and sat on his chest until they suffocated him to death.

Like many other five-year-olds, Amy Burney of New York was prone to tantrums, but her mother and grandmother believed evil spirits were the cause instead. They attempted a home exorcism, tying her down and forcing her to swallow a poisonous mixture of ammonia, vinegar, pepper, and olive oil. They taped her mouth shut so she couldn't spit out the lethal potion, so the little girl died. The police found her body wrapped in a sheet and dumped in the garbage bin outside of the mother's apartment.

Five-year-old Breanne Spickard of Los Angeles was spinning cartwheels around her apartment when her mother and two friends decided to "rid her of the devil." In a bizarre exorcism, the women savagely paddled the girl with a cheese board. Two days later, they beat her again because "their work was not finished." For two hours they whipped her with the cheese board, stripping away layers of her skin. One woman stuffed her foot in the child's mouth to stifle her cries, while another jumped on her back. The women believed they were communicating with God, who ordered them to conduct the exorcism. They were regular users of methamphetamine, and often used a wooden paddle to beat their children when they were high. Weeks before her death, Breanne was enlisted to "help get rid of the devil" and participated in a similar beating of another child.

Jessica Carson of Henderson, Texas, believed that her baby was possessed, so she and her boyfriend Blaine Milam decided to "beat the demons out of" thirteen-month-old Amora Bain Carson. Milam attacked Amora brutally, while her mother looked on. The couple decided that the exorcism had gone badly, so they went to a pawnshop to sell some household tools to pay a priest to perform an exorcism. However, when they came home Amora was already dead. She had sustained a head injury, trauma to her genitals and liver, and multiple breaks in her ribs. She showed signs of strangulation, and her little body was covered in bruises and bite marks.

Many of these exorcisms are home jobs, although in no way are the supposed "professional" jobs safer, or more valid. Bob Larson brags that his exorcisms never result in more than a bruise to the possessed, but not even a bruise is acceptable for an illegitimate cure. Put simply, people who undergo exorcisms aren't receiving the real help they need. It is often the exorcist that needs the help, and there is a broad range of underlying problems, including drug use, mental-health issues, fraud, and dangerously misinformed beliefs. As we can see, attempts to suffocate, drown, or beat out the demons only result in the suffocation, drowning, or beating of the victim, and the exorcism often becomes an execution. The real horror of exorcism is not in the alleged possession, but the exorcism itself.

Diagnosis "Demons"

When the original Rite of Exorcism was written there was no Diagnostic and Statistical Manual of Mental Disorders. Despite a few attempts to have demonic possession listed in the manual as a genuine condition, it is not recognized as a psychiatric or medical diagnosis. However, the underlying causes of the symptoms often are psychiatric or medical, and before the advent of modern psychiatry, demonic possession was the explanation for neurological disorders and mental illness. These conditions are confused as demonic possession because their symptoms resemble the alleged signs of possession. For example, epilepsy can cause convulsions, while schizophrenia can cause auditory and visual hallucinations. One person's mental illness is another person's possession.

How can exorcists tell the difference between demonic possession and mental illness? The Catholic Church claims that medical doctors, psychologists, and psychiatrists work with the Church to rule out these conditions before proceeding with an exorcism. In practice, medicine takes a back seat to belief. If the exorcists do consult doctors, they use Catholic ones who are biased and believe in demonic possession. Church-appointed doctors are like doctors appointed by the prosecution, or tobacco-company scientists. In the end, the decision is supposed to be made by the bishop, but no sufferer, priest, bishop, or even pope is qualified to diagnose. In a no-win situation, if the alleged possession is proven to be an illness, it is often believed that demons caused the illness. If those involved do proceed with the exorcism, some clergy recommend that the person undergoing the exorcism also seeks concurrent psychiatric care, which would be the efficacious treatment.

Sometimes it takes a while for the medical profession to get to the bottom of a case that can mimic possession. Twenty-two-year-old Kiera Echols was suffering from a mysterious disorder that caused fever and severe hallucinations. In her confusion and distress she demanded that a priest perform an exorcism on her. Medical tests eventually revealed that she didn't have demons, she had a rare teratoma tumor growing on one of her ovaries. These tumors contain cells from other organs, and teratomas have grown their own hair, teeth, bones, and, occasionally, eyes, hands, or feet.

No Mother Teresa

Several days after her death in September 1997, it was revealed that Mother Teresa had once undergone an exorcism. She was in hospital at the time when fellow patient Henry D'Souza, the Archbishop of Calcutta, diagnosed her demons. No, she didn't scream because she came into contact with holy water, but she was suffering from insomnia. D'Souza feared she was possessed and ordered an exorcism for her. She was dazed and behaved strangely before the exorcism, but this is unsurprising. She was eighty-seven-years-old and suffering from a heart condition. After the exorcism, she apparently "slept like a baby," but it was probably due to the reassurance, and the drugs.

Some argue that exorcism still offers comfort to the would-be possessed. This is a result of the placebo effect, the psychological and often temporary effect of an inert pill or, in this case, of a ritual. Exorcism that is effective is self-deception on the part of the believer, and often the exorcist. But the placebo effect doesn't work for all complaints. Even if the exorcism is cathartic, it's not worth the risks. Moreover, it is not effective in the way it is described to work.

There is no single explanation for claims of demonic possession. There are as many causes as there are claims. Cases of possession and exorcism aren't documented in any formal way. Diagnoses are informal, and alleged successes of exorcism are anecdotal. However, with no evidence for demonic possession, we are left with the natural explanations. The "possessed" is suffering from a physiological, psychiatric, or psychological condition, or they are affected by the human condition, not a religious condition. It comes down to a choice to understand the natural world, or to believe in a supernatural, demon-haunted world.

Like a Man Possessed

What about the real story that inspired *The Exorcist*? Today, the facts have emerged, and it was a hoax. The actual events occurred in Cottage City, Maryland. The boy had a dysfunctional upbringing in a deeply superstitious family, and it appears he suffered from some psychological issues. Upon closer inspection, the phenomena don't seem so paranormal. The "shaking beds" were on rollers that could be easily moved. The boy's "Latin" only mimicked the Latin phrases spoken by the exorcists. His voice didn't become deep and guttural, and there was no vomiting or urinating. Simply, there is no evidence that demonic possession was involved. This is probably the most significant case of paranormal phenomena of our time, but it has been revealed to be a prank. Yet the alleged events have generated thousands of exorcisms, many of which have resulted in physical and psychological abuses, or even death.

As we saw at the beginning of this chapter, various polls show a strong belief in the existence of the devil and possession. Interestingly, other surveys reveal that while people like to believe in a literal God and heaven, Satan and hell are seen as figurative. Satan is symbolic, and the devil, demons, bad spirits, and other negative entities are only symbols of evil and misfortune. In the end, evil is a part of human nature, and misfortune is a part of the human condition. As Blaise Pascal once observed, "Man made God in his own image." Similarly, we have made demons in our own image too.

Deliver Us from Bob Larson

One of the most infamous deliverance ministers is the Reverend Bob Larson of the Spiritual Freedom Church. He boasts that he is "the world's foremost expert on cults, the occult, and supernatural phenomena." A former disk jockey and rock musician, Larson became a preacher against the evils of rock and roll. Larson is also known for preaching against the discredited phenomenon of Satanic ritual abuse. Ironically, he authored the salacious *Dead Air*, a novel that some call "Christian pornography." With great relish, Larson tells a graphic story of Satanic abuse, rape, pedophilia, and incest. It was later revealed that the book was ghostwritten by Lori Boespflug and Muriel Olsen. He tried to avoid giving them credit, although he has been accused of having affairs with both women. Larson's ministry is wracked by accusations of financial corruption and sex scandals.

Larson is best known today as a deliverance minister, and bills himself as "the Real Exorcist." His ministry's motto is "Do What Jesus Did" (DWJD)—that is, performing exorcisms, not dying for anyone's sins. However, he does plenty of things that Jesus didn't do too. In stark contrast to the claims of the Catholic Church that possession is rare, Larson claims to have performed over 20,000 exorcisms, and that most of us have been or will be possessed at some point in our lives, although not him.

Larson maintains there is a global shortage of exorcists. To meet this demand he founded the International School of Exorcism and has established ministry teams across the country. Larson's dream is that no one would be more than a day's drive away from exorcism. Larson believes that female, teenage exorcists are particularly effective at curing possession, and so he created a team of demon-slaying apprentices. The "teenage exorcists" are a group of precocious protégés, including Larson's daughter.

According to Larson, a spinning head isn't a telltale sign of demonic possession. It's simpler than that. Deliverance ministers see Satan behind everything. Everyday misfortune is caused by demons and curses. These demons manifest as arguments, accidents, car troubles, sickness, or not being able to pay your mortgage. But they're nothing that a quick exorcism can't fix. Larson travels the globe, exorcising people at public seminars and personal sessions. Larson also teaches self-deliverance techniques, so you can do-it-yourself at home, and protective prayer, so you can avoid possession in the first place.

Larson's events are billed as "free," although there's no such thing as a free exorcism. These are really live infomercials for his books, DVDs, anointed crucifixes, counseling sessions, exorcism courses, face-to-face encounters, and real-time online sessions. The seminars are grueling events that last many hours. Larson's high-pressure sales approach is to brainwash the attendees over the course of the night with sermons, theatrical exorcisms, and continual solicitations for donations and sales.

There is no greater persuasion technique than the threat of eternal hell. Larson is notorious for his hellfire and brimstone sermons. At the last event I attended, he told the audience we had been "drafted into the Lord's army in a battle against Satan's army of demons." We needed to become "spiritual warriors" and to fight with our weapons of "warfare prayer." "I'm feared in hell, and you need to be too. My face is on a "Wanted" poster in hell and it's my job to put your picture right there next to mine!"

Larson's public seminars are a form of group ministry, in which multiple people are exorcised in front of an entire audience. He begins by "rebuking the devil," this is often known as "provocation." Unlike Catholics, deliverance ministers taunt the demons, to coax out the devil in all of us. (Similarly, ghost hunters provoke evil spirits in the belief that this captures their voices in electronic voice phenomena.) When they have manifested, the demons can be cast out. Catholics believe that exorcists shouldn't hold conversations with the devil, but Larson banters with them, and they say really mean things like, "I don't like you." They even recognize Larson, as one quipped, "You again?" Recently, a demon swore to him, "This time you'll lose," but he won. However, I recognized these last two quotes, so either Larson or the possessed is a fan of the movie *The Exorcist III*.

Larson wandered about the room, glaring at everyone in an accusatory manner. It was presupposed that we were all possessed. "If you want to get rid of the devil, go to the point of pain. What was the worst thing that ever happened to you?" he asked. We were told to recall our worst fears, sufferings, and hurt to invoke our inner demons, and Larson told us to "let them take over." The congregation was composed of Larson's acolytes, and they all knew the drill. Across the room there was great wailing and gnashing of teeth. People burst into tears, hissed, groaned, moaned, or did other things they thought demons would do. A woman sitting in front of me was so eager to be exorcised that she began growling. She was clearly possessed by the demon of overacting. Larson and his teenage exorcists performed a series of quickie exorcisms throughout the crowd. They touched the "possessed" with Bibles and crosses. They recited prayers and cast out the demons by ordering them to go. Demons won't respond to wishy-washy pleas and politeness; they must be spoken to aggressively and commanded to leave.

The Bob Larson Show

The star of *The Real Exorcist*, Larson is a walking, talking, reality TV show. He chooses the most histrionic performer to be the main entertainment, and parades that individual in front of the audience, where he performs a full exorcism center stage. At this seminar the victim was twenty-five-year-old Ben, who had been dragged along to the event by his mother. The young man was struggling with his faith, relationships, and an alcohol addiction. Larson's ego is bigger than his Bible, and he asked Ben before the exorcism, "Do you know anything about me, Ben? Do you know who I am?" "No!" cried a terrified Ben. "I am . . . the Real Exorcist!" Larson shouted dramatically, as the room erupted into applause and cheers.

Exorcism can be a kind of stage hypnosis. The subjects are bombarded with instructions and terminology and become so overwhelmed that they just go along for the ride. In a Spanish Inquisition–style interrogation, Larson lists a number of demon names and sins, barking these choices again and again, until the flustered victim "confesses" to some of them. At Larson's insistence, Ben admitted to being host to a number of demons, including "hate," "addiction," and "Belial." If that wasn't bad enough, Ben was also the unwitting victim of a seven-generation curse unleashed by a murder! Of course, there was no proof of these claims, only Ben's admissions under coercion. Instead of the rack or iron maiden to force his confession, there was his desperate mother, a frenzied audience, and a hysterical Larson.

None of these demons had the "legal authority" to be inside of Ben, so they had to be exorcised. There is no green pea soup, but Larson's exorcisms are extremely violent events. Three assistants held Ben forcibly as others murmured prayers over him. As he fired verbal abuse at the "demons," Larson jabbed his pointy cross into Ben's chest and slapped him around the head with a Bible. He then insisted his daughter take over the reins of the exorcism. She ordered the demons to "go to the pits of hell," but her persuasiveness was undermined when she asked her father, "What was the demon's name again?" Earlier in the seminar

Larson denounced Harry Potter books as tools of the devil. However, the exorcism suddenly turned into a scene from Hogwarts as his daughter drew a "blood line." She performed a spell to bind and restrain the demons, and break the spiritual bondage. Demons really seem to be into BDSM.

Ben was visibly traumatized by the event. He was shaking, sweating and sobbing throughout the fifteen-minute exorcism. Larson seemed more concerned with sensationalism than salvation. He had a cameraman filming the event, to whom he issued constant instructions on how to get the best angles. And as you and I know, Ben was not "cured" of his addiction. Instead, he probably felt like a stiff drink afterward, but his ordeal wasn't over yet. Ben's mother had scheduled a one-on-one session with Larson for the following day.

Exorcism is a role-playing game. Before they even arrive, most people know what to expect as attendees are prepped by pop culture. They are also primed by Larson, who begins his seminars with footage from his exorcisms, to prepare the audience for their upcoming role. They continue to receive cues and directions along the way. There is a lot of pious peer pressure placed on the possessed to play along, and if the exorcisms don't work, Larson blames it on the victims. They somehow "blocked" the ministry because they were unrepentant, or they harbored unconfessed sins, or they had more demons to be exorcised.

Larson claims that his clients are desperate, and that exorcism is a last resort after conventional medicine has failed. On the contrary, exorcism is often a quick fix. Many of Larson's clients see him as an alternative to a psychologist or counselor. Some undergo regular exorcisms as ongoing therapy, like others might have a massage. Exorcism is also about attention seeking and catharsis. Society ignores Joe Schmoe, but all eyes are on the shaking, screaming man who's important enough for Satan to inhabit! It's easier to shake and scream if one can blame Satan. Believers defer blame to someone or something else so they don't have to take responsibility for their own actions. Satan is a scapegoat.

Larson encourages his audience to develop this victim mentality and to blame demons for the problems in their lives. He teaches that sexual indiscretions are the work of Jezebel, and he compiled his juiciest Jezebel encounters into the saucy DVD, *Casting out Jezebel*. At a previous seminar, Larson exorcised a sixteen-year-old girl. The girl had been pregnant, but she had miscarried the night before and believed she was cursed. The dead fetus was still inside her.

"Who are you?" Larson asked the "demon."

"Jezebel," the girl replied, coached by a film shown earlier in which Jezebel had been named.

"You killed the baby, didn't you?" Larson asked with a leading question.

"Yesssss . . ." she hissed, like she believed she should.

"Say it!"

"I killed the baby!"

"Why?"

Crying and trembling, the girl paused for a long time before saying, "She didn't want it to live!" This false confession was probably driven by guilt, as few teenagers want to be pregnant. Larson then prayed over her, asking the Holy Spirit to "start that heart beating again." Through the ecstatic screams of "Amen!" few people in the audience heard Larson mutter under his breath, "Unless it's God's will that this not happen…"

Chapter 6

Sympathy for the Devil
Satanism

"Better to reign in Hell than to serve in Heaven."
—*Paradise Lost*

At a dinner party, my friend Louise asked the table, "If you had to join a religion, which one would you choose?" Before anyone else could answer, Matthew yelled out "Satanism!" "But you'd have to kill a baby as part of their initiation!" Louise said in shock, as everyone laughed. "No, really!" she said seriously.

We Are Many

There are many different versions of Satan. Depending on your beliefs, he's an angel, a god, a serpent, or a man who walks among us. To many people, he's an adversary, and a fallen angel who was booted out of heaven. So why would anyone worship Satan? Well, he's suave and sophisticated and, as the Rolling Stones say, he's "a man of wealth and taste." He's charismatic and powerful, like the Satan of Milton's *Paradise Lost*. He also personifies pleasure and temptation. Satan is a sex symbol who is often represented as dark, brooding, mysterious, and muscular, even if he is red and engulfed in flames. Satan offers immediate gratification, while Christians must wait for theirs in the next life, but who wants to float on a cloud and play the harp all day long?

Yet in other portrayals, Satan is depicted as a hideous monster with horns, claws, fangs, or hooves. Sometimes he simply wears really unfashionable red pajamas and has a pointy tail. Satan is the CEO of hell, which is a fiery pit where damned souls suffer torment and terrifying punishment. This Satan stands for all that is evil, and you're on the losing guy's team. The devil is deceptive and cunning, so even if you sell your soul to him he can't be trusted. If his promises weren't worthless, fleeting fame and fortune here on Earth are not worth burning in hell for all eternity.

Does anyone really worship Satan anyway? Historically, there are many urban legends of devil-worshipping societies, but there is no proof of their existence. Satan has always been a contrived enemy in times of ignorance and fear, and He is the original scapegoat for disaster, disease, and death. During the tragic witch hunts and trials, numerous individuals were condemned as witches, tortured to secure false confessions, and burned at the stake or hanged. Today, similar crimes continue in Africa, where a belief in the supernatural is still rampant. Fortunately, in most contemporary Western societies, Satan is rarely considered real, but is instead a metaphor for wickedness in the world.

LaVeyan Satanism

Until recently, being a Satanist was mostly an accusation, rather than a reality. That is, until the flamboyant Anton Szandor LaVey saw this as a niche market and turned Satanism into an actual movement. On April 30, also known as Walpurgis Night, the other Halloween, in the *Annos Satanas* 1966, LaVey shaved his head and founded the Church of Satan. This was the first legally recognized satanic organization, and "Doctor" LaVey was dubbed its "High Priest" and the "Black Pope." He held seminars and rituals out of the "Black House" in San Francisco, which was the organization's church but also his home. This was the Church of Satan's only meeting place in the country, but due to its popularity, LaVey allowed for the creation of local groups known as grottos.

However, trying to organize Satanists is like trying to herd familiars, and by 1975 Satanism suffered a schism. In an occult soap opera, the grotto system disbanded over administrative and philosophical disagreements, and also internal family squabbles. This spawned several Satanic sects, including the Temple of Set, the Universal Church of Satan, and the Modern Church of Satan, just to name a few. LaVey died in 1997, and Magus Peter H. Gilmore (just like Jesus H. Christ) was appointed the High Priest of the Church of Satan. The church is now headquartered appropriately in the "Hell's Kitchen" neighborhood of New York City.

In recent decades, America has been gripped by the "Satanic Panic," where Satanists were and still are accused of ritual abuse and inserting subliminal satanic messages into music and advertising. Satanists are blamed for vandalized tombs in cemeteries and cases of animal abuse. They are believed to be members of the Hellfire Club, the Illuminati, and others secret societies. They are linked to Nazism and the Ku Klux Klan, and held responsible for drug crimes and murders. They are vilified by various religious groups and stigmatized by society. For many it is hard to have sympathy for the devil, but Satanists are much misunderstood.

Satanists don't eat babies or kill puppies, but they do wear silly outfits and occasionally say silly things on television talk shows. They are often the subject of gossip and urban legend. There are rumors that various celebrities are members of the Church of Satan, including Bill Gates and George Bush. Proctor & Gamble, McDonald's, and other major companies have been accused of being affiliated with the Church. There are many myths and misconceptions about Satanism, and for the most part, those contrary Satanists like it that way.

The Devil's Advocate

Only a very small band of Satanists actually believe in Satan. Traditional, theistic, or spiritual Satanists believe that Satan is real and not symbolic. Satan is seen as a deity or force, like an anti-God. Communication with God is achieved through prayer and other supernatural rituals, and likewise Satan can also be contacted. These Satanists petition and praise Satan through magic, and usually "black magic," that is, spells that aim to harm enemies. This kind of Satanism is a personal belief system that is rare, and there is no formal religion. LaVeyan Satanists even doubt the existence of these true "Devil Worshippers."

Like the victims of the witch trials, most accusations that people literally worship Satan are unfounded. In the 1890s there were reports of a society of Satan worshippers called the Palladists who were linked to the Freemasons. These Masonic diabolic orders were believed to be in France, and in Charleston, South Carolina. However, these stories proved to be the brainchild of Gabriel Jogand-Pagès, better known as Leo Taxil, who invented the Palladists as part of an elaborate practical joke to mock the Roman Catholic Church. Similarly, there is no evidence for the existence of the thirteenth-century German Satanic cult of the Luciferens, or the nineteenth-century French Society of Lucifer.

More recently, the Yazidi, a Kurdish religious group in Iraq, have been accused of being devil worshippers. The Yazidi venerate an archangel known variously as Melek Taus, Maluk Tus, Tawûsê Melek, and the Peacock Angel. Having so many names is one of the problems here, as the angel is also called Shaytan and Shaitan, which are Islamic names of the devil. Melek Taus is the central figure of faith to the Yazidi, but by some Christians and Muslims he is connected to Satan, the fallen angel. According to the Yazidi, Melek Taus repented and cried for 7,000 years. He filled seven jars with his tears, with which he quenched the fires of hell, so he is considered a redeemed angel. This is simply a case of the gods of one religion being seen as the devils of another.

There is far less theology to the most commonly practiced form of Satanism. In the Bible, Satan is the adversary of God, so people think that the beliefs of Satanism must be the opposite of Christianity. This is not true. Satanism isn't so much a religion as a culture with a set of philosophies that attracts like-minded individuals. Atheistic or modern Satanism is the most common type of Satanist. These Satanists do not practice Satan worship because they don't believe in Satan. Peter H. Gilmore describes Satanism as an "unreligion," because there is no deity and, therefore, no deity to be worshipped. Satan is a symbol of humankind and Satanism is more about worshipping yourself. As LaVey said, "I am my own God." Most Satanists are freethinkers and identify as atheist, agnostic, or secular humanist.

The Satanic Bible
LaVey was the first to write a "how-to" manual of Satanism with his infamous manifesto *The Satanic Bible*. This became his dissertation for

a doctorate awarded to "Doctor" LaVey by his own church. However, this is not the Satanic equivalent of the Bible. It doesn't feature books by Satanic disciples, or any Satanic psalms or parables. However, LaVeyan Satanism does have an answer to the Seven Deadly Sins. The Nine Sins of Satanism include Stupidity, Pretentiousness, Solipsism, Self-deceit, Herd Conformity, Lack of Perspective, Forgetfulness of Past Orthodoxies, Counterproductive Pride, and Lack of Aesthetics. The Eleven Satanic Rules are responses to the Ten Commandments, which includes the Satanic version of "Thou shalt not steal": "Do not take that which does not belong to you unless it is a burden to the other person and he cries out to be relieved."

In some ways, Christianity and Satanism have a lot in common. Satanism operates within a Christian worldview and Satanism is defined in a Christian context. Much Satanic lore comes from Christianity, not Satanism. You can't have Satanism without Christianity. Rather than being the flip side to Christianity, Satanism is a reaction to Christianity and the perceived problems caused by religion. Satanists are more often antireligion than pro-Satan. *The Satanic Bible* outlines LaVey's opinions about Christianity, and questions religious and moral dogma. He denounces religion for being a source of conflict and abuse, and the Bible as an obsolete social guide. More often his criticisms are of the puritanical ideals of Christianity and hypocritical Christian behavior, rather than of any positive aspects of religions. LaVey called Christianity a "guilt-ridden philosophy" that inhibits the natural behavior of humans, causing inevitable sinning and breeding hypocrisy. As LaVey said, "Satan has been the best friend the Church has ever had, as He has kept it in business all these years."

LaVey didn't believe in Satan as much as he didn't believe in God. As he quipped, "man has always created his gods, rather than his gods creating him." Satanists see Satan as a social construct that was invented as a tool for social conditioning. As they see it, Satanists self-condition themselves and therefore don't require the moral guidelines offered by religion and needed by followers. They embrace flaws as a part of human nature, but decry injustice and abuse. Despite their reputation, Satanists are by no means immoral, and their views are often surprisingly insightful, rational, and enlightened. Satanism is more about "vital existence," the here and now, and living this life than the "spiritual pipe dream" of believing there is a next one.

Satanism is a vigilante religion that teaches people to believe in what they want to believe in, and to do what they want to do, unless it would hurt other people. They have a laissez-faire attitude of "live and let live" and "to each his own." They preach "do unto others as they do unto you," but seek vengeance instead of turning the other cheek. They advocate love, kindness, taking responsibility for their actions, and giving respect . . . to those whom they think deserve it. There is also a selfish, spoiled brat aspect to Satanists too. Satan is a symbol of human characteristics favored by Satanists, such as individualism, indulgence, egotism, and the glorification of sexuality. To Satanists, the Seven Deadly Sins are goals because they "all lead to physical, mental or emotional gratification." A few Satanists are in it for the rebellion and the shock value, while they often have the reputation for being pompous and obnoxious. Some are Satanists because they are actively anti-Christian and like to mock religion. In many ways, Satanism is a religion for assholes.

Join Us! Join Us!
Don't worry. Satanic missionaries won't come around to your door preaching their beliefs, or lack thereof, and asking, "Have you found Satan yet?" Satanists don't solicit members. People are drawn to them instead. They read *The Satanic Bible* and recognize themselves in the book. Up-and-coming Satanists often feel they lived the lifestyle before they read the book. LaVey used to say that "Satanists are born, not made." There is no Satanic community as such, as many Satanists just aren't the kind of people to organize a potluck, and probably wouldn't even like each other anyway. Instead, like-minded individuals are urged to become members of the Church of Satan. However, LaVey conceded that one can be a Satanist but not have to be a member of the Church. Anyone can call themselves a Satanist.

At a dinner party, my friend Louise asked the table, "If you had to join a religion, which one would you choose?" Before anyone else could answer, Matthew yelled out "Satanism!" "But you'd have to kill a baby as part of their initiation!" Louise said in shock, as everyone laughed. "No, really!" she said seriously. However, there is no confirmation to become a Satanist. Neophytes don't sell their souls to the devil, or participate in initiation rites involving sexual depravity, unless they want to do so. To become a (red) card-carrying Satanist, there is an application process, and a one-time fee of $200. This admits the person to a lifetime membership, although there aren't any benefits other than bragging rights. When people complain about the fee, they are reminded that many churches charge tithes of 10 percent of a person's annual income.

The application form is to vet applicants and ensure that they're not nerdy Goth kids who just want to piss off their parents, or those who dabble in Satanism for the Halloween costumes and Slayer music. Satanists brand these people pseudo-Satanists, or poseurs, and they hold a lot of disdain for them. The application form contains a lengthy questionnaire, but it doesn't ask for your Satanic testimony. It is more like a form to register for a dating service than a religious society. Here is a sampling of questions the Church asks: *If you were granted three wishes, what would they be? Are you satisfied with your sex life? Describe your ideal of a physically attractive sex partner. How many years would you like to live? What are your food preferences? Tell one of your favorite jokes. Do you drink alcoholic beverages? If so, to what extent? State preferences.*

Once you join, there is a hierarchy in the Church of Satan. Members can simply be registered, or active. Unlike most religions where the congregation stays in the pews, Satanists can be promoted to higher levels in the Church through achievement and contributions to society. Members can progress through the various "degrees" of Satanism: Satanist (First Degree), Witch/Warlock (Second Degree), Priest/Priestess (Third Degree), Magistra/Magister (Fourth Degree), and the highest rank of Maga/Magus (Fifth Degree). Those who hold titles of Priest/Priestess and above may call themselves "Reverend," and the Church's fifth degree merits the title of "Doctor."

For reasons of privacy, the Church refuses to share its list of members. Peter H. Gilmore claims they have some high-profile members who would lose their jobs if they were exposed as Satanists, such is the bigotry of the public. According to urban legend, just about every rock star has been tagged a Satanist, but a few of them actually are, such as heavy metal musician King Diamond and Marilyn Manson, who is an honorary Reverend. The Church occasionally awards honorary memberships to celebrities and scholars, to attract the type of people they want. Sammy Davis Jr. is famously cited as a member of the Church, and this is true. He was granted an honorary membership as a Warlock. However, he had previously converted to Judaism, and he eventually resigned from the Church of Satan, joking that he was "only into it for the chicks."

The Church is also evasive about its membership numbers, stating that if people think there are too few of them, they won't be taken seriously, but if people think there are too many, they will be seen as a threat. LaVey once bragged that the Church of Satan had hundreds of thousands of members, but various sources estimate that there are several hundred to several thousand Satanists in the United States today.

A Devil of a Job

The Church of Satan in New York is the only Satanist church in existence. There aren't any branches, and the system of grottos has been phased out. Since most modern Satanists don't practice Satanic worship, there isn't a need for a house of worship anyway. Satanic practices are based in the performance of rituals instead. For a few Satanists, they believe these magical rituals affect change in the external world. For most Satanists, rituals are "psychodramas" acted out for theatrical or cathartic effect. They are often performed to purge fears, phobias, inhibitions, and repressions.

Satanic rituals are classified as a type of left-hand path magic. The left hand is roughly synonymous with "black magic" or the occult, and the right hand with "white magic," although Satanists reject these labels. LaVey said that there is no "good" or "bad" magic, there is just magic, as every practitioner thinks that he or she is doing the "right" thing. Left-hand path magic is more about personal gain and the self, while right-hand path magic is about spirituality and submission to a higher power. Left-hand path magic is also about rejecting strict morality and dogma. These ceremonies aren't the stereotypical Satanic rituals involving the drinking of blood, human sacrifice, and sexual abuse. Like the occultist Aleister Crowley's "magick," these rituals are anti-Christian, not criminal.

Satanic rituals don't involve anything illegal or immoral, although they often incorporate taboo elements, such as nudity, masturbation, and sex, and they always seem to end with an orgy . . .

LaVey always maintained that Satanic rituals are for the purposes of psychodrama, but one of his Eleven Satanic Rules is: "Acknowledge the power of magic if you have employed it successfully to obtain your desires. If you deny the power of magic after having called upon it with success, you will lose all you have obtained." Whether they are believed to work supernaturally or psychologically, Satanic rituals are used for a number of purposes. Most commonly they are designed to curse, charm, banish, or protect. Satanists also conduct more traditional rituals, such as Satanic weddings, funerals, and baptisms. Christenings don't involve sacrificing babies or drinking blood, but are instead a celebration of life. The first ever Satanic baptism was of LaVey's daughter Zeena, when she was three years old. LaVey acknowledged that baptisms are for the parents, so he also created a ceremony for adults to be baptized as Satanists.

That Spells Trouble

LaVey's *Satanic Bible* contains three basic rituals. There is one to attract a sex partner, one to enlist help or attract success, and another hoped to cause the destruction of an enemy. As a companion to his *Bible*, LaVey wrote *The Satanic Rituals*, a compendium of an additional nine rituals. His rituals were inspired by, but don't always acknowledge, the writings of other authors, including Aleister Crowley, H. G. Wells, Ayn Rand, and Friedrich Nietzsche. Some of these rituals are about as convincing as "mirror, mirror, on the wall." Others are too complex and arcane to be reproduced, but if they could be it would prove they don't work anyway. The Law of the Trapezoid (*Die Elektrischen Vorspiele*) calls for a Tesla coil, neon lights, strobe lights, a Hammond organ, and a human skull, while the invocations are recited in German to the tune of Richard Wagner music. Clearly, most rituals are just created for the drama, such as the Call to Cthulhu, intended to raise the creature that we all know is based on H. P. Lovecraft's mythology.

Individuals can perform Satanic rituals, although they are often performed in a group, which reinforces the perceived power and adds to the spectacle. Unlike the stereotypes, these rituals are unlikely to be performed in a cemetery or around a bonfire in the middle of a forest at midnight. Unless you're invited to a Black Mass with Peter H. Gilmore at the Church in New York, Satanic rituals are most commonly performed in the homes of practitioners. They are conducted in a special room dedicated to these rituals, known as the ritual chamber. All outside lighting is blocked, and the chamber is lit by candles. All black candles are used, except for a single white candle representing "the hypocrisy of white light magicians."

There will be an altar covered in a black cloth that holds the ritual tools. In clear view is the sigil of Baphomet. This is the Satanic logo that features the face of a goat in the center of a pentagram, a five-pointed star. Some say that the goat mocks the "lamb of God," while others say it represents carnality. LaVey claimed that the Baphomet was "used by the Knights Templar to represent Satan." This isn't true, but the symbol became known during the Inquisitions of the Middle Ages, where inquisitors linked the Baphomet to members of the Order during forced confessions under torture. The participants in the ritual all wear necklaces with Baphomet or pentagram pendants (as sold by the Church of Satan's Emporium).

Satanic rituals are an opportunity for the participants to play Halloween dress-up. LaVey often wore a costume featuring a bright red cape and a face mask complete with little horns growing out of his head. His fellow Satanists sometimes wore pig, goat, or cat masks, so you couldn't be sure if they are on their way to a bondage and discipline session, or were about to rob a bank. Those who are really into the lifestyle get vampire-fang veneers on their teeth, or style their eyebrows into arches like devil's horns.

The practitioners wear hooded black robes, unless you're a female participant, and therefore expected to dress in garments that are "sexually suggestive"—that is, unless the woman is to serve as a nude altar. The naked woman lies spread-eagled across a platform and is used as a human candleholder. Her arms are outstretched into a cross, and she grasps a black candle in each hand. She might have "666" painted across her breasts, or she may be dressed up as a whore, with heavy makeup, gaudy jewelry, and high heels. She is dressed, or rather undressed, ready for the unbridled orgy that will ensue after the ritual.

To begin the ceremony the air is "purified" by the ringing of a bell. Then the priest recites the "Invocation to Satan," a prayer-like request that Satan manifest the desires of the practitioners. Satan's "infernal names" are then called, taken from a long list of adversarial figures from folklore, such as Pan the Greek god of lust, and Lilith the Hebrew female devil. Those relevant to the ritual are listed, and the names are repeated by the congregation. The priest then takes a drink from the "Chalice of Ecstasy." The chalice should ideally be silver, but it can be made of anything but gold, which is the color of white-light religions. The chalice is filled with the "Elixir of Life," that is, the alcohol of the priest's choice. The priest takes a sword or dagger and directs it to each point of the compass, and he calls forth the "Princes of Hell": Satan from the south, Lucifer from the east, Belial from the north, and Leviathan from the west. The priest then performs benediction, but he doesn't use his hands, or a blessing cross. To make the sign of the cross the Satanic priest uses a penis-shaped object or other phallus.

The priest then reads aloud the appropriate incantation for the desired effect. There are many Satanic rituals to be found in books and online. These are often taken from existing rituals in grimoires, the Necronomicon, books by Aleister Crowley or LaVey, and modified passages from the Bible, the Qur'an, or other sacred texts. As a personal belief system, Satanists are also encouraged to create their own meaningful rituals. These rituals may use fragments of magical languages such as Latin or Hebrew, because being ancient is a magical qualification. The invocations may also be accompanied by music and singing. LaVey seemed to like classical music or organ music, as he was formerly an organist.

Satanic rituals are heavily influenced by pagan, Voodoo, and Hoodoo spells and sympathetic magic. They may include the use of magical incense, herbs, and oils. For curses and rituals intending harm, photographs, sculptures, or dolls made from cloth, wax, wood, or other materials are used as an effigy of the victim, and these are burned, or stuck with pins. Sounds, smells, or images that invoke the victim will be used, such as the person's perfume. Graphic pictures that depict a victim's intended fate are worked into the ritual, such as a drawing of a man falling down and breaking his leg. The desired outcome is also written down and read aloud. This message is then burned in the flames of a candle to make sure it comes true. As LaVey says, "To insure the destruction of an enemy, you must destroy them by proxy! They must be shot, stabbed, sickened, burned, smashed, drowned, or rent in the most vividly convincing manner!"

The Satanist can use visualization to imagine the desired outcome, or even enact this event through role-playing. Movies or songs that describe this eventuality can be played to intensify the ritual. LaVey says that prayer is "useless," but he recommends the desire be stated in an impassioned, affirmation-like manner. If the request is sincere enough, it will manifest. Showing true emotion such as shedding tears or screaming in emotional pain will empower the ritual. If it is a ritual to attract love or sex, LaVey recommends the use of sex magic, in which the alleged power and energy of an orgasm is harnessed to bring about the desired result.

The incantations are often followed by the reading of an appropriate Enochian Key. These are a set of calls or chants written in the potent Enochian language. LaVey claims that Enochian is the "magical language used in Satanic ritual," although he frequently uses bits of Latin, French, and German elsewhere. There are nineteen keys, each with its own meaning. For example, "The Seventh Key is used to invoke lust, pay homage to glamour, and rejoice in the delights of the flesh." Enochian is allegedly an angelic language discovered by sixteenth-century seers John Dee and Edward Kelley. LaVey claims that Enochian is older than Sanskrit. However, Enochian has been debunked as a language invented by humans, not angels. It is a kind of made-up speaking in tongues that steals from English syntax and sounds.

"Shemhamforash" is another magical word used in Satanic rituals. Derived from a Hebrew phrase meaning the seventy-two names of God, it is corrupted by Satanists to refer to the names of seventy-two demons. Shemhamforash is used like a Satanic "Yours Sincerely" in letters and e-mails, and is uttered at the end of a ritual. "Hail Satan!" is the Satanic equivalent of "Amen." Whenever these words are uttered by the priest, the other participants repeat them in a chorus, and then a bell is sounded. When the ritual is over the priest utters "So it is done." In many rituals, this is followed by a gang bang with the female altar.

Black Sabbath

The most infamous Satanic ritual is the Black Mass. Far from being a tradition of Satanism, it has its roots in Christianity, and is a profane parody of the Roman Catholic Mass. In a medieval conspiracy theory, it was believed that Catholic priests conducted these ceremonies surreptitiously to place curses on their enemies and perform other dark deeds. According to legend, the Black Mass was typically held in a disused church late at night. Sacramental bread was stolen, or black bread, black leather, or a slice of turnip was consecrated by the priest instead. This "body of Christ" was then desecrated, by being burned or stabbed. Crosses were spat on, stepped on, or defiled in other ways. In a spoof of the wine that becomes the blood of Christ, the congregation would drink a concoction of human or animal blood, urine, semen, and vaginal fluid. Many of the rituals were a reversal of the Catholic Mass. The Lord's Prayer was recited backward and crosses were worn upside down. "God" was substituted with "Satan" in prayers, and "good" with "evil." Sometimes a Mass for the Dead would be recited for a living enemy, in the hope it would cause their death. The sacrilegious ceremony culminated with the sacrifice of an unbaptized infant, leading to the modern myth that Satanists sacrifice babies. In true Satanist style, the Black Mass ended with an orgy.

The Black Mass took an even more sinister turn when it was associated with the Witches Sabbath and used as "evidence" in allegations of witchcraft. Suddenly the Black Mass was not only about mocking God, but also about worshipping Satan. In these stories, the Mass was presided over by Satan, or a goat-like creature to whom the witches would pay homage. This was followed by the obscene kiss, where the witches kissed the devil's bottom. All along they blasphemed against God and Jesus Christ. Of course, a baby was sacrificed, and offered to Satan. Again, the ritual would be followed by fornication. However, there is no reliable evidence that Black Masses ever took place, and the reports fit the profile of an urban legend. These claims tend to do the rounds though—for example, the Romans accused early Christians of child sacrifice.

In *The Satanic Rituals* LaVey devised a modern-day version. *Le Messe Noir* is performed to purge oneself of "inhibiting guilts imposed by Christian dogma," or for fun. In his usual grandiose style, LaVey claimed his ritual is modeled after one performed by the nineteenth-century French group the Society of Lucifer (a group which never existed). In truth, it is a blend of folklore, while the incantations are based on the fictional Black Mass in the French novel *Là-Bas*. LaVey's Latin and French are full of mistranslations and grammatical errors.

LaVey's Black Mass is a pompous paranormal pageant. The clergy and congregation are dressed in hooded black robes, except for a woman dressed as a nun in a habit and wimple, and the requisite nude woman serving as the altar. The ritual begins by invoking Satan and his demons. The celebrant recites lengthy incantations full of praise for the Lord (of Darkness), including the Satanist's version of the Lord's Prayer.

> Our Father which art in Hell, hallowed be Thy name. Thy kingdom is come, Thy will is done; on earth as it is in Hell! We take this night our rightful due, and trespass not on paths of pain. Lead us unto temptation, and deliver us from false piety.

At one point the "nun" lifts her habit and urinates into a chamber pot. A phallic object is used as an aspergillum, which is dipped into the pot and the urine sprinkled about as a substitute for holy water. If that wasn't obscene enough, the "body of Christ" is consecrated by insertion into the altar's vagina. Then it is taken out and trodden upon. The "blood of Christ" is usually wine supped from a human skull. This ritual is intended for theatrical effect only, but LaVey saw it as an outmoded practice, so it was rarely performed.

Surprisingly, LaVey's version isn't as outrageous and full of eroticism as other contemporary versions. The *Missa Niger* was devised by an author who uses the pseudonym Aubrey Melech. This version directs the congregation to finish the Mass by "fornicating indiscriminately, without regard to privacy, sex or relationship with their partners." During the Black Mass written by the Order of Nine Angles, the priestess masturbates the priest, who ejaculates over the sacramental bread symbolizing the "body of Christ." This is trampled upon by the congregation, and followed by an orgy. In the *Missa Solemnis* ritual the celebrant masturbates the "altar" with the "body of Christ." He later masturbates in front of the congregation and presents his semen to Satan as a sacrificial offering. His semen is then poured into a chalice of wine and he drinks the contents.

All Hell Breaks Loose

The witch trials and the legend of the Black Mass are precursors to a contemporary mass hysteria. Satanists are tarnished by the folkloric reputation that precedes them. The creation of the Church of Satan turned Satanism into a reality, and has inadvertently given a common enemy to Christianity. Satanists are stereotyped as sadists, reprobates, and criminals. Satanism has been blamed for real and perceived crimes, such as placing hidden Satanic messages in music and advertising, and the vandalism of cemeteries and houses of worship. Most heinously, Satanists have been accused of so-called Satanic ritual abuse, involving animal and human sacrifice, incest, and the sexual abuse of children.

The 1980 autobiography *Michelle Remembers* reveals a horrifying story. Michelle Smith began having sessions with psychiatrist Lawrence Pazder for depression. Under hypnosis, Smith began recovering some terrifying memories. In 1954, Smith's mother became a member of the Church of Satan. At the age of five, Smith allegedly participated in numerous rituals that involved sexual assault, torture, and murder. These experiences culminated in an eighty-one-day ritual in which Satan himself was summoned. Fortunately, Jesus, the Virgin Mary, and the Archangel Michael intervened. They healed Smith's physical scars and removed her memories "until the time was right" for them to be recovered. This was only the beginning of the modern witch hunt that became known as the Satanic Panic.

In 1983 a mother of a student at the McMartin preschool in California reported to the police that one of the schoolteachers had sodomized her son. She also claimed to see this teacher fly. The claims triggered a large-scale investigation of schools across the country. A frightening array of allegations emerged from hundreds of children, including reports of sexual abuse, torture, cannibalism, orgies, human sacrifice, and necrophilia. Children were reputedly forced to watch pornography and animal abuse. They were force fed urine, blood, semen, feces, and fetuses. They were raped with knives, sticks, forks, and magic wands, and they saw witches fly. Beyond the schoolyard, adults were also reporting forgotten memories of Satanic ritual abuse.

The theory emerged that a network of Satanic cults were behind these crimes, and that they were part of a worldwide conspiracy to breed children for sacrifice, drug trafficking, prostitution, and pornography. However, when all of these claims were investigated, the authorities found no evidence of the crimes. When adults testified in court, they claimed their memories were impaired because they had been drugged by cult members. If children were being kidnapped and raped with knives, we would expect to find some proof, but no corroborating evidence was ever found. In their investigations the authorities often overlooked evidence to the contrary.

These adults and children weren't victims of Satanic ritual abuse, but of something called false memory syndrome. During the witch trials, confessions of witchcraft were elicited by means of torture. False accusations of Satanic ritual abuse were elicited by manipulative questioning and therapeutic techniques. The "inquisitors" were therapists, social workers, lawyers, police, and child-protection advocates. Their methods included coercion, repressed (or recovered) memory therapy, and the use of leading questions and suggestion. Pseudoscientific tests were devised to "prove" cases of abuse, such as the "wink response" test, in which the anus was swabbed to see if there was a reflex to demonstrate that someone had been sodomized. All of these procedures are now discredited.

Folk legend, rumors, and pop culture were clearly at play too. Some of the allegations included clear elements of fantasy, such as children's reports of flying witches, riding in hot air balloons, witnessing a giraffe, a rabbit, and an elephant being killed, and being molested by magic wands. In a photo lineup, one boy identified Chuck Norris as an abuser. The emergence of the Church of Satan brought about a cultural awareness of Satanism, and for many people, its existence seemed to give credence to the strange claims.

Furthermore, the foundational claims for Satanic ritual abuse were baseless. The mother who started the scandal in schools was later revealed to have suffered from paranoid schizophrenia, and she died of alcoholism halfway through the trial. Most tellingly, it seems that Michelle Smith of the book *Michelle Remembers* had misremembered. Her mother had allegedly joined the Church of Satan fifteen years before it had even been established! Her "repressed" memories were really false memories, implanted by her doctor (and later husband) during six hundred hours of hypnosis.

Even though the allegations were proven false, there were some serious real-world consequences. The McMartin trial lasted seven years, at a cost of some $15 million. The interrogations and prosecution was overzealous, and the interviews, "therapy," and trials caused psychological damage to countless adults and children. Several victims spent years in trial, or even years in jail—charged with crimes that never even happened. Others lost their jobs or businesses, and their careers and relationships were ruined. Children were wrongfully taken from their families and put into foster care. Millions of dollars were paid to "victims" in undeserved settlements. The events also led to the victimization of Satanists and calls for Satanism to be banned. Regardless of whether we sympathize with their beliefs or not, Satanists were not at fault for this panic.

"Here's to My Sweet Satan"

Schools and teachers weren't the only targets during the Satanic panic. The music industry is no stranger to Satan. Rock-and-roll music is labeled an instrument of the devil, and there are many urban legends of musicians making deals with the devil in exchange for their talents. When the Beatles started experimenting with backward-recording techniques, reports of subliminal Satanic messages soon followed. It was feared that musicians, working in conjunction with the Church of Satan, were implanting demonic messages into music to promote Satanism and to encourage teens to have sex and take drugs. Fundamentalist Christians such as Pastor Gary Greenwald spread these beliefs, leading to record burnings, death threats, boycotts of band tours, and proposed anti-backmasking legislation.

Most famously, Led Zeppelin's "Stairway to Heaven" allegedly features the backward message, "Here's to my sweet Satan." Jimmy Page was an Aleister Crowley enthusiast, and so clearly, the band must have entered into a Faustian pact with the devil for its success. Played in reverse, Styx's "Snowblind" supposedly says, "Satan moves through our voices." Electric Light Orchestra's "Eldorado" reputedly reveals the hidden message, "He is the nasty one. Christ you're infernal. He said we're dead men. Everyone who has the mark will live." Band member Jeff Lynne's appropriate response to the allegations was "Skcollob."

AC/DC's *Highway to Hell* supposedly conceals the message, "My name is Lucifer." Serial killer Richard Ramirez claimed that the song "Night Prowler" from the same album inspired him to commit his murders. The man dubbed as the "Night Stalker" professed to be a Satanist and argued that he was only following Satan's orders. He drew a pentagram on the thigh of an eighty-three-year-old victim after he murdered her. He forced another victim to cry repeatedly, "I love Satan," as he raped her. During his trial he yelled "Hail Satan!" and flashed a pentagram drawn onto his palm. However, Ramirez was living a Satanist lifestyle as much as predatory priests are living a Christian life. The infamous serial killers David Berkowitz, Robert Berdella, Larry Eyler, and Tony Costa also claimed to be Satanists. For people with serious emotional problems the popular stereotypes of Satanism have a certain kind of magnetism.

The backmasking claims inspired many popular bands to place hidden messages in their music deliberately. This was not in support of the Church of Satan, but for the purposes of creativity, comedy, or to agitate the Fundamentalists. When played backward, the intro of Slayer's *Hell Awaits* features the chant "Join Us!" Iron Maiden were sick of being labeled devil worshippers, so at the start of "Still Life" they inserted drummer Nicko McBrain's impression of Idi Amin, "Don't meddle with things you don't understand," followed by a burp. Taking a leaf out of the mythical Black Mass, Cradle of Filth's "Dinner at Deviant's Palace" features the Lord's Prayer recited backward.

Sometimes it's the music played forward that's the problem, and song lyrics are misinterpreted to implicate a band as Satanic. According to urban legend, The Eagles are Satan worshippers and their classic song

"Hotel California" was written to inaugurate the Church of Satan. Another rumor says that the song was about Boleskin House, Aleister Crowley's former mansion in Scotland. The song's "Beast" apparently refers to Satan, while "the Master" is LaVey. It is also claimed that LaVey featured on the album cover, appearing in a window, but in reality, a female model had posed for the shot.

Rock, heavy metal, and punk bands are often accused of being in league with Satan because of their hellish names, morbid lyrics, and hardcore sounds. Satanism is only a persona for bands such as Slayer, Kiss, and Mötley Crüe. Ozzy Osbourne once denied being a Satanist and explained, "It's only an image. It's like Halloween for me every night when I'm on the road." He added, "I'm not a Satanist. I'm a likeable loony."

Mark of the Devil

Being labeled "Satanic" may be a public relations boost for rock stars, but it's a PR nightmare for politicians, authors, and corporations. Several major companies have famously been accused of tithing to the Church of Satan, or even being owned by them. A persistent urban legend is that designer Liz Claiborne appeared on a television talk show and brazenly admitted she donates a portion of her company's profits to the Church of Satan. This same accusation has also been leveled at McDonald's and Proctor & Gamble. This isn't the only Satanic speculation to plague Proctor & Gamble. During the 1980s its "man in the moon" logo came under scrutiny. It was claimed that the decorative curls in the character's beard represented "666," the "mark of the beast." The origin of the rumor is unknown, but its spread was traced to Amway, the company's competitor. The accusations continually dogged the company, so it retired the historic symbol in 1985 after 103 years of use.

Seeing Satanic images in symbols and hearing Satanic messages in music are both the result of pareidolia, the phenomenon of detecting meaningful patterns in random stimuli. Like Satanic ritual abuse, other crimes that are attributed to Satanists are also unfounded. Acts of vandalism and cruelty to animals are often related to drug abuse. Some occurrences of animal sacrifice can be linked to religious rituals, such as those practiced in Santeria, Candomblé, and Voodoo. Like the Richard Ramirez case, where an individual claims that his or her actions are performed in the name of Satan, the person's behavior is often the result of a psychological or psychiatric disorder, and is in no way connected to the Church of Satan.

Satanists don't harm animals or children. In fact, two of the Satanic "Rules" include: "Do not kill non-human animals unless you are attacked or for your food," and "Do not harm little children." A vengeful Satanist would be more liable to kill the child abuser. As LaVey once said, "the only time a Satanist would perform a human sacrifice would be if it were to serve a two-fold purpose; that being to release the magician's wrath in the throwing of a curse, and more important, to dispose of a totally obnoxious and deserving individual." The Church of Satan dislikes religious hypocrisy and believes that religion breeds repression. Ironically, the cases of child sexual abuse that have been proven haven't been the allegations of Satanic ritual abuse, but abuses committed by Catholic priests and Christian ministers.

Well before the birth of the Church of Satan, Satanism has been a scapegoat. Most of the evil committed in relation to Satanism has not been committed by the Satanists, but by their accusers. We often think of persecution as something that only happens to religious or ethnic groups, but the Satanic ritual abuse scandal qualifies as the persecution of Satanists. Satanists certainly have their faults, but they have been unfairly stigmatized and victimized for crimes they didn't commit. The fear of Satanism is far more dangerous than Satanism.

However, Satanists say they like to take responsibility for their actions, and there is some obvious fault to admit here. If you're going to adopt the name of the world's most diabolical character, who personifies evil, wickedness, and sin—a name that is given to Adolf Hitler, Osama bin Laden, and other "Antichrists" of our time; a name that is synonymous with words like adversary, opponent, and archenemy; a name for a figure that is portrayed as a fallen angel cast out of heaven; the very name of the Devil—then you have to expect that you are going to attract some negative attention . . .

He's Not Satan—He's a Very Naughty Boy!

The "Black Pope" had a very colorful career. He was born Anton Szandor LaVey, to parents Joseph and Augusta LaVey. At a tender age he was introduced to the supernatural by his Transylvanian Gypsy grandmother. He played second oboe at age fifteen for the San Francisco Ballet Orchestra, and was the youngest musician in the history of that institution. Soon thereafter he joined the Clyde Beatty Circus as their lion tamer and calliope player. Then he became an organ player for a burlesque theater in Los Angeles where he met a young Marilyn Monroe, with whom he had a passionate affair. He also had a steamy fling with Jayne Mansfield, who was a card-carrying Satanist and died at the hands of a curse that LaVey placed on her lover, Sam Brodie. LaVey was a technical adviser for *Rosemary's Baby*, Roman Polanski's movie in which the heroine unwittingly gives birth to the spawn of Satan. LaVey bragged that he was a multimillionaire with homes across California, a convent in Italy, a château in France, a yacht, and a fleet of luxury cars.

However, it seems LaVey was less diabolical and more of a conman. All of these sensational claims are untrue. As proof of his dalliances with Monroe, LaVey had a pinup calendar of her that read, "Dear Tony, How many times have you seen this! Love, Marilyn" This was autographed personally . . . by LaVey's former wife. Diane LaVey had forged Monroe's handwriting. LaVey never even met Monroe. However, he did meet Jayne Mansfield, who even posed with him for a series of tongue-in-cheek photographs of a Satanic ritual. However, they never had an affair. LaVey was smitten with Mansfield, although she didn't take him too seriously. She once said of him in an interview, "He had fallen in love with me and wanted to join my life with his. It was a laugh."

LaVey's birth certificate shows he was bestowed with the considerably less exotic-sounding name Howard Stanton Levey, born to parents Michael and Gertrude Levey. The lies continued after his death. LaVey's original death certificate states that he died on October 31, 1997, a suitably sinister date for the devil. An investigation conducted by the City of San Francisco revealed that he actually died on the less notable October 29. LaVey was probably dressed for the occasion, but the Halloween date had been written illegally on the document.

The Church of Satan is more of a cult of personality than a Satanic cult in the popular sense of the term. The cult revolved around LaVey during his lifetime, and now revolves around his memory—or his myth. LaVey's public life was its own psychodrama, and a carefully crafted legend. As he admitted in the posthumously published book *Satan Speaks!*

> I'm one helluva liar. Most of my adult life, I've been accused of being a charlatan, a phony, an impostor. I guess that makes me about as close to what the Devil's supposed to be, as anyone. It's true. I lie constantly, incessantly. Because I lie so often, I'd really be full of shit if I didn't keep my mouth shut and my bowels open.

Satanists are credited with far more power than they have ever had. They have been much maligned, and aren't guilty of Satanic ritual abuse, skinning cats, worldwide conspiracies, or the many other charges that have been leveled against them. However, Satanists are often guilty of selfishness, greed, hedonism, egotism, and misanthropy, but these are charges they won't deny.

Chapter 7

It's All in Your Head
Dianetics and Scientology

**"Fuck those people! There's no way I'll ever get involved
with that son-of-a-bitchin' group. All they want is my money."
—Elvis Presley**

*We approached an empty office appointed in gold and encased in glass. It
was worthy of a pharaoh's tomb, if it wasn't for the E-Meter. This was an
altar dedicated to Hubbard. "We keep an office for L. Ron in every church,"
Harry explained reverently. "We have it set up so he could walk right in and
continue his work."*

From Self-Help to Religion
In 1950 Lafayette Ronald Hubbard published *Dianetics: The Modern
Science of Mental Health*. This revolutionary self-help book promised
to cure illnesses of the mind and body without medication or therapy.
This was a curious career change for a science fiction writer who was
deeply influenced by the works of Aleister Crowley, but who had
no training in psychiatry. After all, the first draft of the theory was
published in *Astounding Science Fiction*. Dianetics was rejected by the
medical community. The American Psychological Association reviewed
Hubbard's theories and claims and concluded they were "not supported
by empirical evidence," while fellow author Isaac Asimov branded

the book "gibberish." Nevertheless, the book and its methods rapidly developed a following.

Hubbard soon discovered that humans are "thetans." These are spirits or souls that inhabit a "meat body" and are ageless beings that reincarnate. Dianetics is designed for the mind, so he created Scientology for the spirit (although some cynics say that he was suffering financial and copyright problems and needed a new money-making project). The newly founded Church of Scientology became the institutionalization of Dianetics. The two are meant to be complementary, although they are mostly interchangeable, and form a unique blend of therapy and theology. Hubbard's new teachings were published as *Scientology: The Fundamentals of Thought*, which is a kind of combination of the Bible and the Diagnostic and Statistical Manual of Mental Disorders. The Scientologist becomes both a patient and a parishioner. However, Scientologists are militantly antipsychiatry and refuse to accept labels such as "psychotherapy" for their practices.

The benefits of most religions are in an afterlife. Scientology promises benefits here on Earth (or Teegeeack, as the case may be). Scientology affords ambiguous aims to improve your spiritual well-being, achieve your goals, and reach your full potential in this life, and the next (and the next). The Church offers numerous books, DVDs, courses, and treatments to help you get there. Scientology is not overly spiritual in tone, but to his many followers Hubbard's word is gospel, even if those words are confusing at times. Hubbard devised an entire meta-language for Dianetics and Scientology that is so extensive it fills two full-sized dictionaries. He wrote obsessively, penning over two hundred works of fiction, forty books, and numerous documents, and he produced thousands of recorded lectures on Scientology. Allegedly, Hubbard even had a posse of assistants who followed him around to record his every word.

Hubbard "dropped his body" (Scientology-speak for the thetan deciding to continue its research without the burden of the meat body) on January 24, 1986. After a power struggle, David Miscavige became "COB" (Chairman of the Board), although Scientology is more famous for its famous members. For their abilities to promote and financially support the Church, Scientology actively recruits television and film stars through its "Celebrity Center," a kind of Scientology Studio 54. Scientology is seen as Hollywood's religion, with a cast of followers including Tom Cruise, John Travolta, Kirstie Alley, and Priscilla and Lisa Marie Presley, although Elvis was clearly on to the organization.

Elvis was not the only one. Scientology's status as a "Church" is controversial. Not many religions brand their beliefs, practices, and terminology with registered trademarks. Scientology maintains that it is a religion, sometimes, or alternatively, Scientologists argue it is an applied religious philosophy, a system of ethics, or a science of the mind. Many outsiders brand Scientology as a scam and a cult, but Scientologists don't take too kindly to criticism, and are known to attack and harass their critics. Scientology is known more for its litigation than its liturgy. Regardless of this threat, former members, journalists, politicians, and activists speak out about the Church's abuses and generate a lot of negative publicity for Scientology. However, the most negative publicity still comes from within the Church itself.

There's No Such Thing as a Free Personality Test

Scientology is a homegrown religion. Hubbard opened his first church in New Jersey in 1953. Now it is a worldwide organization with some 8,500 churches, missions, and outreach groups in 165 countries. Scientology claims to have millions of members and to be the fastest growing religion in the world. However, various sources report it may have as little as 30,000 adherents, although not through lack of trying.

A few years ago, a friend was about to walk into a supermarket in Denver when he noticed a man chasing after him, waving a book in the air. "Hey buddy, did you drop this?" He asked, revealing a tattered copy of *Dianetics*. "No. It's not mine," he admitted. The guy then shifted gears. "Can you spare any change?" My friend replied with the expected response, "No. I can't." "Which is precisely why you need to read this book!" he enthused. He handed my friend a business card and said with a smile, "Call us. Come to some classes. It'll change your life."

Scientologists are known for their enthusiastic (and evasive) evangelism and their aggressive tactics to recruit "raw meat," as they like to call potential members. Representatives appear at conventions, farmers markets, and shopping malls, and approach passers-by outside their churches. They are charming and well-dressed, but initially, they won't tell you who they represent. These are the persistent peddlers of the "free personality tests," which are the only thing free about Scientology, or so it seems at first . . .

This is the Oxford Capacity Analysis test. It doesn't have anything to do with Oxford University, although Scientologists hope you'll be confused enough to think so, and it is not scientifically recognized. The questions resemble those from a quiz in a women's magazine, while the answers will allegedly enable you to "discover things about yourself that can help you gain a happier life." The test asks two hundred questions, and the sheer length of the test is somewhat disorienting to the subject, and renders them more suggestible to the sales pitch that follows. Some of the questions include: *Are you likely to be jealous? Have you any particular hate or fear? Do you tend to be careless? Do you enjoy activities of your own choosing?* Even though these are subjective questions about the human condition, the answers will be marked as "correct" or "wrong." Regardless of your responses, you are a deeply troubled individual who would benefit greatly from purchasing Scientology's books, multimedia, seminars, classes, training, and counseling. Scientologists claim their method will help you increase your intelligence, improve your hearing and eyesight, enhance your communication skills, reduce stress and anxiety, deal with grief, decrease accidents, overcome irrational fears, and treat illnesses of the mind and body. What is this miraculous panacea? To Scientologists, the answer is: Dianetics.

Of Two Minds

The Dianetics theory of the brain turns neuroscience on its head. Hubbard taught that there are two parts of the brain, the *analytical mind* and the *reactive mind*. The analytical mind is like a computer that stores information and solves problems. The reactive mind is a mental archive of every incident involving emotional or physical pain. These incidents are called "engrams."

An engram is not a memory. It is a recording of a traumatic moment that is recorded in the exact color, sound, feel, and taste of the actual experience. Engrams are created when we are somehow in a weakened and vulnerable state, that is, when someone is under anesthetic, rendered unconscious after an accident, in a state of shock, or on prescriptive medication. During these times, the analytical mind is on pause, but the reactive mind is busy recording the surrounding sights, sounds, and smells occurring around the incapacitated individual. The Scientology Web site provides the following example of how an engram is created.

> A woman is knocked down by a blow to the face. She is rendered "unconscious." She is kicked in the side and told she is a faker, that she is no good, that she is always changing her mind. A chair is overturned in the process. A faucet is running in the kitchen. A car is passing in the street outside.

These surrounding stimuli install hidden commands, like hypnotic suggestions, that control the way we think, act, and feel. Our painful past affects our present, and a moment of pain may be replayed in unrelated situations in the future, when the engram is "restimulated." So, in the case of the example above, if the woman experiences an environment similar to the one during which the engram is created, the engram awakens and triggers psychosomatic symptoms, such as a headache or anxiety.

Our reactive minds affect our analytical minds and our bodies. Engrams are believed to be the root cause of most of our problems, including mental illness, addiction, homosexuality, sexual deviancy, irrationality, behavioral disorders, and crime. Engrams are behind ulcers, arthritis, asthma, allergies, cancer, dermatitis, the common cold, hearing difficulties, and even the need for reading glasses. According to Hubbard, these conditions are all psychosomatic.

Engrams are also created in the womb. The baby-to-be is affected by every little thing that mom does, or anything that happens to her during pregnancy. Prenatal engrams can be caused by mother's constipation, stress, sickness, sneezes, arguments, sexual activity, and the birth itself, so Scientologists advocate a "silent birth." Old Mother Hubbard must have suffered many terrible accidents when she was pregnant with Ron. Engrams are created not only by incidents in our past, but also by those that occurred in our past lives. As we can see, just about anything can create an engram, including events that we don't even remember, yet they are the source of most of our problems.

Have I Made Myself Clear?

Engrams link unrelated events and are heavily embedded in the psyche, so how are they diagnosed? Scientologists detect engrams using a device called an electropsychometer, known popularly as an E-Meter. The subject grabs on to two cylindrical electrodes, while a trained Scientologist asks a series of questions, noting the verbal responses and monitoring the activity of the device. The subject is invariably diagnosed with numerous engrams and requires immediate treatment.

Advertised as a "free stress test," E-Meter readings are often offered in conjunction with a "free personality test" to recruit new members. The E-Meter looks sciency, but it only measures the subject's galvanic responses—that is, the device reads the person's sweat and grip and is a kind of mini lie-detector test. Everyone "has engrams" because everyone responds physically to hot-button questions. My friend Bryan once underwent one of these tests at a conference. Understanding the science behind the device, he attempted to thwart the reading. In his own words, "I relaxed my grip on the handles and thought of puppies" and the E-Meter flatlined. The Scientologists looked at him as though he was either dead, or the reincarnation of L. Ron Hubbard. They finally told him, "the machine is broken. Can you come back tomorrow?"

In the end, it really doesn't matter what the response is, as the results will be interpreted subjectively. Once it has been established that the subject is riddled with engrams, they must be removed. The only way to eliminate engrams is through a process called auditing or processing. This is "spiritual counseling" with the goal of deleting the engrams from the reactive mind. The audit is conducted by a trained Dianetic therapist known as an auditor, while the engram-affected person being audited is known as a "pre-clear" (PC).

At the start of a session a "key incident" is selected for auditing. The subject is hooked up to an E-meter as he or she relives this moment, retelling the story again and again until the event's "charge" is nullified according to the device. The audit isn't as innocuous as it sounds at first. If the subject can't think of an event to audit one may be recalled through intensive questioning. The auditor issues endless commands and the subject is forced to repeat verbal routines for hours on end, placing the person in a suggestible state. An audit is no more than an interrogation.

Sometimes the "key incident" never even happened. Auditing is a kind of regression therapy that allows for the creation of false memories. Over the course of numerous audits the subject is regressed back to birth to remove the "prenatal engrams." Then the subject is regressed back further still, to remove engrams created in past lives. A person's entire life history across space and time is known as the "whole track." Herein is a new kind of threat: body thetans. These are itinerant spirits that have attached themselves to a human and come along for the ride, causing even more physical, psychological, and behavioral problems. This type of regression and questioning, coupled with these beliefs, can induce fantasies and delusion and implant false memories created by the auditor and the person being audited.

The auditing session is a kind of confessional, and the pre-clear reveals highly sensitive information about his or her career, finances, family, and sex life. Scientologists who are disciplined for bad behavior must write-up their sins known as "overts and withholds." This procedure is a voyeuristic penance where they must confess lies and secrets, including every sex act they have either thought of or committed. In their characteristic paranoia, Scientologists run occasional "security checks" on their members. These are interrogative audits to compel their colleagues/congregation to fess up about things they didn't know they did. They are asked hundreds of questions, such as, "Do you have a secret you're afraid I'll find out?" and "What has someone told you not to tell?" Unlike the confession given to a Catholic priest, records are kept of all audits, security checks, and overts and withholds, and potentially used for blackmail purposes. Of course, the Scientologist is charged a pretty penny for this confession.

Over time, Scientologists must audit all of their engrams and body thetans. Hubbard estimated that the average person has over two hundred engrams. Of course, this requires many sessions of processing, and each audit costs anything from $150 to $2,000. If there are any errors or oversights in the auditing, a costly "review audit" must be undertaken to correct these mistakes. Alternatively, the Scientologist can undergo expensive and emotionally grueling training to be able to self-audit. This requires the purchase of a personal E-Meter that retails for $3,500. It is recommended that each auditor own two devices, in case one breaks down during a particularly sensational audit. Scientologists are encouraged to undergo both processing and training for auditing, so they can self-audit and help others. "Field auditors" counsel others as a full-time job and charge thousands of dollars per session.

The engram-free Scientologist is then labeled a "Clear." His or her reactive mind is totally erased, as though the brain has undergone a reformat. Becoming a Clear is reaching the Nirvana of Scientology, and the Clear is considered a kind of superhuman. Clears are said to be free of physical and mental illnesses, so they won't even catch a cold. Hubbard claimed they would have increased intelligence, perfect eyesight, and a photographic memory. Various sources estimate conservatively that the cost of auditing required to reach this status is $50,000. Scientology's goal is to "Clear the planet."

Hubbard provided an example of the "world's first Clear" during a lecture to 6,000 people in Los Angeles in 1950. The Clear was a student of physics by the name of Sonya Bianca. She was presented as someone with "full and perfect recall of every moment of her life." However, in answering a set of questions, she failed to remember a single physics formula, and couldn't remember the color of Hubbard's tie when his back was turned. At that point most of the audience stood up and left the lecture theater.

Road to Nowhere
Scientology doesn't end when you're a Clear. Even superhumans have room for improvement. A Catholic is a Catholic, but there are different levels of Scientologists. After becoming a Clear, the next step is to reach the level of Operating Thetan (OT). Scientologists not only undergo numerous sessions of auditing to become Clear, but then complete a dizzying array of courses to progress through the levels of OT. There are eight levels that form the "Bridge to Total Freedom." The word is that

Hubbard created even more levels, and the Church dangles this prospect like a carrot, saying that followers must wait for their release until more people are brought into the Church.

The spiritual path to OT is said to be well worth the wait. Hubbard taught that when Scientologists reach the level they can alter matter, energy, space, and time (MEST) at their will, control others, and even create their own universe. There are higher echelons still, and Scientologists can become members of the inner elite group the Sea Organization, but they must sign a one-billion-year contract, promising to continue to serve Scientology into future lives. The Sea Org's motto is, "We Come Back."

Scientology is a kind of religious pyramid scheme. Each level costs thousands of dollars to complete, and the route from "raw meat" to the "whole bridge" is estimated to cost some $350,000. There is a reason why the Church of Scientology is often abbreviated to Co$. To lure you in, the initial courses are cheap, then the prices skyrocket. If you can't afford them, don't worry, you can become a member of staff and recruit others as you work your way across the bridge. But don't expect to party with John Travolta and Kirstie Alley. Celebrities receive preferential treatment in Scientology, because they promote and fund the religion. They roll out the red carpet for Tom Cruise, and they held "auditions" when they needed him to find a Scientology-friendly wife. However, life as a staff member isn't as glamorous. The pay is low, the conditions are poor, the hours are long, and you'll have to meet strict targets each week, or else.

Shocking information has come to light about the severe punishments metered out to members of the "Sea Org" who commit real or perceived violations. Sometimes these alleged crimes are detected by E-Meters. Offenders are assigned to the "Rehabilitation Project Force." This program has been likened to prison, boot camp, concentration camp, or a gulag forced-labor camp. The Sea Org itself has been likened to the Hitler Youth. Ex-members provide horrifying accounts of enduring physical and psychological abuse for months to years. They were guarded constantly, only allowed to speak when spoken to, and fed a diet of rice, beans, and water. Their days are filled with strenuous manual labor and degrading jobs and their nights are spent sleeping on the floor, sometimes in cockroach and rat-infested areas. They are forced to undergo hours of auditing, training, and security checks, and are refused access to their spouses and children. Not only is Scientology a pyramid scheme, but it is a cult.

They're Coming to Take Me Away

One of Hubbard's main motivators for creating Dianetics was his distrust of psychiatry. Scientology has a number of front groups to wage war against the medical field, including the Citizens Commission on Human Rights (CCHR), founded by Scientologist psychiatrist Thomas Szasz. The organization argues that mental illnesses do not exist, that treatments are ineffective and dangerous, and that psychiatry is a pseudoscience driven by profit. The CCHR comprises a group of activists who launch campaigns against psychiatrists, psychiatric organizations, and pharmaceutical companies.

Their main office in Los Angeles houses "Psychiatry: An Industry of Death." This is a Scientology-sponsored "museum" that is a bombardment of antipsychiatry propaganda. Rooms are decorated as padded cells, with gory exhibits of controversial practices, including electroconvulsive therapy and lobotomy. They delight in parading an onslaught of vintage paintings and photographs of agonized victims in asylums, eerie institutions, and patients held in restraints or undergoing primitive procedures. Psychiatry is accused of kidnap, rape, torture, and murder, and blamed for the deaths of Ernest Hemingway, Marilyn Monroe, and Kurt Cobain. They promote conspiracy theories, citing psychiatry as the cause of the Columbine shootings, the September 11 attacks, Jonestown, Pearl Harbor, and the Holocaust.

Scientologists fear that psychiatry has infiltrated education, government, courtrooms, churches, and homes as part of some kind of "master plan." David Miscavige has his own plan, to achieve "the global obliteration of psychiatry." Dianetics is Scientology's answer to psychiatry. It teaches that mental illnesses are merely psychosomatic and caused by engrams and body thetans, and that they are curable through auditing. Additional techniques exist as alternatives to psychiatry, including their detoxification programs. Hubbard believed that drug residues are stored in fat for years, and that these are released on occasion, causing the person to experience the effects of the drug and leading to addiction. Narconon is Scientology's drug rehabilitation program that advocates the use of extreme exercise, saunas, diet, and high doses of vitamins known as "drug bombs" to flush out these toxins. The program costs about $23,000.

Narconon is based on Scientology's Purification Rundown, a detox regime that recommends the use of, you guessed it, exercise, saunas, diet, and vitamins, and costs about $1,500. The program is outlined in Hubbard's *Clear Mind, Clear Body* and recommends that patients spend up to five hours a day in a sauna and take high doses of vitamins. Hubbard claimed incorrectly that a Nobel Prize was won in 1973 for "curing insanity with niacin," and as part of these programs mega doses of niacin are administered as medication. The Food and Drug Administration's recommended daily allowance is 16mg for men and 14mg for women, while the Scientology programs start on 100mg and steadily increase up to 5,000mg. The patient is literally overdosed on niacin, causing itching, dizziness, and a flushing sensation of the skin. Hubbard believed that these were positive side effects that purged sunburn, radiation, and toxins from the body. The Purification Rundown is yet another cure-all that will allegedly lower cholesterol and weight, treat anxiety and depression, increase intelligence, and alleviate symptoms of cancer, heart problems, and AIDS—all with the added benefit of allowing the patient to survive a nuclear war.

Out of Touch

"Touch assist" is another treatment described in Hubbard's *The Scientology Handbook*. A touch of Scientology supposedly treats earaches, heals broken bones or infected boils, and relieves dental pain, but its applications are "unlimited." This is Scientology's version of faith healing and is a kind of laying on of fingers. Taking one finger the patient is instructed to "feel my finger" as the healer touches various "nerve channels" on the body that supposedly store the pain. This puts the patient back in communication with the affected area and promotes healing. The procedure can be used on sick or injured animals too. Scientology missionaries are trained to use this technique in disaster regions, and touch assists were used on victims after the 9/11 terrorist attacks in New York and in Japan after the 2011 earthquake and tsunami. John Travolta once used a touch assist to heal musician Sting of a sore throat before a performance, although Sting can't remember the incident.

Hubbard also devised other "assists" that are known as forms of "locational processing." "Contact assist" is designed to remove pain from an injury or accident. In a sort of physical audit, the patient is instructed to role-play the incident again and again until the pain is gone. There is a "how to make a person sober assist" that involves telling the intoxicated individual to focus on various items in a room until they are no longer drunk. The "unconscious person assist" is used to bring someone back from a coma or unconsciousness by instructing them to "feel that bedspread" and "feel that pillow," among other commands. Scientologists believe that a trained "tone" of speech can be used as a tool of persuasion to convince a stubborn boss, to handle a fight with a spouse, to placate a grumpy child, or to even bring back the dead.

Lowering the Tone

Hubbard reports, "A child had died, was dead, had been pronounced dead by a doctor, and the auditor, by calling the thetan back and ordering him to take over the body again brought the child to life." The healer has about three to four minutes to raise the dead person back to life. They are to command them with, "Come back and bring this body to life!" or order the corpse to "Come back here and pick up your body! At once! Pick it up! I order you! Right now!" If these techniques don't work, try "coaxing" the person back, by pleading with them to think of their families and friends. One auditor failed with these phrases but finally had success with the appeal, "Think of your poor auditor!" upon which the deceased woman came back to life.

This type of command is known as "tone 40" and is learned during a Scientology Training Routine (TR). These are drills designed to improve communication skills. Scientologists practice tone 40 on an ashtray, commanding it to move by intention, but they learn how to walk before they can levitate. Lower-level routines involve staring at a training partner for hours on end, without movement, excessive blinking, or loss of attention. In another routine, the coach yells and screams at a student who must learn how to sit still without being distracted or reacting in any way. These training routines have been criticized for having a strong hypnotic effect and causing hallucinations, rendering the students more susceptible to directions from Scientology.

With all of this "training," Scientology members become self-proclaimed experts in psychology and psychiatry. Their stable of celebrities become spokespeople for a topic they know nothing about. Tom Cruise is known for his zealous outbursts against psychiatry during interviews. He publicly blasted Brooke Shields for taking medication for postpartum depression. During an interview with Matt Lauer, Cruise claimed to "know the history of psychiatry." He denounced the medication Ritalin and denied the existence of ADHD. Kirstie Alley credited Narconon for her recovery from a cocaine habit, although she never actually underwent the program.

Scientology claims that autism is a "fake" illness, but it was speculated that John Travolta's son Jett suffered from the condition. The boy's sickness was instead explained as Kawasaki disease and blamed on environmental toxins from household cleaners and fertilizers. Sadly, Jett died at age sixteen during a seizure, which is a common occurrence when autism is left untreated. After Jett's death, Travolta finally acknowledged his son had autism. Many Scientologists refuse treatment for their mental and neurological conditions, or they are refused treatment by their colleagues.

Psychiatry is an imperfect science, with a past of experimental treatments and patient abuses, but Dianetics is not a viable alternative. Scientology demonizes psychiatry to promote its own agenda. Ironically, Scientologists don't believe in psychotherapy, yet Dianetics is just another type of psychotherapy, and a pseudoscience. It has been revealed to be ineffective at best and dangerous at worst. This is when Scientologists switch from the secular to the spiritual and claim the benefits are a matter of faith. In fact, Hubbard's books contain disclaimers that these are religious rituals, and not medical treatments, although these were forced on them by the government. As the warning label on E-Meters says:

By itself, this meter does nothing. It is solely for the guide of Ministers of the Church in confessionals and pastoral counseling. The Electrometer is not medically or scientifically useful for the diagnosis, treatment, or prevention of any disease. It is not medically or scientifically capable of improving the health or body function of anyone and is for religious use by students and Ministers of the Church of Scientology *only*.

In the Beginning

By now you may be wondering, where is the religion in all of this? Since 1954 Scientology has been declared a "religion," although the organization has been accused of declaring this for the tax-exemption status that it has held, on and off. There is a lot of overlap between Dianetics and Scientology, but the latter operates within a religious framework. However, the religiosity is mostly in the terminology. Scientology introduces the concept of the "thetan," or spirit, and that Jesus Christ was a Clear. Scientology books are relabeled as "scripture." Scientology presents auditing as "spiritual counseling," its central religious practice, that is performed to achieve spiritual salvation. The Scientology auditor is reframed as a "minister" and the subject being audited becomes a "parishioner." Auditors are all ordained ministers in the Church of Scientology.

To reframe themselves as a religion, Scientologists incorporate the use of an eight-pointed cross, and their practices draw parallels to the established rites of other religions. Their centers become "churches" or "missions" where they conduct Sunday "services." There they present Hubbard's poems as prayers, his science fiction stories as sermons, and perform a session of group auditing as a kind of devotion. They occasionally toss in the word "God" or "Supreme Being," although sometimes that appears to be Hubbard. He taught that we are all gods who can recover our powers through Scientology courses and training.

Most belief systems have a story that explains the origins of the universe, whether it's Genesis of the Old Testament or the dreamtime legends of the Australian Aboriginal people. Scientology is no different. Its creation myth is the story of Xenu, also known as Incident 2. It is a space opera so fantastical that you would think it was penned by a science fiction writer.

Once upon a time, 75 million years ago to be more precise, there lived an evil alien dictator named Xenu, the Satan of Scientology. He ruled over a galactic confederation of seventy-six stars. Faced with the problem of overpopulation, he devised a kind of Final Solution. Billions of different species of aliens were rounded up and imprisoned. A group of psychiatrists paralyzed these aliens using a compound of alcohol and glycol. In this state they were packed into spaceships that looked like DC-8 airliners without engines. The aliens were then transported to Teegeeack, today known as "Earth." Xenu parked the ships around volcanoes, and then detonated hydrogen bombs. The aliens all died, but their souls were released into the atmosphere.

Xenu recaptured these "thetans" using electronic beams, and they were shipped to Hawaii and Las Palmas in the Canary Islands. There they were seated in an intergalactic cinema and exposed to thirty-six days of movies that implanted the knowledge we have today. The Judeo-Christian–centric Xenu programmed the thetans to believe in Jesus and God. They were also commanded to go forth and do "bad things" in society, accounting for our original sin. These brainwashed thetans were finally set free. With nowhere else to go, they formed clusters and attached themselves to local life forms. Xenu was eventually captured and imprisoned on a hidden planet where he remains a prisoner to this day. These wretched thetans still linger on Earth, where they attach to modern people as body thetans, causing spiritual harm and sickness.

Climbing Mount Impossible

David Miscavige claims the story of Xenu isn't a belief of contemporary Scientology. However, secrecy is part of the game of Scientology. The scriptures of other religions are made freely available. Their beliefs are preached in houses of worship, and fervent missionaries spread the "good news," but in Scientology doctrine is restricted knowledge. The organization's beliefs are withheld from the neophytes. Scientology's scriptures are sold and its tenets are trained, over a period of time.

Like the "milk before meat" of the Mormons, Scientology releases its doctrine in "gradients," to make its more controversial aspects palatable. The Xenu story is only revealed when the Scientologist reaches the level OT III, known as the "Wall of Fire." In a 1972 court case, a former

Scientologist revealed that he was forced to sign a waiver to not hold Scientology responsible for anything that might happen during his progress through OT III. Those who become enlightened are discouraged from revealing this top-secret scripture to lower level Scientologists. Hubbard issued a kind of curse that if unauthorized people read these stories before their time they would become ill with pneumonia. This strange doctrine was veiled in secrecy until the Internet enabled the dissemination of this information to the public.

This bizarre revelation of Xenu even destabilized Tom Cruise, who distanced himself from Scientology for awhile when he learned this tenet of the Church. Why would anyone believe this tall tale? Upon reaching OT III, Scientologists have progressed many years into the program, and may be subject to the sunk cost fallacy because they have invested a large amount of time and money into their beliefs. They are coerced by their leaders, who threaten to blackmail them with their guilty secrets accumulated over many hours of auditing, to "stay in the fold, or else." They have isolated themselves from their friends and family and rational influences. They have been indoctrinated and brainwashed for years, and their critical thinking skills have been eroded. They are discouraged from questioning the doctrine. Some accept the story of Xenu as no crazier than the belief that Jesus raised the dead and arose from the dead himself. Others see the story of Xenu as Scientology's version of the Old Testament.

Most of all, by the time Scientologists reach OT III, the space opera seems plausible because in a sense, they have undergone similar personal experiences. At this level, the subject has been regressed to numerous "past lives" during auditing. As is common with past-life therapy, some subjects believe that they were once famous or notable people. Many Scientologists report that they were once Jesus. Hubbard presents a collection of "case histories" in his book *Have You Lived before This Life?* Hubbard himself claimed that in a former life he had been the intrepid traveler, politician, and mining magnate Cecil Rhodes, the founder of De Beers diamonds. Rhodes was clearly a man after Hubbard's own heart. Ironically, it is widely believed that Rhodes was homosexual, and Hubbard was a staunch homophobe who preached that homosexuality is an illness or a perversion.

The process of auditing eventually regresses the subject through the "whole track" of their alleged lives, for those with enough money. In reliving these "former lives" many Scientologists report memories of a more extraterrestrial nature. They tell graphic details of their adventures as captains of space ships, being killed by "zap guns" and living in robot bodies on other planets. They emerge from their auditing sessions believing they have conquered universes and saved entire planets from destruction. Just like those who claim to be victims of Satanic ritual abuse and alien abduction, these people are reporting false memories, not former lives. These are not implants by Xenu, but fantasies implanted by the auditor and products of their own imagination. These "memories" prime them to believe the Xenu story and become evidence to support the claims of Scientology.

These false memories are influenced by pop culture, and especially Hubbard's writings. There are strong similarities between his science fiction and the narratives of Scientology doctrine. However, in Hubbard's universe the line between science fiction and fact is blurred. Hubbard believed that science fiction is really an unconscious recollection of real events and real past lives that took place millions of years ago. Hubbard completely rewrote the history of the universe in *A History of Man*, which is alleged to be an account of the last sixty trillion years of existence. He claimed the existence of now-extinct alien civilizations, including Helatrobus and Arslycus. In events known as "key incidents," evil aliens invaded Earth, and posing as gorillas, bears, and wearing other disguises, they hypnotized humans and implanted them with false memories, all with the goal of limiting our abilities. By reading this book, Hubbard promises that, "the blind again see, the lame walk, the ill recover, the insane become sane and the sane become saner."

Scientology has even devised a "security check" to investigate the actions of members during their past lives. The suspect is forced to undergo auditing to reveal crimes they allegedly committed against Ron in former lives, and interrogated with hundreds of questions, including: "Have you come to earth for evil purposes?" "Have you ever enslaved a population?" and "Have you ever made a planet or nation radioactive?" When people buy into Scientology, their lives become a science fiction plot. Treating Dianetics and Scientology as guides for physical and spiritual health is like taking advice from Isaac Asimov's *I, Robot*.

Down to a (Pseudo)Science

Hubbard's books are essentially about self-improvement. However, they are not as innocuous as *How to Win Friends and Influence People*. Dianetics and Scientology involve some extremely dangerous beliefs and practices. Here are just a few victims of this "religion."

Thirty-six-year-old Lisa McPherson of Clearwater, Florida, was a Scientologist who suffered from an undiagnosed psychiatric illness, but her condition was denied by the Church. Following a psychotic episode that landed her in hospital, fellow Scientologists checked her out of there and into a hotel, for some "rest and relaxation." Instead, they subjected her to an "introspection rundown." They isolated her and "muzzled" her, so that no one supervising her was allowed to speak. This silence was broken up by intensive sessions of auditing. Lisa's supervisors administered vitamins and illegally prescribed drugs to her. After several weeks of this "treatment," she suffered a pulmonary embolism. Still alive but gasping for air she was driven past several local hospitals and taken to a Scientology-friendly doctor who pronounced her dead on arrival. Her entire body was covered in what appeared to be bug bites and severe bruises, and she was seriously underweight and dehydrated. At the time of her death Lisa was considered a Clear.

Fifty-four-year-old Elli Perkins was a senior auditor for the Church of Scientology in Buffalo, New York. Her son Jeremy began hearing voices and believed he was Jesus Christ. Following a brush with the law, a court-ordered psychiatric exam revealed that he was suffering from schizophrenia. In accordance with Scientology doctrine, Elli denied that he had a mental illness and refused to allow him treatment with anti-psychotic medication. Instead, she took him to an osteopath and fellow Scientologist who diagnosed that Jeremy was suffering from chemical toxins and recommended vitamin therapy for him. Elli forced her son to take vitamins, and in his psychosis, he believed she was trying to poison him. Untreated and unstable, he made an attempt at suicide. When this failed he then fatally stabbed his mother seventy-seven times.

Many people go into serious debt believing the promises of Scientology. Roxanne Friend was not feeling well, but as a Scientologist, she was taught that illness is psychosomatic and can be cured by auditing. She spent $80,000 on auditing, but she still wasn't feeling well. She was externally diagnosed with cancer, but Roxanne was kept under house arrest by fellow Scientologists and refused medical treatment. In the meantime, her cancer became incurable. She left Scientology and sued them for these abuses. The Church settled out of court for "nuisance value," but Roxanne died soon thereafter.

Scientology's social programs report astounding success and low recidivism, although the Church's claims are unsupported by research. Alternatively, there are many stories of abuses. Patients are told that the Purification Rundown can cure liver disease, but Jerry Whitfield suffered permanent liver damage while on the program, while Christopher Arbuckle died of liver failure. Narconon has been at the center of many controversies, including a lack of medical care, while members of staff have been accused of being on drugs, selling drugs, refusing to administer patients' medication, or providing drugs in exchange for sex, leading to cases of overdoses and patient deaths. Narconon patients Patrick Desmond, Stacy Murphy, Hilary Holten, and Gabriel Graves died because of alleged negligence. Narconon centers have been closed down in France, Italy, and Canada for similar abuses.

It's Off to Jail We Go
Probably the most notorious Scientology scandal is that of Operation Snow White. In the 1970s, Hubbard became convinced that Scientology was under attack from various organizations, so he launched a counterattack. A group of Church members, led by his then-wife Mary-Sue, became involved in espionage. They infiltrated government agencies and private companies critical of the church, and they ransacked offices, and copied, modified, or stole documents that contained information about Scientology. This was the Watergate of Scientology. These crimes led to wide-scale convictions of theft and obstructing justice, and Mary-Sue took the fall for Hubbard and spent five years in jail.

Scientology is unable to abide criticism. The Church plays the religion card and positions legitimate criticisms as acts of discrimination. However, it does not turn the other cheek, but instead it retaliates. The Church's tactic is to "attack the attacker." Ex-members, journalists, known as "merchants of chaos," and others who speak out are labeled "suppressive persons" (SPs) who become "fair game" for its policy of "dead agenting." This is smearing people with lies or rumors to discredit them. The Church is in the habit of overwhelming a critic with lawsuits, harassment, threats, and smear campaigns. It likes auditing so much it reports enemies to the IRS as tax cheats to have them audited. It isn't afraid to tackle governments and companies, and it has taken on *Forbes* magazine, the Better Business Bureau, the American Medical Association, the American Psychiatric Association, and the IRS. In a battle with the Cult Awareness Network, it bullied its critics so much that the network went bankrupt and, ironically, Scientology bought it up.

Agencies, authors, and defectors aren't the only suppressive persons. In a practice called "disconnection," Scientologists are forced to sever contact with anyone who criticizes the cult, including friends, family, and colleagues. They are coerced to abandon their parents and children and leave their spouses if they disparage the religion, and they liken this to the Amish practice of shunning. This is an effective way to isolate the member and draw them more deeply into the fold.

Despite the threats, many individuals and organizations have raised awareness about Scientology, proving there is strength in numbers. These people include former members turned activists Gerry Armstrong, Tory Christman, and Lawrence Wollersheim, and actor Jason Beghe, who admitted that Scientology is "very dangerous for your spiritual, psychological, mental, emotional health and evolution." *South Park* creators Trey Parker and Matt Stone parodied Scientology in the episode "Trapped in the Closet" that is famous for providing the best explanation of the Xenu story. Authors Jon Atack and Janet Reitman have written exposés of Scientology, while Paulette Cooper fought the Church's harassment for fifteen years until her book *The Scandal of Scientology* was taken off the market. Thanks to the efforts of Andreas Heldal-Lund of Operation Clambake, Mark Bunker of Xenu TV, and the online collective known as Anonymous, many of Scientology's secrets have been made publicly available on the Internet. Most damning of all are insider stories from the family members of Scientology's figureheads, including the criticisms from David Miscavige's niece Jenna Miscavige Hill and from L. Ron Hubbard's great-grandson Jamie DeWolf. One of Scientology's biggest critics was Lafayette Ronald Hubbard, Jr., Hubbard's son. He changed his name to Ronald DeWolf to avoid any associations with his father, whom he referred to as "one of the biggest con men of this century."

Sci(fi)entology

Hubbard is depicted as an explorer, a medical pioneer, a scientist, a humanitarian, a philosopher, and a war hero. He was none of these things. In reality, he was an eccentric who liked to repeat urban legends and other people's experiences as personal stories. Hubbard was a dropout, a bigamist, and a charlatan. He was deeply involved in the occult and black magic. He had a criminal record for crimes of theft and fraud, and he was named an unindicted co-conspirator for Operation Snow White, which led him to spend the rest of his life in hiding from the law.

The biggest Clear of them all was far from superhuman. Dianetics and Scientology never cured Hubbard's obesity or his chain-smoking habit, and didn't prevent or treat his many illnesses, including a pulmonary embolism, chronic pancreatitis, a heart attack, or the stroke that killed him. Clearly, they didn't get to him in time to "tone 40" him back from death. For all of his rabid criticisms against psychiatry, Hubbard died with Vistaril in his system, a drug used to treat anxiety. His son Ronald Jr. once admitted during an interview that his father was a hypochondriac and addicted to cocaine, amphetamines, barbiturates, and even peyote.

Hubbard created an intricate world of science fiction that he preached as fact. Dianetics and Scientology are both obvious works of fiction. Of course, self-help and spirituality are more lucrative than peddling pulp science fiction, especially when you're not very good at it (despite the positive reviews one sees on Amazon today that are clearly written by Scientologists). As Hubbard once said, "Writing for a penny a word is ridiculous. If a man really wants to make a million dollars, the best way would be to start his own religion." And so he did.

The Holy Ghost

I visited a Church of Scientology in Colorado to attend its Sunday service. From the outside the building looks like a Masonic Hall with its esoteric Freemason-like symbols. On the inside, it is a cross between a tourist information center and Times Square. Large flat-screen TVs constantly ran promotional films. It also looked like a Barnes & Noble specifically built for Hubbard, as it was full of his numerous books in a range of languages. The decor was modern and slick and could be confused for the trendy offices of an advertising company, if it wasn't for the portraits, posters, statues, and logos of L. Ron Hubbard everywhere.

I walked in and was confronted by a woman at the front desk. She greeted me enthusiastically, but seemed a little surprised. Passersby usually fall into their web and are dragged in, yet here I was walking in off the street. She immediately asked me to sign a guest book and complete a form with my personal details. "How did you hear about us?" she asked. "Who hasn't heard of Scientology?" I joked, at which she laughed—too hard. An older gentleman approached and introduced himself as Harry. He was dressed like a maître d' and wore a white shirt and rust-colored satin vest under a black suit. "I'm here for the service," I explained. "Excellent! I'll be the one holding it!" he beamed.

Harry led me around the room. The first stop was a bright orange E-Meter on display with a sign above saying, "SEE YOUR THOUGHTS." "Is this used for therapy?" I asked. "We would object to that term," he said sternly. Harry gave me a demonstration, but I used Bryan's trick, so the needle barely moved. He seemed perturbed and swapped the handles to no avail. "I think this one's broken," he muttered.

"How about you watch some videos instead?" He led me to a screen and started a documentary about Hubbard. This was a glowing biography that portrayed Hubbard as an explorer, a sportsman, a scientist, an author, and a hero of war. However, every accolade stopped short of telling the truth. Yes, he attended George Washington University . . . but he dropped out. Yes, he was an officer in the Navy during World War II . . . but during his service he was demoted and soon discharged due to an ulcer. I continued to watch infomercials about the Purification Rundown, Narconon, the Citizens Commission for Human Rights, and

Criminon, a program to rehabilitate criminals. My eyes glazed over with the relentless propaganda. Scientology seemed to have an answer to all of life's problems.

Living up to their waiter-like uniforms, Harry and other members of the Scientology staff kept checking in on me. Ostensibly, this was to see if I had any questions, but it also seemed as though they were keeping an eye on me. Soon, another staff member appeared and began snapping photos of me without my permission. "These are just for promotional purposes!" he assured me, before disappearing.

Harry approached me again, suddenly wearing a gold cross that was pinned to his lapel in his transition from curator to minister. "It's time for the service!" he announced. As I walked through the halls, I asked, "How many people attend the service?" "A family usually attends, but they are busy today," he explained as he led me into an empty chapel. It was opulently decorated with marble walls and an intricate mosaic inlaid on the floor. Various symbols covered the walls. The Dianetics logo is a sliced pyramid, "modeled after the Greek letter delta." The Scientology symbol features an "S" interwoven with two triangles, with the upper triangle representing knowledge, responsibility, and control, and the lower triangle symbolizing understanding.

Scientology is a church in name only. After the Church of Scientology International (CSI) had its tax-exemption status revoked (for the first time) in 1967, it began incorporating religious symbolism into its rituals, especially that of the golden "eight-point cross." One of these crosses was featured on the podium, and an enormous cross was center-wall behind the stage. Hubbard's paraphrased commandments covered the walls on large scrolls, but strangest of all, there was a large bust of Hubbard on the stage. "What is Hubbard to the Church? Is he a prophet?" I asked. "No," Harry chuckled. "He was our founder." However, the displays put him somewhere between messiah and dictator.

With Harry at the podium, I was the only person in the audience. There were fourteen empty chairs in the chapel, although the building was brimming with staff members who weren't attending. Unfazed, Harry proceeded to present a service to a congregation of one. "I'll give my sermon to a full room . . . or to a single person," he said nobly. He began by reading the Church's creed that had more references to mental health than spirituality, and then he read Hubbard's appalling short story "The Golden Ball" as a sermon. Then he announced, "Now we're going to do some group processing." This was called an "ownership session." He asked me to take two fingers to measure the size of my head and then to pull back my fingers slowly to view this estimated size. In turn, he asked me to repeat this process for my eyes, nose, mouth, ears, and feet.

Then Harry issued a lengthy series of commands: "Find the floor. Find the chair. Focus on something in the room. Focus on something else in the room. Think of a person you can talk to. Think of someone else you can talk to. Think of a person who can talk to you. Think of someone else who can talk to you." He went back and forth with these phrases and many similar directions. Then he asked me to imagine a series of ideas. "Have the idea that you own your body. Have the idea that your mother owns your body. Have the idea that your father owns your body. Have the idea that your grandparents own your body. Have the idea that someone else owns your body." He toggled back and forth between these and other statements, and then the concepts became more abstract. "Have the idea that the government owns your body. Have the idea that you won your body in the lottery. Have the idea that your body was left to you in a will. Have the idea that you bought your body from Tiffany's." He always returned to the phrase, "Now have the idea that you own your body." These relentless commands continued for forty minutes. This "group processing" was clearly an audit, and an attempt at hypnosis. The procedure was disorienting, and very annoying.

The service finished with a recitation of the Scientology "Prayer for Total Freedom." At the end of the prayer I inquired, "This building is full of other people. Why didn't they attend the service with us?" Harry seemed insulted that I would even ask. "They are all busy doing their jobs!" he exclaimed. These men and women, also wearing black suits and vests, rushed about the place, giving the semblance of being incredibly busy. They all had smiles plastered on their faces, and they seemed artificially happy. I walked past one room and a man grinned and waved at me like he was whizzing past on a miniature train at Disneyland. Posters around the halls advertised, "Auditors wanted. Awful pay. Tough Preclears. Impossible hours. But we groom staff auditors into the smoothest auditors in the world and you're close in on the greatest push in the last 2,500 years."

Harry gave me a tour of the premises. This was the first church I'd been to that also had a bookstore, café, video kiosks, offices, therapy rooms, a gym, and a sauna. "This is our 'Purification Room,' where we can detox. It's important to get rid of those toxins!" advised this portly, red-faced man. I approached an empty office appointed in gold and encased in glass. It was worthy of a pharaoh's tomb, if it wasn't for the E-Meter. This was an altar dedicated to Hubbard. "We keep an office for L. Ron in every church," Harry explained reverently. "We have it set up so he could walk right in and continue his work," he said, almost as though he expected Hubbard to do just that.

The staff spoke of "L. Ron" as though he was still alive. As a constant presence throughout the building, Hubbard is certainly the "Holy Ghost" of Scientology. He is a legend to his followers. In the future, there is a very real danger that Hubbard will be deified and worshipped as a messiah who could heal the sick and bring back the dead. Hubbard is a god in the making, if he isn't a god already.

Chapter 8

Something Old, Something New
New Age Spirituality

"God knows, Anything goes."
—Cole Porter

"Find that perfect place, that silent place, that God within. But if 'God' is an uncomfortable word for you, you can stick another word in there, like 'Spirit,' 'Power,' 'Presence,' or 'Love.'" "God works for me, but I grew up going to church in Texas!"

The Coming of the New Age

New Age Spirituality encompasses a diverse array of beliefs and practices. It is a fusion of theories, ideologies, rituals, and customs. These are plucked from a wide range of historical religions and drawn from philosophy, psychology, self-help, science, alternative medicine, the paranormal, and much more. There is something for everyone. New Age Spirituality is a catch-all title for this metaphysical movement with no other unifying name because it interweaves anything and everything. It is a pluralistic belief system where anything goes.

There is no clear history of the movement because it is so eclectic. It is often thought that New Age Spirituality arose with the appearance of hippies during the 1960s. Others think it goes back to the mediumship and séances of Spiritualism. Some believe it has its origins in the medieval era and its growing fascination with astrology and alchemy. New Age Spirituality has no single founder, unlike Joseph Smith of the Mormons or George Fox of the Quakers. However, there are a number of early key figures who influenced the movement, and they were all Renaissance men and women. Emanuel Swedenborg (1688–1772) was a Swedish engineer, astronomer, and Christian mystic who talked to angels and demons. Franz Mesmer (1734–1815) was a German physician, astronomer, and psychotherapist who promoted his theory of animal magnetism and gave us the word "mesmerize." Helena "Madam" Blavatsky (1831–1891) was a Russian scholar of ancient teachings and formed the Theosophical Society, which is dedicated to studies of the esoteric. Her magnum opus *The Secret Doctrine* came out well before the modern bestseller *The Secret*.

New Age Spirituality was popularized in the twentieth century, especially by its endorsements from celebrities. Shirley MacLaine went out on a limb to promote her beliefs about reincarnation, astral projection, and UFOs. Celebrities often become missionaries for their beliefs. If you loved their movies and music, now try their religion. The Beatles introduced Transcendental Meditation to the Western world. George Harrison converted to Hinduism and had everyone singing "Hare Krishna." Madonna made the Kabbalah trendy, as she wore its braided red-string bracelet as an evil eye. Richard Gere promotes Buddhism and is close friends with the 14th Dalai Lama. George Lucas describes himself as a "Buddhist Methodist." Tom Cruise is the poster boy for Scientology. Yoga buff Sting has everyone still believing the urban legend that he enjoys six-hour sessions of tantric sex.

New Age Spirituality is broad and fragmented, so the movement gives rise to the emergence of new religions, sects, and cults. In 1986, psychic medium Sylvia Browne founded the Society of Novus Spiritus. However, this spiritus isn't so novus. Browne's church refers to itself as Gnostic Christian, but it also includes aspects of Buddhism, Hinduism, and paranormal beliefs. Despite its name, the New Age is age old and there is little that is original or new about it. It's something old, something new, something borrowed, and something blue, that is, if you believe in "indigo children." New Age Spirituality goes back much further than psychedelic music and lava lamps. It is formed from the accumulation of human knowledge and folklore across cultures and time.

Coexisting Beliefs

New Age Spirituality has its roots in history, but it is a thoroughly modern religion—that is, if you want to call it a religion. To some, it is a religion because it includes elements from traditional religions. To others, it's not a religion because it is unstructured. New Age Spirituality is more disorganized than organized religion. Whether it is just another religion or not is in the (third) eye of the beholder.

New Age Spirituality offers a modern alternative to the historical religions and fills the void left by their loss of power and the growing secularization of society. Spirituality can be a noncommittal, secular belief system for those not yet ready to give up the trappings of religion. It is a replacement for religion, for those who want to swap their Bibles for Buddha statues. For some people, the path toward spiritual enlightenment is also the path to letting go of religion. Candles and incense are the spiritual nicotine gum for weaning oneself off religion. In some ways, New Age Spirituality is the religion, or nonreligion, of the future.

New Age Spirituality is a do-it-yourself belief system. It is a personalized theology, and people pick and choose to believe whatever makes them happy. As Joseph Campbell said, "Follow your bliss." If you don't like it, simply don't believe in it. With no fixed theology, people can afford to go spirituality shopping for beliefs that suit their individual wants and needs. For some, enlightenment is an elusive holy grail, and the search never ends. People try everything, and discard what doesn't work for them or doesn't suit their biases. Sylvia Browne best encapsulates the ethos of New Age Spirituality with her motto, "Take what you want and leave the rest behind."

My Sweet Lords

New Age Spirituality may or may not be considered religion, but it can include religion. Followers cherry pick from assorted beliefs and practices of the world's major religions. Western and Eastern traditions are typically merged, and spirituality blends aspects of Christianity and Judaism with Islam, Hinduism, and Buddhism. Sikhism, Jainism, Zoroastrianism, and Confucianism are popularly interwoven. The older and more obscure, the better, and New Age Spirituality also takes from pantheism, Gnosticism, animism, shamanism, and other pre-organized religions. Indigenous beliefs, folklore, and mythology are likely to be added to the mix too.

The New Age belief system might be monotheistic. The deity could be God, Elohim, Allah, a Supreme Being, or another personal god. God may be known by ninety-nine other names, or a name that cannot be spoken, or pronounced. He might be a She, or the believer might be a God or Goddess. The deity can be a demigod, animal, or hybrid. The believer might be polytheistic and worship a number of deities. Instead of a god or gods, there may be a power or impersonal life force, such as the Divine, All Powerful, Absolute, Cosmos, Creation, Mother Nature, Chi, Prana, Energy, Love, Light, Truth, or some other entity with a capital letter.

There is no focus on Jesus in New Age Spirituality—that is *so* Judeo-Christian-centric. Jesus is just one of many spiritual teachers, including Krishna, Buddha, Babaji, and Imam Mahdi. Benjamin Crème claims these are all cross-cultural names for the same world teacher, whom he calls Maitreya. Others worship saints, spirits, bodhisattva, mahatmas, avatars, and other Ascended Masters, enlightened ones who once lived on Earth. They might also believe in angels, fairies, ghosts, or extraterrestrials, or that we are aliens. The spiritual being doesn't have to be a single entity. Esther Hicks channels Abraham, who is explained as a collective or council of spirits. The teachers don't have to have a track record over millennia either, and they can be recent discoveries. Hicks has only been channeling Abraham since 1989.

New Age Spirituality promises that the follower will reach Nirvana, Enlightenment, Consciousness, Connectedness, Awareness, Oneness, Allness, Wholeness, or Mindfulness. Life is a personal spiritual quest to find your true self, or to become part of the Greater Whole, or the Overmind. Not everyone believes in the harps of Heaven and the fiery pits of Hell. Alternatively, there is a choice between "the Light" and the "Left Door." There is a holding room instead of purgatory, and the void or limbo of the Left Door leads lost souls to wander aimlessly throughout eternity. There is no Judgment Day, but there is karma, and everything you do and say goes on your Akashic Record, the cosmic encyclopedia of all existence.

Anyway, some New Agers believe we don't die. Instead, our souls, spirits, or essences are merely in transition. Sylvia Browne says, "There's no such thing as death," while Deepak Chopra tells us that we can cure death with reincarnation. Regression therapists teach that we have had many past lives that affect our present and our future lives. If you don't want to live forever, reports of near-death experiences supposedly prove that there's a spirit afterlife for us. Having passed on and crossed over to this Other Side, our loved ones await us there, according to psychic mediums who claim to talk to the dead. Our deceased friends and family watch over us and protect us, accompanied by our guardian angels and totem animals.

Curiously, nontheism and New Age Spirituality are not mutually exclusive. Not everyone wants to self-identify as an "atheist," even if they are one. Unfortunately, the label is saddled with negative connotations. As an alternative, some call themselves "spiritual." Atheism can be compatible with spirituality for those who simply practice the cultural elements, such as alternative healthcare and self-improvement. Some New Agers are only in it for the "Om."

The Gospel Truths

Just as Jesus is only one of many spiritual teachers, the Bible is just one of many scriptures, and as holy as the Torah, the Qur'an, the Vedas, and the Egyptian Book of the Dead. However, it doesn't have to be ancient to be a sacred text. God hasn't come out with any good books of late, and it's not cool to read Leviticus over a latte. People will stay away, thinking you're about to start quoting Bible passages. To win friends and influence people you should read something by Suze Orman, or Dr. Andrew Weil. The doctrine of New Age Spirituality is whatever self-help book is currently on the *New York Times* Best Seller list.

Followers say that the good thing about New Age Spirituality is that there is no dogma. It is a religion without a rule book. As a whole, the movement is composed of diverse communities that often defy structure and classification. However, the New Age has its own brand of dogma. There are the many different styles of yoga, systems of astrology, and schools of energy healing. The neophyte must learn the origins, theories, traditions, terminology, and approaches. Authors create their own guidelines, steps, methods, pillars, and programs. The Ten Commandments become the lucky seven: Deepak Chopra's *Seven Spiritual Laws*, Wayne Dyer's *Seven Principles*, and Steven Covey's *Seven Habits of Highly Effective People.*

A jumble of icons and symbols coexist happily in New Age culture. The New Age decorator might display figurines of Buddha, Anubis, and the Moai statues from Easter Island. There will less likely be crosses, unless it's a Celtic cross, and more likely ankhs, peace signs, and Yin and Yang and Om symbols. Walls will be galleries of St. Germain and Krishna, and prints of angels, astronomy, and animals that are seen as spiritual, such as wolves, bears, and eagles. Tibetan flags, inspirational banners, and dream catchers blow in the breeze. Mirrors, wind chimes, and dragons are strategically placed around the rooms, in accordance with Feng Shui principles. Instead of collectibles from the Franklin Mint, there will be Himalayan salt lamps and Native American art. The New Age house will smell of patchouli and sandalwood instead of supermarket-bought air fresheners.

New Age Spirituality doesn't have a single house of worship, but there are plenty of metaphysical stores and festivals. There are towns known as spiritual Meccas, including Sedona and Taos, or bohemian "hippie" enclaves like Berkeley and Boulder. There are even a few New Age churches, where the sermons are presented by psychics and psychologists. However, the spiritual can be found anywhere, at any time, including the yoga class and the wellness retreat. There isn't Mass; but there might be hot stone massage. There aren't hymns and psalms, only chants and mantras. Instead of a church choir or a little old lady playing piano there will be Native American flute players, crystal singing bowls, and community drumming. The blood of Christ is replaced by kombucha. The confessional becomes primal scream therapy. You won't be forgiven your trespasses, but your chakras will be aligned.

Spirituality is also a process by which people connect with the divine, but you don't need to get down on your knees to get with God. No one really hugs trees, but naturalists might walk a labyrinth or take a hike instead. Others communicate with spirits via mediumship, automatic writing, and divination. Yoga and meditation are used to experience a one-on-one connection with a divine force. Prayer isn't the only way to petition God, or the Universe. There are many different tools of intention. Some use spells, candle burning, and other forms of folk magic in an attempt to get what they want in life, but there are several modern incarnations of incantations. You can use visualization to realize your cosmic goals. Visualizing is rehearsing the future in your mind; just imagine your dream result, stay focused on this, and it will manifest. Affirmations are verbal talismans that aim to attract abundance. They're also amulets that protect against destructive negative thoughts. Positive affirmations, inspirational words, and Confucian quotes are carried like charms, taped to the refrigerator, or recited to the bathroom mirror.

A Not-So-Free Spirit

There are no priests or popes of New Age Spirituality, but there are many spiritual leaders. There may not be a God, but there are godmen and gurus, yogis and swamis, such as Sai Baba and the Maharishi Mahesh Yogi. If they're not demigods, they're demagogues, like the motivational mentors Zig Ziglar, Bob Proctor, and the fire-walking Tony Robbins. These self-help gurus include authors, academics, psychics, and psychologists. Dr. John Gray, Dr. Wayne Dyer, and Dr. Phil are prophets with PhDs.

Some spiritual leaders are actual spirits. They let the mortals do the talking for them, or they talk through a medium. When experimenting with an Ouija board during the early 1970s, Jane Roberts began channeling a spirit named "Seth" who could soon communicate through her voice, or via a typewriter. Seth generated a collection of metaphysical texts known as the Seth Material that are mostly a hodgepodge of Christian and Eastern beliefs. In the 1980s, J. Z. Knight began channeling the 35,000-year-old spirit warrior named Ramtha, although his English is pretty good for someone from the Pleistocene Ice Age.

Sylvia Browne channels her spirit guides Raheim and Francine, who help her give psychic readings. Browne is one of the world's most famous psychics, but unless her predictions are vague, her accuracy rate is poor. She predicted that missing twenty-nine-year-old Eve Brown was alive and well in Florida, but tragically, she had been murdered. Browne predicted that missing twenty-three-year-old Holly Krewson was working as a dancer in a strip club in Hollywood, but six years before, Holly's remains had been found in San Diego and she had been buried as a Jane Doe. Browne told the parents of missing eleven-year-old Shawn Hornbeck that their son had died, and his body would be found near jagged rocks. Thankfully, she was wrong. Shawn had been kidnapped and was soon found by police and returned to his family.

Amanda Berry went missing from Cleveland, Ohio, on April 21, 2003, a day before her seventeenth birthday. In a 2004 episode of *The Montel Williams Show*, her mother, Louwanna Miller, sought out Sylvia Browne to find out anything she could about her missing daughter. Browne had a devastating prediction. "I hate it when they're in the water. She's not alive honey," she said bluntly. "Your daughter's not the kind who wouldn't call." Fortunately, Browne was dead wrong. Berry was alive. She had been kidnapped, along with two other women, and held captive by Ariel Castro. Berry had been missing for ten years when she finally escaped on May 6, 2013. Sadly, Miller died in 2006, believing that her daughter was dead.

James van Praagh becomes possessed by a posse of different spiritual guides. Sister Theresa was a nun from the Sisters of Mercy order, Golden Feather was a Native American, Harry Aldrich was an English medical doctor, and Master Chang was a spiritual teacher. Sometimes the spirits are holy. Over the course of four years, Annie Kirkwood received daily messages from Mother Mary (who told her that she wasn't a virgin). Neale Donald Walsch has conversations with God, while Helen Schucman was the scribe for Jesus when He wrote *A Course in Miracles*.

Your Body Is a Temple

New Age Spirituality ministers to more than the spirit; it is concerned with the mind, body, *and* spirit. Medical doctors Andrew Weil, Mehmet Oz, and Deepak Chopra focus on not only spiritual health, but also physical health and personal well-being, and are spokespeople for alternative, complimentary, and integrative therapies. Chiropractic, acupuncture, iridology, homeopathy, naturopathy and traditional Chinese medicine are popular practices for those who are disillusioned by mainstream medicine. Despite their wide acceptance by the public, these therapies are unproven, if not entirely disproven.

Complementary and alternative therapies are also favored by people who want their health care to be a spiritual experience. Most of this is in the aesthetics. There isn't a cold, clinical doctor's office with bright white walls and a sterile smell. Instead, the room is dimly lit and filled with the calming scent of aromatherapy candles, while soothing meditative music plays softly in the background. There are no intimidating lab coats, disposable medical gloves, or an embarrassing surgical gown through which your bottom peeks out. There isn't a doctor with a bad bedside manner who keeps checking the clock, but a caring person you know on a first-name basis who offers you a cup of herbal tea and listens carefully to what you have to say.

Alternative therapies are holistic, so practitioners will not only treat diseases of the body but will also stop negative cycles and eliminate physical, emotional, and etheric blockages. They will boost your immune system, purify your blood, cleanse your dysfunctional liver, restore the vibrations of your energy field, recalibrate your DNA, and rejuvenate, re-energize, recharge, and rebalance you. They will cure you of illnesses you didn't know you had. There is no uncomfortable examination, and while there might be a bitter herbal remedy, there are no painful injections, toxic drugs, or invasive surgery. They won't even touch you, unless it's a relaxing reflexology foot massage. They can heal you remotely, so you don't even need to be in the room with them.

Empaths and medical intuitives claim to diagnose and treat patients using psychic abilities, either in person or via absent healing. Edgar Cayce (1877–1945) pioneered this technique. Known as the Sleeping Prophet, he entered into a trance under which he diagnosed people and suggested treatments for their ailments. These homespun remedies were snake oils, such as peach-tree poultice for convulsions, or beef broth for everything from gout to leukemia. People who smoked moderately were told that their habit was harmless. Some are still popular today, such as castor oil for relief from back pain. Some treatments were less appealing. To cure breast cancer Cayce instructed one patient to slaughter a rabbit and place the fresh warm skin on the affected area. He became so popular that he received thousands of letters from patients, and it often took him years to address each request. In several cases, by the time Cayce replied he had performed readings and suggested cures for people who were already dead.

Spiritual healing is the New Age version of faith healing. However, you don't need to repent to be healed, because alternative therapies simply return the body to its natural state of health. There are many different kinds of this "energy medicine," including Reiki, aura healing, therapeutic touch, crystal healing, and Qigong. New fad therapies are always coming out. Take Braco, for example, who is a spiritual healer with a difference. He is a "gazer," that is, he stands on a podium and simply gazes at his audience. Braco makes no claims, he doesn't even talk in public, but his fans do make claims. They believe that his gaze brings good luck, life transformations, healings, and miracles. According to testimonials, Braco has cured cancer, restored someone's sight, healed a paraplegic woman, and cleared someone's blocked nostrils. However, his powers are so potent that his shows carry the warning that to avoid being "overburdened," we shouldn't view his gaze for more than seven seconds, including looking at videos and photos of him. For their safety, people under the age of eighteen and pregnant women should avoid his gaze altogether.

Take It with a Grain of Salt
Eating food can be a religious experience, whether it's receiving the blood and body of Christ during Holy Communion or participating in a Zen Buddhist tea ceremony. For New Agers, a spiritual experience with food might involve ethical consumerism, and ensuring they buy organic, fair trade, cruelty free, and locally produced. You are what you eat, so nothing with preservatives, additives, or hormones, and no junk food. Dining can also be a spiritual act too, especially if the food is shared with family and friends. The meal might begin by saying grace, showing gratitude by thanking the Universe, or thanking the food. Don't waste anything, and be sure to recycle afterward.

New Age Spirituality is about exploration, especially when it comes to nutrition. New Agers often like to feed their temples with fad foods. Shots of spirulina and wheatgrass are popular in the juice bars, but the more exotic the better, like acai juice and Tahitian noni juice. Himalayan goji berries and chia seeds are branded antiaging miracle foods, while the humble oats and oranges have enjoyed a revival as superfoods. Yerba maté and other herbal teas are touted as wonder tonics. Some prefer their nutrients in capsule form, and their pantry becomes a veritable apothecary of vitamins and the latest nutritional supplements. Online self-diagnosis and treatment is popular, while the adventurous experiment with megadoses of vitamins.

New Agers trial diet pills and extreme diets to achieve weight loss. Cabbage, grapefruit, low fat, low carb, and low GI diets go in and out of vogue. Some diets are as famous as the celebrities who swear by them, including the Beverley Hills, Atkins, South Beach, Pritikin, and the Paleolithic diets. Sometimes the diet guru isn't as healthy as they'd like us to believe. Pastor George Malkmus invented the Hallelujah Diet, based on vegan raw foods that God intended us to eat in the Garden of Eden. Malkmus claims the diet healed him of cancer. There is no evidence to back this up, but there is evidence that he is on medication for stroke and high blood pressure.

Most religions have foods that are forbidden in some way. Jews eschew pork because it's believed to be unclean, Hindus avoid beef because the cow is sacred in Hinduism, and Mormons are not allowed to drink alcohol or caffeine. New Agers go on the latest restrictive diet, be it vegan, macrobiotic, raw foods, or fruitarian, which limits the diet to only fruits, nuts, and seeds. Some fruitarians refuse to eat even seeds because they contain future plants, and choose to only eat foods that fall naturally off plants and have given themselves up to the world to be eaten. Many people try detoxification with apple cider vinegar, juicing, or colon cleanses. These diets aim to flush out toxins, even though we have a liver for that. Some fast for weight loss, or in the long-held spiritual tradition in the footsteps of Jesus and Gandhi, they fast as a purification ritual to cleanse the body and mind.

Pull a Fast One

Alternatively, they eat nothing at all. Breatharianism, otherwise known as inedia, is the alleged ability to live on light rather than food. The leader of the movement is an Australian woman, Jasmuheen, who was born with the less spiritual-sounding name Ellen Greve. She claims that she hasn't eaten since 1993, when her final meal was a lightly fried falafel ball. Since then Jasmuheen has lived on pranic nourishment, cups of tea, and the occasional piece of chocolate or cheesecake if she's bored—or so she says. A journalist once caught her ordering the vegetarian option on a plane.

The Australian television program *60 Minutes* challenged Jasmuheen to demonstrate her dietary claims. The TV crew found her house stocked with food, although she argued it was for her husband. They began the test in a hotel room, and within two days Jasmuheen was showing signs of dehydration, stress, and high blood pressure. She complained that pollution from traffic outside was preventing her absorption of nutrients from the air. They moved the test to a mountainside retreat, but it didn't make any difference. After four days of fasting Jasmuheen's body was failing. The doctor monitoring the test urged her to stop, which she did, but this hasn't deterred her devoted followers. Some of these people weren't so lucky, and four deaths have been linked to breatharianism. Jasmuheen dismisses these deaths, saying her victims hadn't "found the light" that would nourish them. Fifty-three-year-old Lani Morris died after ten days of starvation, and Jasmuheen stated that the woman was "not coming from a place of integrity and did not have the right motivation."

Motivational speaker James Arthur Ray is known for using dangerous training methods at his retreats and seminars. They are like fraternity initiations, involving fire and glass walking, sleep deprivation, and fasting. One woman shattered her hand after being pressured into a martial arts exercise to break a block of wood. During another exercise, a man was injured after he was ordered to jab his neck with an archery arrow. Ray is infamous for his sweat-lodge ceremonies, especially one that took place in October 2009. Sixty-four people attended his Spiritual Warrior Retreat in Sedona, where each attendee paid almost $10,000 for the pleasure of fasting for thirty-six hours and enduring two days without water. Then they were locked in a sauna for a "spiritual cleaning ceremony," and when people tried to leave the room, they were blocked by guards. Eighteen attendees were hospitalized after suffering burns, dehydration, and kidney failure, while three people died. Ray was found guilty of negligent homicide, and spent two years in an Arizona state prison.

Some New Age treatments are more like punishments. Colloidal silver, urine therapy, ear candling, cupping, oleation, purgation, and colonic irrigation are so bad they must be good for you. However, any treatment is dangerous if medical science is neglected. New Age therapies are not only sought out by people disillusioned by mainstream medicine, but also by those who are desperate. Alternative therapists claim to be able to cure the incurable and prey on vulnerable patients. When Apple cofounder Steve Jobs was diagnosed with a less aggressive case of pancreatic cancer, he wasted precious time by attempting to treat his condition with alternative medicine. He had formally been a fruitarian and decided to try a diet plan devised by Dr. Dean Ornish. After a fruitless nine months, his cancer had progressed to the point where conventional treatments were rendered less effective than they might have been immediately upon diagnosis, and Jobs died in 2011.

In early 1984, comedian Andy Kaufman attempted to cure his advanced lung cancer with a vegetarian diet. When that failed to make a difference, as did some last-minute radiotherapy, he traveled to the Philippines for a six-week course of psychic surgery with the Reverend Jun Labo, who claims he channels Jesus during his surgery. This form of spiritual healing is usually a last resort for hopeless patients with terminal conditions. It is a graphic, bloody procedure involving a bare-handed operation to extract what appears to be the offending tumor. There is no anesthetic, no incision, no wound, no pain, and no results. Psychic surgeons are frauds known for using sleight-of-hand techniques, with chicken entrails and blood as props. Kaufman had two cancerous "tumors" removed, but within two months of returning to the United States, he died.

God Helps Those Who Self-Help Themselves

People believe the axiom that God helps those who help themselves, but that phrase isn't even in the Bible. Religion is more about providence and preordination, and accepting one's lot in life. New Agers believe in fate and destiny, when it suits them, but they don't wait for God's will to be done. A third eye cures that blind faith. They consult psychics, sensitives, astrologers, and tarot readers to get a glimpse into the future. Nostradamus and the Bible code provide them with ancient prophecies and warnings about modern times. They don't pray for God's intervention. They cut out the intermediary and tell the Universe what they want.

Religion often seems to be about the power over us. Instead, New Age Spirituality promises to empower us and affords a sense of control over the world. Rather than discovering God, spirituality has an emphasis on self-discovery and personal development. It is a religion of self-help that preaches to its parishioners about alternative medicine, aging, activism, diet, environmentalism, relationships, art, music, career, peace, politics, psychology, science, sexuality, quality of life, the afterlife, and our past lives. Spirituality is less about what is holy and more about being holistic.

Religion offers salvation for the soul, but spirituality offers *Chicken Soup for the Soul*. Books about spirituality can be found in the New Age, Alternative Medicine, Self-Improvement, Psychology, and Philosophy sections of the bookstore. Within their pages, the Road to Damascus becomes the road to wealth, health, and happiness. New Age Spirituality aims to be proactive, offering practical advice and life tools. Jesus had some valuable teachings, but He can't help you lose weight. However, spirituality has all the answers to our immortal and mortal questions: how to lose weight, quit smoking, develop confidence, read body language, interpret dreams, boost brain power, self-hypnotize, develop inner peace, cope with a demanding boss, develop ESP, overcome stress, navigate gender differences, have better sex, cure impotence naturally, balance yin and yang, and look ten years younger.

Unlike Catholic initiation, there are no lengthy rites of passage for the New Age. Your baptism is buying the book. Spirituality is instant karma, and your life will supposedly improve in the time it takes to say "Om" or to read books like *Enjoy Life and Be Happy in 30 Seconds* and *Spontaneous Happiness*. New Age books are filled with two-cent philosophy and quick fixes that satisfy the spirit, until the next book is released. Promoters promise that reading their books and attending their lectures will be a life-changing experience . . . for a price. The spiritualist congregation is comprised of consumers, and there is much more money to be made out of spirituality than can fit into the collection basket.

Do You Want to Know a Secret?

Religious beliefs are presented as good news to be spread from door-to-door or from the pulpit. Bibles are usually complementary, and you'll find one in your hotel room should you forget to pack your copy. New Age Spirituality isn't always free, but is sold in seminars and infomercials. The promoters have a "we-know-something-you-don't-know" attitude, but they are prepared to sell you this knowledge.

However, there is a government cover-up, or a Big Pharma conspiracy. Like Kevin Trudeau's series of books, this is stuff "They" don't want you to know. This information has been carefully guarded, and the keepers of the secret have been silenced, until now. Their books and lectures will unlock these truths and reveal enigmas, lost mysteries, and hidden knowledge. For example, the maker of the Magnetic Qi Gong reports that a "Tennessee mountain man discovers missing link to eternal youth, previously known only to China's Yellow Emperor and an anonymous Tibetan sage!"

Then there is *the* secret. *The Secret* was a movie that became the subject of a book by Rhonda Byrne (2006). This "secret" is also known as the Law of Attraction. This is a principle of the New Thought movement that teaches the ideas that "thought creates" and like attracts like. Whatever happens to us, good or bad, we have attracted through our thoughts. However, we are on this Earth for abundance, prosperity, success, and health, which can be achieved with positive thinking and positive language. All it takes to manifest our desires is visualization and positive affirmations, such as "I am worthy of love" and "I have all the money I want."

The movie features a number of other proponents of the theory, including Michael Beckwith, Jack Canfield, and James Arthur Ray, just a few years before his negligent homicide. The movie is a glorified infomercial, full of sound bites, simplistic magical thinking, and nonsensical references to quantum physics. It is a spiritual pyramid scheme with a few gurus at the top making the money out of merchandising.

However, the secret is not such a secret after all, and New Thought isn't so new. Numerous authors have peddled these ideas for centuries. James Allen was an early proponent of these self-help theories with his book *As a Man Thinketh* (1903). The title is taken from the biblical passage, "as he thinketh in his heart, so he is" (Proverbs 23:7). William Walker Atkinson was another pioneer of the New Thought movement and wrote over one hundred books on the subject, which were also penned under the names Yogi Ramacharaka, Swami Bhakta Vishita, and other metaphysical-sounding pseudonyms. In his seminal book *Thought Vibration or the Law of Attraction* (1906) Atkinson coined the phrase "like attracts like."

Other forerunners to these theories are Wallace Wattles' *The Science of Getting Rich* (1910) and Napoleon Hills' books *The Law of Success* (1928) and *Think and Grow Rich* (1937). More recently, the Law of Attraction has been influenced by various psychotherapies, including neurolinguistic programming. Modern adherents wrestle with each other over ownership of these ideas—for example, Abraham Hicks advertises "It All Started Here!" In typical New Age style, everything old is new again.

Way Out There

In learning the secrets of the universe, some New Age proponents come to believe that we are not alone. UFO religions incorporate extraterrestrials, flying saucers, and science fiction into their beliefs. Scientologists believe that humans are thetans who've lived numerous past lives on other planets. Raëlians believe that humans were genetically engineered by scientifically advanced aliens. Members of the Aetherius Society believe that Jesus, Buddha, and Krishna came to Earth from other planets to teach lessons to humankind. According to Aetherians, a messianic leader will soon arrive upon Earth in a UFO, and spiritual healing, yoga, and prayer will help prepare us for his coming.

Members of the infamous religious group Heaven's Gate believed that we are extraterrestrials. The doomsday cult was founded by Marshall Applewhite after he claimed to have a near-death experience. He taught that the world was about to be destroyed. The only way his followers could survive was to board an alien spacecraft following the Hale-Bopp comet that was then passing by Earth. On March 26, 1997, his thirty-nine followers committed suicide in the belief that their souls would teleport to that spacecraft and be saved.

Most UFO religions believe in ancient astronauts. In *Chariots of the Gods*, Erich von Däniken popularized the belief that ancient aliens visited Earth thousands of years ago. Proponents of this theory believe that early humans were too stupid to have constructed most ancient monuments. So, the advanced aliens either built or taught humans how to build marvels such as Stonehenge, the Great Pyramid of Giza, Machu Picchu, and the Moai statues on Easter Island. Supporting evidence for these claims are examples of ancient art such as the hieroglyphs, the Nazca Lines, and cave paintings from around the world that supposedly depict aliens and spacecraft.

One of the major supporters of the idea of ancient astronauts is conspiracy theorist David Icke. He also lets us in on *The Biggest Secret* of them all. According to Icke, the world is controlled by a secret group known as the Babylonian Brotherhood. These are shape-shifting, blood-drinking reptilian humanoids from the Alpha Draconis star system. Human beings were developed in a breeding program by these evil reptilians. Members of this underground group include prominent people in society, including the Rockefellers, the British monarchy, and former U.S. president George W. Bush and his family.

Benjamin Crème also believes in UFOs and they are a central belief to his faith. He teaches the "good aliens" theory, although "space people" is the preferred name because "aliens" and "extraterrestrials" are slurs. I was once branded a racist by his cronies for referring to "little green men." Crème believes we have a wider family of "space brothers and space sisters." These space siblings come from Venus and Mars (so he must have read Dr. John Gray's *Men Are from Mars, Women Are from Venus*). These benevolent aliens have a spiritual mission to protect and watch over us. They are technologically superior to us and reduce the impact of human destruction. The evidence for their existence is the numerous sightings of UFOs; this is when these spacecraft lower their vibrations so we can see them temporarily. Crop circles are further evidence. They are "love letters to humanity" that are created within seconds by space ships. According to Crème, this activity all heralds the reappearance of Christ, that is, Maitreya.

Others claim to have more than mere sightings. Contactees are people who believe they have been abducted by aliens. They never bring back physical proof of their visits to other planets and aboard spaceships, but they bring back plenty of anecdotes. As real as they seem, these experiences can be caused by hallucinations, sleep paralysis, or regression therapy. Alien abduction therapists plant ideas into their clients when they are under hypnosis and create false memories of alien encounters and anal probes, which are also influenced by pop culture. However, natural explanations simply aren't exciting enough for many people.

Blinded by Science

New Age Spirituality places great emphasis on personal experiences. It has been scientifically proven that echinacea doesn't prevent or treat colds and influenza, but regardless, the herb is still one of the world's most popular remedies. Whether it's the placebo effect, or a matter of timing, people conclude, "It works for me." Correlation is powerful personal proof. Urban legend is also treated as science, and testimonials from friends, family, and gurus appear to be convincing proof. Anecdotal evidence is preferred to scientific evidence. For example, a ghost sighting may be explained as a hallucination, but the supernatural explanations are preferred to the natural ones. The witnesses argue that their personal experiences are real, and you weren't there. You don't know what they saw. You're too afraid to accept the truth. You are closed-minded, and there are more things in heaven and earth than are dreamt of in your philosophy . . .

New Age Spirituality is not only unscientific, but is also often antiscience. Science is perceived as unchangeable, cynical, reductionist, and materialist. Scientists are accused of only being interested in making money. People can be suspicious of science, and inaccurate beliefs and conspiracy theories are widespread. Activists spread panic about genetically-modified foods, and deny that global warming exists. Often, these misconceptions are dangerous. Antivaccination lobby groups believe that vaccinations contain toxins that cause autism, ADHD, brain damage, and cancer, and that pharmaceutical companies have financial incentives to promote them. These pressure groups organize fear-mongering campaigns, and the public listens to these impassioned yet misinformed pleas. As a result, people neglect to vaccinate their children, leaving communities susceptible to measles, mumps, whooping cough, and other highly contagious and harmful yet preventable diseases.

In the contradiction that is characteristic of New Age Spirituality, science can have credibility too. Many New Agers strive to be viewed as scientific, although they're scientifically illiterate. They speak about their evidence of ghosts, believing that anecdotal evidence is evidence. Surely numerology is as scientifically valid as urology because they are both "ologies." Reflexology is confused as a branch of podiatry. Homeopathic preparations are sold in pharmacies. The workplace offers aromatherapy inoculation as an alternative to flu shots. The body lotion contains aloe vera, so it must be safe and natural. The beautician wears a lab coat and uses words that sound sciency. Traditional Chinese Medicine has been around for thousands of years, so it must work. The only thing that supersedes science is the exotic; if the belief or practice is ancient, foreign, and preferably Eastern, it has immediate authority and wisdom. This kind of New Age Spirituality endeavors to be complementary to science, but its theories often contradict science. It endeavors to explain the unknown and seems to fill those gaps of knowledge, but often it undermines what is known. New Agers mightn't believe in the Theory of Relativity, but they believe in the mythical "lost" civilizations of Atlantis and Lemuria. However, science is about what is true, whether you want to believe in it or not.

New Age Spirituality often appears to be the mainstream. People visit their chiropractors weekly. Businesses consult Feng Shui masters to decorate their offices, while spirit workers are hired by realtors to bless and cleanse houses that won't sell. There are Reiki tax guides, and psychic financial advisers. Recognizable and trusted titles portray spiritual practitioners as professionals. There are psychic surgeons, psychic detectives, angel therapists, spiritual advisers, intuitive counselors, and psychic forensics. Unconventional practices are portrayed as conventional, such as Ayurvedic "medicine" and homeopathic "vaccines." Spurious science sells.

Science is name-dropped in *The Science of Success*, *The Science of Getting Rich*, *The Science of Happiness*, and *The Happiness Hypothesis*. Movements appear to be scientific with names like Religious Science, Christian Science, and the Church of Scientology. Dianetics and Raëlians blend science fiction and fringe science into their beliefs. Pseudoscientific therapies and theories are often framed as science. Parapsychology and postmodernism have the facade of being scientific fields. The New Thought movement sounds like a type of psychotherapy. Numerology and sacred geometry appeal to mathematics to support their claims. Neuro-linguistic programming is conflated with neuroscience and linguistics. Astrology aligns itself to astronomy. Birth chart declinations, fancy graphs, and diagrams have the convincing semblance of science. Electromagnetic readers and Geiger counters are scientific tools that are used irrelevantly for ghost hunting. However, the beliefs and practices of New Age Spirituality don't use the scientific method, and their approaches are metaphysical, not empirical.

A number of scientists actively attempt to bridge science and spirituality. Stanton Friedman and Claude Swanson are both physicists who believe in UFOs and twist their scientific knowledge to fit their pseudoscientific theories. Physicists John Hagelin and Fred Alan Wolf feature in the movies *What the Bleep Do We Know!?* and *The Secret*. However, no one wants to listen to them speak about Newton's Law of Gravity; instead they want to hear about the Law of Attraction. Both scientists invoke theories from quantum mechanics to support their controversial beliefs. Quantum entanglement, wave function collapse, and the Heisenberg Uncertainty Principle are reinterpreted to mean that things aren't always what they seem, and anything is possible.

"Quantum" has been appropriated by the New Age community in general, along with "energy," "vibration," "frequency," "consciousness," and other technical terms. They are bandied about because they sound convincing and lend credibility, but also because they are little understood by consumers, and often little understood by the proponents too. Deepak

Chopra's *Quantum Healing* uses quantum concepts to support bogus claims about healing, antiaging, and immortality. He later admitted that his usage of "quantum" has nothing to do with quantum physics. Similarly, I once interviewed Frank Sumption, the inventor of the Frank's Box. This is a radio device that he claims can be used to talk to aliens, angels, and the dead. In explaining how it functions, he said, "It works on the quantum level." I asked him to clarify this, "What do you mean by 'quantum'?" He replied, "I don't know," and shrugged his shoulders.

Every Little Thing We Do Is Magic

What is seen as spiritual is subjective. It is about what affects someone personally, and in their opinion, moves them closer to what they perceive as spiritual. New Age Spirituality is a religion of lifestyle, and some see spirituality in any experience. Author Natalie Fee says, "Every action, whether it's cooking for the kids, resolving problems with a partner, cleaning toilets, if done with awareness is a spiritual experience." Spirituality is accessible to everyone, and people assign spiritual significance to everyday acts. Personal practices can be perceived as spiritual, such as caring for the "temple" that is the body through diet, exercise, yoga, massage, meditation, and alternative therapies. New Age music, collectibles, crystals, and candles are tools used for being spiritual and accessing the divine. Humanitarianism is also seen as spiritual, especially vegetarianism, environmentalism, activism for peace and equality, and performing charitable work and other acts of human kindness. Spirituality is humanism with a halo.

People find spiritual meaning in human experiences. Emotions become insightful "gut feelings," "intuition," and "knowing." An idea is reinterpreted as an epiphany, a vision, or a revelation. Thoughts become magical messages from the universe or from beyond the grave. Animal whisperers and pet communicators are believed to have mystical connections with animals. People thank God for their achievements and successes. Beating the odds or surviving an accident is viewed as a religious experience. Birth is a miracle, and death is not an end, but a new beginning.

New Age Spirituality gives a sense of cosmic vanity. It is believed that there are no coincidences, but there is synchronicity, and everything happens for a reason. Our partner is our soul mate, the person we were meant to be with. It is destiny, fate, and written in the stars. Negative experiences are "life lessons" we're supposed to endure for our own spiritual growth. Alternatively, we choose our destiny. Indigo children are born with gifts of intuition and they select their parents. Negative thinking manifests bad luck, while positive thoughts attract our desires. People tend to observe the hits that appear to confirm their beliefs and ignore the misses that contradict them.

Some people find spiritual meaning in nature. We wish on stars and rainbows, and a shooting star means good luck. A hurricane becomes an act of God, a solar eclipse is a bad omen, and a full moon drives people mad. We derive immense emotional satisfaction from physical phenomena. The magnitude of monoliths and mountain ranges and the expanse of oceans fill us with awe. Sunrises, sunsets, and night skies inspire romance, wistfulness, and hope. The beauty and complexity of nature is interpreted as evidence for a creator, an architect, or a designer. People find spiritual experiences to be profound and deeply meaningful, and they are—to us. These feelings are powerful, humbling, and moving. They can be so overwhelming they seem to come from beyond, but they come from within. Spirituality is made by us.

And Now for Something Completely Different

Religious Science or Science of the Mind was pioneered by Ernest Holmes (1887–1960) and his book *The Science of the Mind* (1926). Unsurprisingly, it aims to merge science and religion. In practice, this New Age religion blends beliefs and customs from around the world, including Christianity, Buddhism, the spiritual healing elements of Christian Science, and theories from the New Thought movement that claim we can use our minds to create change.

I paid a visit to the Mile Hi Church, which is officially a church or "center" of Religious Science. The church is interfaith and welcomes people of all backgrounds—in fact, the more cultural influences the merrier. The church offers services, but also holds workshops and retreats to empower people, lead them to their personal potential, create life transformations, and promote centeredness and inner balance. These activities aren't held only by ministers, but also by self-help gurus, psychologists, and psychics. Upcoming events included a workshop on alternative therapies for pets and a pilgrimage to Abadiânia, Brazil, to visit psychic surgeon John of God.

The Mile Hi Church is a series of buildings that includes a sanctuary and a labyrinth. When you enter the lobby the walls are lined with quotes from the founder Ernest Holmes and inspirational sayings from Picasso and Dr. Seuss. Unlike most churches, the Mile Hi Church features a New Age gift shop. The store sells meditative music and self-help books, including titles by Ernest Holmes, Eckhart Tolle, Deepak Chopra, and Shirley MacLaine. It also displayed smudge sticks, essential oils, Buddha figurines, magnetic bracelets, and other metaphysical paraphernalia.

I attended the "Sunday Evening Rejuvenation Hour," which began with "oneness meditation," a personal quiet time to connect with "Spirit." The darkened room was lit by candles, and I was struck by the overwhelming stench of patchouli incense. Soon, a woman emerged onto the stage wearing a silk scarf, slippers, and large bohemian-style earrings that caught the light and jiggled when she moved. She was dressed like a fortune-teller, but this was the Reverend Ruby.

The evening's theme was "It's Your life. Live It with Love." The service began with a positive affirmation. Ruby instructed, "Say after me, 'I am a winner!'" The room echoed the affirmation, but this wasn't convincing enough. We were ordered to repeat the statement again, and then again, with growing conviction until we were shouting with our fists in the air. It felt like a pep talk from a coach before a football game. Ruby then prayed that we may all achieve awareness, and when we do, she reminded us to "give gratitude, and ask Spirit to move within you." She finished her speech with the words, "And so it is." This phrase soon revealed itself to be the "Amen" of the New Age Church.

Chad was seated at a piano onstage. Between Ruby's messages he performed inspirational songs with such passion that he sounded like a frustrated Broadway musical star. After a musical interlude we were told to close our eyes and, "Find that perfect place, that silent place, that God within. But if 'God' is an uncomfortable word for you, you can

stick another word in there, like 'Spirit,' 'Power,' 'Presence,' or 'Love.'"
"God works for me, but I grew up going to church in Texas!" she joked.
Accompanied by Chad's tinkling piano sounds, Ruby led us in guided
imagery. We were instructed to breathe deeply, and to repeat silently to
ourselves, "God is all around me. God is inside me. God is all there is.
There is only God. I am so grateful. Life is good. I am so blessed. I am
love. I am lovable. And so it is."

It was now time for some "storytelling." "This is what I call practical
spirituality. I'm going to tell you a story from the Bible," Ruby said
apologetically, and then she shared the parable of the prodigal son.
Incredibly, she told the story completely in New Age–speak. By asking
for his inheritance before his father's death, the younger son had "sinned,
that is, he made a mistake," Ruby explained. After squandering his money,
the son is reduced to feeding pigs, during this time he "meditates" and
finally reaches "a state of awareness." He returns home and "stood in
gratitude" when his father "held him in love and light" and welcomed
him back. The moral of this story is, "Love is all there is. And so it is."

After another jaunty tune from Chad, Ruby spoke about the
importance of controlling our thinking, and quoted Holmes, "Daily we
must control all thought." She is an elementary teacher at the school on
the premises. As training in controlling thought, she teaches her students
how to cloud burst, that is, to dispel clouds with the power of the mind.
Ruby instructed us to practice this at home too, but to be sure to express
gratitude by saying, "Thank you cloud for disappearing!" When the
clouds disappear it is proof that our thoughts create change. Therefore,
we should think and say positive things to attract abundance in our lives.
"After all, it's your movie. What do you choose?" she paraphrased from
The Secret.

The church's motto is, "It's different here," but it is really only
about variations on a theme. There were affirmations instead of prayer,
inspirational songs instead of hymns, and storytelling instead of sermons.
Like in traditional churches, its members certainly passed around the
donation basket, after we recited the catchy congregational affirmation,
"I am a gift to life and life is a gift to me. My giving enriches my living."
This certainly ensures abundance for the church, if no one else. In

conclusion, Ruby asked us to look at a handout we had been given. It read: "I have seen what they do but I will love them anyway. Biblical verse." Ruby read aloud the quote. "And that's from the Bible!" she said smugly.

"And so it is . . ."

Chapter 9

Friends in High Places
The Quakers

"I get by with a little help from my friends."
—*The Beatles*

After forty minutes of silence, I started thinking like I used to do during an exam, and lyrics from really annoying yet persistent songs began whirling around my head, including "9 to 5" and "Islands in the Stream." I tried to quieten my mind to receive a revelation, but I simply couldn't hear the "Light," unless God is Dolly Parton.

Sowing Wild Oats

Quakers are an enigma to most people. To many, Quakers are a brand of oats. Those who have heard of the Quakers think they wear bonnets or beards, reject technology, and address everyone as "thee." Some know them as peacemakers, while others argue, "You know, Richard Nixon was a Quaker!" They are confused with Puritans and the Amish, or they are not viewed as a religion at all. Many Quakers don't even see themselves as belonging to a religion, but more of a religious society or community. There are many misconceptions about Quakers, but their influence is widespread, if not always recognized.

The Quakers were founded in seventeenth-century England during the English Civil War. At that time, most people were still arguing about whether they were a Roundhead or a Royalist. However, a young man by the name of George Fox (not the clown, Methodist minister, musician, or baseball player) was questioning his religion instead. In those days, the clergy were social counselors as much as they were spiritual leaders, so Fox consulted several priests about his crisis of faith. According to his journal, their advice wasn't always useful, or relevant. One priest advised he take up smoking and sing psalms as a cure, while another performed bloodletting on him. Fox fell out with yet another church because it believed that women didn't have souls. During a visit with a priest who had a green thumb, Fox accidentally trampled on a hallowed flowerbed as they walked and talked, and the angry priest did the Renaissance equivalent of "get off my lawn!" Fox became seriously disillusioned with the Church of England.

This quest for self-discovery led Fox to a spiritual awakening, although his religious ideas were radical. At a time when it was believed that God only talked to priests, vicars, and bishops, Fox decided that anyone could have a direct religious experience, *without* the clergy. The Church was closely linked to the government and authority of the country, but Fox believed in the separation of church and state. It was mandatory to attend church, at houses of worship on consecrated premises, yet Fox believed that God was everywhere and could be worshipped anywhere. He believed that doctrine and rituals could be dispensed with, such as communion and baptism. It was law to pay taxes to the local church, but Fox refused to tithe. Rather than following a strict interpretation of the scriptures, Fox preached that people should follow their own "inner guide"—that is, their conscience.

On a secular level, Fox's social ideas were considered extremist too. In those days of slavery, and when women were considered the property of their fathers and husbands, Quakers believed in the equality of all humankind. When kings were thought to be appointed by God, Quakers treasonously refused to swear oaths of allegiance in court. When politeness toward those of a higher social standing was convention, Quakers refused to address their superiors as "Mister" or to take off their hats. They opened their businesses on Christmas Day and the Sabbath. In a time of wars and religious upheaval, Quakers opposed conflict, refused military service, and promoted religious tolerance.

Don't Mess with a Missionary Man

The Quakers were branded heretics, but they were certainly rebels. In their attempts to convert others, Fox and his followers would burst into Anglican church services to preach their word. They yelled in the streets and banged pots and pans to get attention so they could proselytize. A few brazen men and women stripped off their clothes in public to demonstrate their lack of desire for material things, but worse still, women were allowed to be Quaker ministers too.

There were already many breakaway Protestant sects, but anyone who was not Anglican was persecuted, including Catholics, Lutherans, and Anabaptists. As troublemakers, the Quakers were harassed and persecuted worst of all. Quaker homes and meeting houses were torched, vandalized, or confiscated in incidents similar to Kristallnacht, the "Night of Broken Glass" when German Nazis attacked Jewish residences and businesses. Quakers were spat on for not bowing to their "betters." The public and the police subjected them to brutal physical assaults. They were regularly beaten by churchgoers for disrupting their worship, and George Fox was once given a bloody nose by a priest who whacked him with a Bible to silence him. For peacemakers, they certainly attracted a lot of violence.

A number of Quakers claimed that they were able to create biblical-style miracles, and Fox published a *Book of Miracles* containing two hundred such reports, although the manuscript has since been lost. This branded them as practitioners of magic and witchcraft. They were even accused of causing the Great Plague of London, an outbreak of bubonic plague that killed about 100,000 people. Fox and thousands of his followers were frequently fined or imprisoned, where many died as a result of mistreatment or poor conditions. No good deed goes unpunished. Quakers were often arrested when they were on errands of mercy as they ministered to the sick and poor.

When they weren't in jail, Fox and his followers traveled across the country, throughout Europe, and to the United States to preach their beliefs. A few brave (or foolish) Quaker missionaries traveled to the East to convert Muslims. Three Quakers arrived in Constantinople (Istanbul), the seat of the Ottoman Caliphate, where in Quaker style they interrupted worship, in a mosque. They were punished with three hundred blows on the soles of their feet, but this didn't stop them. However, having their hands and tongues chopped off, their eyes bored out, and stakes driven into their bottoms did stop them.

In the 1650s, Quakers began immigrating to the North American colonies to escape persecution, but it followed them. There they were jailed, whipped, tortured, banished, and even executed by the Puritans, who, ironically, had earlier fled to the Americas to escape religious persecution. Fox spent so much time being punished that it was said that "the pillory served George Fox for his pulpit." In the early 1680s, famous Quaker William Penn founded Pennsylvania with a land grant from King Charles II. The colony was formed as a safe haven for the Quakers, who were finally able to live in peace in the New World.

Any Friend of Yours Is a Friend of Mine

Quakers weren't always known as Quakers. In fact, this name was once an insult. Followers initially called themselves "Saints," "Seekers of Truth," or "Friends of the Truth," and then simply "Friends." "Friends" comes from a statement by Jesus: "You are my friends if you do what I command you" (John 15:14). There are a few theories about the origins of "Quaker." In 1650, Fox was charged with blasphemy, and he appeared before magistrate Gervase Bennet. During his trial, Fox warned him to "tremble at the word of the Lord," so Bennet mockingly branded Fox and his followers "Quakers." Rather than rejecting the term, they embraced it. Another theory has it that followers physically "quake" when they have a religious experience. Today, they are still known as Quakers, or Friends, who belong to the Religious Society of Friends. There are about 350,000 Quakers worldwide, with approximately 110,000 members in the United States. They are also found in England, Japan, South Africa, Kenya, New Zealand, Australia, and Canada.

There are many misconceptions about Quakers. For the most part, they don't dress like the Amish or avoid technology. They are not Quakers because they breed Quaker Parrots, and while Quaker families are behind such well-known companies as Cadbury chocolate, Barclays bank, and Clarks shoes, Quaker Oats is *not* owned by the Quakers. The man on the cereal boxes is not William Penn, but a fictional character named

Larry. As the Quaker Oats company explains, "His image is that of a man dressed in the Quaker garb, chosen because the Quaker faith projected the values of honesty, integrity, purity and strength."

Based on those early values promoted by George Fox, modern Quakers are committed to peace, equality, integrity, simplicity, and truth. In fact, Quakers place more emphasis on values than beliefs. Opposing beliefs have caused many schisms within the community, leading to the formation of numerous different branches over the centuries. Quakerism is still evolving, while some Quakers seem to be evolving out of religion.

An Atheist by Any Other Name

There is great variance in the beliefs of Quakers across the United States. There are two main traditions in Quakerism, the Conservatives and the Liberals. In Ohio, Iowa, and North Carolina, there are a few small branches of "Primitive Friends," such as the Wilburite Quakers, who conserve the older beliefs and traditions. They believe in the Holy Trinity, in heaven and hell, and that Jesus is the son of God. Also known as Plain Friends, they live the plain life, wearing plain dress like the Amish and using plain language, such as the archaic pronoun "thee" to address others. Many Quakers don't even regard these Quakers as Quakers.

Conservative Quakers, often called Wilburites after founder John Wilbur, and Evangelical Quakers, often called Gurneyites after Joseph John Gurney, make up the majority of modern Quakers. The two main organizations include Friends United Meeting and Evangelical Friends International. These groups arose in the nineteenth century over splits over doctrine. In their practices, these Quakers are just like any other mainstream Protestant church. However, the nonevangelical Liberal Quakers are a small but growing group of Quakers that we will mostly focus on here.

Since there are so many Quaker branches and beliefs, it is difficult to write a description that is acceptable to all Quakers. Liberal Quakerism is less about what Quakers believe and more about what they don't believe. These Quakers often reject scripture, symbolism, and sacraments, and they have no creed, dogma, or doctrine. There are no Quaker idols or saints. There are no Quaker priests or ministers, because clergy get in the way between the believer and God. Quakers take personal responsibility for their beliefs, and they prefer a direct experience with God. There is no Quaker Bible; in fact, there is little emphasis on sacred texts. The Bible is not regarded as the Word of God, but as just another inspirational book. There are no Quaker churches; they have meeting houses instead. There are no services, no hymns, no prayers, and no rituals. God can be found in everyday life, as much as during worship. Quakers don't believe in heaven and hell; they concentrate on this life rather than pondering what happens after it. However, you can't judge a Quaker by his or her cover. Quakerism is a personal religion and can't be put in a box. Beliefs vary at the individual level, so there will always be exceptions to these descriptions.

Are Quakers Christian? All Quakers share common roots in Christianity, and Quakerism contains Christian elements for historical reasons. Conservative Quakers are Christocentric, although opinion is divided among Liberal Quakers, where there are as many beliefs about God as there are Quakers. Some identify as Christian, but usually not in the sense used by the majority of Christians in the United States. Some Christians consider Quakers to be heathens. Disappointed with the lack of a strict theology, many ex-members seek out more traditional denominations. Alternatively, disgruntled with the inflexibility and ritual of church services, Quakerism appeals to many former Christians. However, there is one belief that is fundamental across Quakers. This is George Fox's assertion that "there is that of God within everyone." However, there are many different interpretations of this phrase. Some Quakers understand this as the presence of God in everyone, while others see this as a metaphor for equality or humanity.

Is Quakerism a religion? Many Quakers object to the word "religion," and as their full name suggests, they prefer the term "religious society," committee, or council. Quakers are broken down into independent national, regional, and local groups known as "meetings." Attending a Quaker meeting can be a grab bag of beliefs; you're not sure what you'll find until you get there. However, Liberal Quakers are very tolerant and there is great religious diversity at many meetings. A Quaker meeting might be attended by those who identify as Buddhist, Pagan, Muslim,

Jewish, Humanist, and nontheist, as much as those who see themselves as Christian. Quakerism is uniquely compatible with other beliefs and even nonbelief.

Fox taught the importance of freethinking and the search for truth. Like Fox's spiritual quest, Quakerism is a search for enlightenment. This search has led many Liberal Quakers to reject theism entirely. As strange as it sounds, atheism is popular among Quakers. You'd never have an admitted Catholic atheist, but some Quakers call themselves Nontheist Quakers or Atheist Quakers. Similar to secular Judaism and nontheistic Buddhism, these Quakers are in it for the philosophy, values, and culture. When I grew up in Australia there was an advertisement campaign for the nonalcoholic beverage Claytons, which was promoted as, "The drink you have when you're not having a drink." Likewise, Quakerism is often the religion you have when you're not religious.

Nontheist Quakers are more interested in the natural than the supernatural. They do not believe in any kind of Supreme Being, and God is seen as a symbol of human values. They translate Quaker theistic language into nontheistic terms. "There is that of God in everyone" is still a motto, but is reinterpreted as an analogy for the equality of humankind. Nontheistic Quakers follow a kind of Einstein-like interpretation of God as a metaphor for nature. In fact, Einstein had a fondness for the Quakers, and once said of them:

> I consider the Society of Friends the religious community which has the highest moral standards. As far as I know, they have never made evil compromises and are always guided by their conscience. In international life, especially, their influence seems to me very beneficial and effective.

To Liberal Quakers, it is not important to share the same beliefs. Beliefs don't make a Quaker, but participation in the Quaker community does. They don't believe in the divinity of Jesus, but they follow his moral teachings. Quakerism is less about the spiritual and more about the social. Instead of concentrating on beliefs, Quakers focus on their practices.

The Quaker Testimonies

As we have seen, Quakers have no doctrine. Instead they are guided by "testimonies" to their faith. This isn't the same thing as eyewitness testimony in court, or giving passionate testimony of Christian conversion to the congregation's cries of "Amen!" The Quaker testimonies are not beliefs, but the values by which Quakers live. The main testimonies are peace, equality, simplicity and truth, while some Quakers would include social justice, integrity, love, and stewardship.

These testimonies are not only values, but also actions. Quakers are activists who want to make the world a better place. For people who are against fighting, they are certainly always fighting for human rights. In many ways, Quakers are true to the stereotype of the charitable religion. Some of the testimonies arise from the moral teachings of Jesus, and Quakers are "Doing What Jesus Did" more than the Reverend Bob Larson, who champions this motto.

The Peace Testimony is the Quakers' commitment to peace. In a 1661 declaration to Charles II, Quakers vowed to "Utterly deny all outward wars and strife and fightings with outward weapons, for any end or under any pretence whatsoever." Nothing has changed in all this time. Known as a "peace church," Quakers oppose war and are against the use of weapons. They aim to ultimately eliminate causes of war. Quakers believe that violence breeds more violence and they prefer peaceful solutions to conflict. Many Quaker men fought in World War I and II, although others sought conscientious objector status and refused to serve. They are famous for their wartime protests. Sometimes they go to extremes. In 1965, Quaker Norman Morrison protested the war in Vietnam by burning himself to death in front of the Pentagon, directly below Secretary of Defense Robert McNamara's office.

Quakers are often criticized for resisting war taxes and protesting the Pentagon budget, but they are praised for their widespread aid and charity. Quakers were involved in setting up several prominent campaigning and relief organizations, including Oxfam, Greenpeace, and Amnesty International. Quakers prefer the term peacemakers to pacifists, and their efforts are anything but passive. Quakers have gone into the trenches as aid workers and become involved in mediation and reconciliation. The Quakers are recipients of the Nobel Peace Prize. It was awarded in 1947 to the British and American Friends societies for their relief work during the two World Wars and their aftermath. Unlike religions that are charitable to the in-group only, the Quakers make no distinction between allies and enemies.

Quakers are widely known as peaceful people, but, ironically, disgraced former U.S. president Richard Nixon, who invaded and bombed Cambodia and instigated the Watergate political scandal, was a Quaker. Given his hostile actions, Liberal Quakers sought to have him "disowned," the Quaker version of excommunication. However, Nixon was born into a Conservative branch of the Quakers, who fiercely supported him. In general, Quakers believe in consulting one's "inner guide"—that is, one's conscience—as to what is right and wrong, and they rarely discipline their members. In the case of Nixon, the Conservatives proved to be more tolerant than the Liberals, and they accepted Nixon's bad judgment as conscience-driven and accepted his mistakes as human. Although Nixon is not considered an exemplary Quaker by most members, this disagreement only served to further divide the different branches of Friends.

A Friend in Need

The Equality Testimony is the Quakers' commitment to equality, egalitarianism, and social unity. Since there is "that of God in everyone," Quakers value all people equally. Things weren't always so equal. At one time Quakers practiced endogamy and were disowned if they married outside of the community. Today, they aim to remove social inequality, which they view as an underlying cause of conflict and war. Quakers headed abolitionism in the United States and also helped many enslaved people escape to their freedom. In the days when women were considered soulless chattels, the Quakers were pioneers in the movement for equality between the sexes. In more modern times, Quakers headed the women's suffrage movement, and they have worked to achieve equality for the LGBT community. Quakers protect the environment and campaign for animal rights. For some, "Thou shalt not kill" extends to all living creatures, and many Quakers are vegetarian or vegan. Quakers have also worked hard to seek prison reform and find solutions to poverty, hunger, and homelessness.

When the Quakers were founded, England wasn't too far removed from the feudal system of lords and serfs. There was still a strict social hierarchy, with little mobility for those in the lower classes. At this time, "Mister" wasn't the common honorific that it is today. It was a title to address men of "higher" social standing, and this politeness was enforced by society. However, Quakers didn't recognize social hierarchies or worldly honors, so they refused to salute, sit, or bow before others. This behavior was seen as subversive, and the Quakers presented a threat to the established order, for which they were often rewarded with jail time or beatings by the police. As a mark of democracy, Quakers began using "plain speech." To avoid honorifics and status distinctions they began used the equalizing pronouns "thee" and "thou" to address others. This has mainly fallen out of vogue, because using formal, pompous-sounding "thee" would set them apart today in the very way they'd hoped to avoid. "Thee" is now reserved for William Penn's birthday, otherwise known as "Talk Like a Quaker Day."

Quakers once wore "plain dress," just like the Amish and Mennonites. This was a preference for simple clothes in nondescript colors of grey, black, and white, that is, for those men and women who didn't go naked as a statement. This was part of their commitment to the Simplicity Testimony. Quakers try to "live simply, so that others may simply live." As we have seen, only a few Quakers choose to wear plain apparel nowadays, but still the spirit of simplicity is carried on. Quakers probably don't wear Prada. They buy for practicality rather than status and are more likely to wear fair-trade clothes or second-hand items from charity shops. Quakers fear that consumerism and unequal access to resources are another source of conflict. They are usually ethical consumers who buy fair trade, cruelty free, organic, recycled, and local, if possible. To further bear witness to their simple living, many Quakers do not gamble, smoke, take drugs, or drink, or they consume alcohol only in moderation. Historically, Quakers would have been disowned for drunkenness, especially since the Quakers were at the helm of the Temperance movement.

The Truth Testimony is the Quaker's commitment to truth at all times and to the seeking of truth. A person's conscience is his or her moral compass. Quakers refuse to swear oaths in court, based on the biblical verse, "But above all things, my brothers, swear not, neither by heaven, neither by the earth, neither by any other oath: but let your yes be yes; and your no, no; lest you fall into condemnation" (James 5:12). Quakers don't like the implication that if they were not sworn to tell the truth, they might otherwise lie. Truth is truth, so there aren't two standards. Instead, Quakers prefer affirmations, a kind of legal declaration.

For their values, Quakers developed a reputation for honesty and fairness, especially in their business dealings. In the days where sellers would charge a high price and then haggle with the customer, Quakers began setting fixed prices. As part of their persecution, early Quakers were prevented from careers in the government and from higher education, so they started their own businesses and opened their own schools. Quaker entrepreneurs became innovators and inventors who enjoyed success in the iron, steel, and engineering industries, and in banking, brewing, pharmaceuticals, food, and tea. They especially seem to like manufacturing chocolate, as Quakers founded Cadbury, Rowntree, Terry's, and Fry's. They were also good employers, offering fair conditions and fair wages, and today, they are still concerned with trade justice. The Quaker name is used by unrelated companies such as Quaker Oats and Quaker State motor oil, to imply fair dealings.

Quaking in Your Boots

Quaker meetings are a core practice for Quakers. Conservative Quakers hold "programmed" or "pastoral" meetings, meaning there is a set schedule for their worship. These more orthodox meetings grew out of the desire of some Quakers for cohesion and leadership, and they are really no different to attending mainstream Protestant churches. Their houses of worship are "churches." They hold services with preachers and do readings from the Bible. They have a choir, and they play music and sing hymns. They hold baptism, communion, and other sacraments.

Liberal Quakers hold "unprogrammed" meetings that are vastly different to programmed meetings. There is no liturgy because they follow the Bible verse, "Where two or three are gathered together in my name, there am I in the midst of them" (Matthew 18:20). Unprogrammed meetings are not held in churches, but in meeting houses, unadorned by crosses, candles, altars, or organs. There are no holy books. Instead, they have copies of *Quaker Faith and Practice*, a book of Quaker organization and inspired writings that are revised every generation.

There are no preachers in unprogrammed meetings. Quakers are very democratic and believe that paid ministers wield too much power that can be abused. Instead, they have clerks and committees. Worship is not only or always about paying tribute to a higher power, but it is also about seeking advice, doing business, and decision making. Without a priest at the pulpit anyone can speak at unprogrammed meetings, and to that end they try to discourage passive laity and encourage everyone to participate. Everyone is equal before God, or each other.

There are no sermons, hymns, or prayers in unprogrammed meetings. This is where it gets really different. Quaker worship takes place in complete silence. "Waiting worship" is time for silent prayer and reflection and to invite God's presence. It is also waiting and listening for a message, revelation, guidance, or inspiration, from a source variably known as: the Light, the Light Within, the Inner Light, the Truth, the Inward Christ, the Holy Spirit, the Inner Teacher, the Seed, the Word, the Universe, Wisdom, Jesus, the Lord, God, or the "still, small voice of God within." Some believe they are waiting for God. Alternatively, Nontheist Quakers interpret the "Light" as thought, ideas, insight, or human reason.

These revelations might be a verse of poetry, lyrics from a song, a line from a book or movie, a passage of scripture, an observation, or any other thought. Often the message is private, but sometimes it is intended for the community. This is when the "Light" manifests in the Quaker, who feels moved, literally, to share the message. The Quaker stands up, while some claim they're standing before they know what they've done. Others describe this as a feeling of being pushed out of the seat. As we know, some suggest that the name Quaker derives from the physical shaking that sometimes occurred during this experience. Like temporary prophets, they are led by the spirit to share aloud what the "Light" is saying to them. This is called "vocal ministry." Without a minister, all members share the responsibility to minister to the group.

There is a difference between members and "attenders" of meetings. If someone wants to join the Quakers, they are urged to first attend six months of meetings. Even though God can be reached without an intermediary, there is an intermediary to joining the Quakers. If a person wants to become a Quaker, it requires more than consulting their conscience; they must apply for membership. This formal application is processed by a "clearness committee," which will determine whether or not the applicant is "clear" to join. This Scientology-sounding process is really only an interview in which the "applicant" answers questions about his or her decision to join, to ensure it is for the right reasons. Anyone from any religious background can attend Quaker meetings without becoming a member. However, those who want to join must first leave their prior religion and provide a letter proving that they are now free to become a Quaker. Similarly, leaving the Quakers requires a resignation letter and exit interview.

Sounds of Silence

When I lived in the Bay Area I used to drive past Quaker meeting houses in several cities and wonder what they were. Of course, "quake" has different connotations in California. I was curious about the Quakers, and few people seemed to know anything about them. Unlike the early Quakers, Liberal Quakers don't proselytize in public. Unlike the Evangelical Quakers, Liberal Quakers don't advertise or actively seek new members. "Birthright Friends" are those who were raised as Quakers, such as Nixon. Most Quakers are "Convinced Friends" who come to them. Everyone is invited to attend their worship, so I visited an unprogrammed meeting at a local meeting house in Colorado. These meetings are held on Sundays, for the convenience of members, not because this is the Sabbath or a holy day for Quakers.

The exterior of the Quaker meeting house looked like a cross between a church, a home, and a school. The building was topped with the Quaker symbol of an eight-pointed star. Inside was a simple, barely furnished hall. Instead of uncomfortable rows of pews, the room was lined with facing benches covered with soft cushions. There was no pulpit, cross, or Bible in sight—only a library of historical books. A crowd of people wearing name tags had already gathered. I knew that part of the meeting was to take place in silence, but for now they chatted as they hugged cups of coffee. Just in case you were wondering, no one was eating bowls of oats.

As one might expect, the Friends were incredibly friendly and welcoming. I was barely through the door when Gene approached me and introduced himself. He eagerly offered to answer any questions, so I took the opportunity to ask him about the meaning of the "Light" and "that of God in everyone." Clearly I'd asked the hard questions. He uncomfortably gave me some esoteric answers and added, "Ask everyone else here and each person will give you a different answer!" He denied that Quakerism is a religion, stating that it is more of a way of life. Then he handed me a stack of literature. "For people with no doctrine we sure like to write!"

By now the room had packed out to about sixty people. I was told that they are steadily outgrowing their meeting house, and sometimes people have to sit on the floor during silent worship. The Quakers aim to be diverse and inclusive, and they are. A good cross section of society was represented: male and female, young and old, and people from a variety of ethnic backgrounds. They weren't wearing their Sunday best, nor was anyone in plain dress. Most people were in the everyday American uniform of jeans and a sweater.

"What do we do next?" I asked Gene for guidance. "Just follow everyone else," he said with smile. There is no set order to the meeting. An elderly man sat down, and others began following suit. This was the signal for everyone to take a seat, and for silence. I just followed the social cues and sat down quietly. Several people were unfashionably late, and it took at least twenty minutes for everyone to settle down. The room suddenly fell silent—that is, as silent as human bodies can ever be. The silence quickly drew attention to the occasional throat clearing, coughs, sneezes, sniffs, scratches, and stomach rumbles.

There were unavoidable distractions, such as the noises of cars passing outside and the members' children who were playing upstairs. Cell phones would occasionally ring, to disapproving looks and crossed arms. A few people sat with their eyes closed in a kind of meditation, although many Quakers deny vehemently that this is meditation, instead claiming that silent worship is about listening. Some Quaker groups offer separate meditation, yoga classes, and "healing circles," where the group gathers around a sick member or a surrogate for another, and they lay hands on the person, "sending loving, healing energy." Some Liberal Quakers have an interest in New Age Spirituality, including astrology, visualization, communication with the dead, and other paranormal and pseudoscientific beliefs and practices.

We were now about thirty minutes into the silence, and a few people took the silent worship as an opportunity for a catnap. Gene had warned me beforehand that he might nod off and start snoring. Others lowered their heads, looked at the floor, or stared vacantly into the distance. I would occasionally look around the room to see what everyone else was doing, or not doing. A woman across the room caught me in the act and scowled as if to say, "You shouldn't be looking around!" even though she was guilty of this offense too.

I was warned that it was rude to read during worship, although I saw a woman thumbing through a copy of *Awakening Loving-Kindness* by Tibetan Buddhist Pema Chödrön. A man seated across from me was reading *Autobiography of a Yogi* by Paramahansa Yogananda. At the risk of pissing off the woman across from me, I glanced around the hall again, and for all intents and purposes it looked like a doctor's waiting room, or a branch of the DMV, without the despair.

After I overcame the awkwardness of being in a room full of silent strangers, I became worried about laughing inappropriately at the absurdity of the situation. Like a mind wandering during bad sex, I started thinking about cleaning the house, and I formed a mental list for grocery shopping. After forty minutes of silence, I started thinking like I used to do during an exam, and lyrics from really annoying yet persistent songs began whirling around my head, including "9 to 5" and "Islands in the Stream." I tried to quieten my mind to receive a revelation, but I simply couldn't hear the "Light," unless God is Dolly Parton. I had no urge at all to stand and give vocal ministry to the group, but I hoped someone else would. I wanted to see it for myself.

It is not uncommon for a meeting to be entirely silent. Gene told me this was a particularly "vocal" group, but clearly this was an off-day. A man nearby occasionally nodded and murmured "um-hum" to himself in personal revelation, but no one was moved to speak. Instead, a few people were moved to go to the restroom. After fifty minutes without speech, the children were led into the room, and their soft chatter could be heard until they settled down with books. Finally, a woman broke the silence. She stood up and addressed the room. Her voice and body did indeed quake as she announced, "I've had lyrics going around in my head, from the song 'Sing 'Til the Power of the Lord Comes Down.' Suddenly, the Lord's power *did* come down, when the children came into the room."

Despite the song's religious theme, this didn't seem any more a "revelation" than me thinking about song lyrics from "9 to 5." Sometimes Quakers stand up and talk about the pretty sunset they saw the night before, or they marvel about the beauty of the world. This is known derisively as "daffodil ministry." Much vocal ministry seems to consist of "a funny thing happened on my way to the Quaker meeting" style revelations that involve social and political commentary, or a retelling of the news. Quakers are critical of this kind of ministry and say that it is not led by the spirit. Of course, these everyday messages are coming from the same source as the scripture passages and song lyrics, and are a loose definition for the voice of God.

The woman sat down and the room fell silent again. It is also considered rude to speak immediately after someone has given vocal ministry. It is etiquette to observe a period of silence of at least a few minutes, to contemplate the message in case it becomes a "seed" for the meditation of others. Periods of silence are also a part of Quaker weddings, funerals, and business meetings, during which people may also stand up and give vocal ministry.

No one else spoke for the remainder of the meeting. I wondered how the close of silent worship would be signaled. I had heard rumors that the meeting would be ended with hugs and handshakes, but only the last part was correct. Martha, the clerk of the meeting, held out her hand to a woman seated beside her. They shook hands in what is known as the sign of peace, a modern version of the "holy kiss" favoured by Amish and Mennonite groups. The women wished each other "good morning." This prompted everyone in the room to turn to their neighbors, shake hands, and wish each other "good morning."

The clerk announced that it was time for "joys and sorrows." This is where everyone is invited to share personal stories about the ups and downs of life. A man announced that the day before he had listened to his unborn baby's heartbeat. A woman spoke of her sudden remission from chronic anemia, making it sound like it was a miraculous healing. Another woman announced her son's seventh birthday, and we all sang "Happy Birthday" to him. Newcomers were then invited to speak, so I stood up and introduced myself, to a chorus of "Welcome!" Quakers believe that worship and action are one, so there were announcements about lobbying to political groups and local efforts of activism. Instead of passing around the collection plate for donations for a new steeple, they finished with coffee and cookies, and no, they weren't oatmeal cookies.

Friend or Foe?

Liberal Quakerism is clearly the odd one out in this entire book. Quakers have their own strange practices, such as silent worship and vocal ministry, but they don't practice polygamy or animal sacrifice, and they don't handle snakes or wear sacred undergarments. However, there is a thin vein of hypocrisy in their ideology and actions. Quakers promote peace, equality, and unity, yet they haven't achieved these within their own community. Diversity is Quakerism's strength, but also its flaw. The fundamental differences have created severe tensions between the traditions. Across the wildly conflicting beliefs and practices that exist under the Quaker label, Quakers are less like Friends and more like rivals.

Liberal Quakerism operates within a religious framework, but there is little about it that is religious. Older Quakers seem to believe in something akin to God, while younger generations are reinventing Quakerism as atheism, where "God in everyone" and the "Light" are metaphors for humanity and human thought. Neophytes seem to be more attracted to Liberal Quakerism's ethics than its theology. Quakerism has so many freethinking and humanist elements to it. However, if it had more skeptical elements, Quakers may question some of their New Age beliefs and mystical practices out of existence.

Liberal Quakers have shown that people can be good without God. They demonstrate purpose, compassion, community, ethics, and morality, mostly without the impetus of religion and without theistic trappings. They truly practice what they preach. To its followers, Liberal Quakerism is seen as a society or community, rather than a religion, and many members have no belief in God. So why have the semblance of religion? Quakers have always been progressive and their beliefs are fluid. Perhaps future Quakers will be able to break free of superstition entirely, to perform their good works in the name of humanity, rather than religion.

References

Chapter 1—Modern-Day Prophets and Polygamists

Adams, Brooke. 2006. Warren Jeffs: A Wanted Man. *Salt Lake Tribune*. May 10.

Adams, Brooke. 2007. A Single Misstep and Musser's World Comes Apart. *Salt Lake Tribune*. April 29.

Adams, Brooke. 2008. Polygamous Sect Picks Tiny, Secluded Colorado Town for Grandmas' Refuge. *Salt Lake Tribune*. August 6.

Bentley, Paul. 2011. Warren Jeffs Sentenced to Life Plus 20 Years in Prison as Picture Emerges of 50 Brides, Bred to Worship the Polygamous "Prophet." *Daily Mail*. August 9.

Bentley, Paul. 2011. Sleazy Rider: Photos Show Polygamist Warren Jeffs on the Run with His Favourite Bride . . . Riding on a Harley Davidson. *Daily Mail*. August 11.

Burton, Greg. 1999. When Incest Becomes a Religious Tenet. *Salt Lake Tribune*. April, 25.

Bushman, Richard Lyman. 2005. *Joseph Smith: Rough Stone Rolling*. Knopf.

CNN Transcript. 1998. Larry King Live. Gordon Hinckley: Distinguished Religious Leader of the Mormons. http://www.lds-mormon.com/ lkl_00.shtml

228 • REFERENCES

The Church of Jesus Christ of Latter-Day Saints. What Do Mormons Believe? http://www.mormontopics.org/eng/home

Deseret News. 1997. Obituary: Alma Adelbert Timpson. April 4.

Dobner, Jennifer. 2007. Caretaker for Polygamous Sect Looks for Wife, Child. *Associated Press*. May 20.

Dougherty, John. 2005. Wanted: Armed and Dangerous. As the FBI Chases Polygamist Prophet Warren Jeffs, Work Continues 24/7 on His Religion's Foreboding New Texas Capital. *Phoenix New Times*. November 10.

Dougherty, John. 2005. Inbreeding among Polygamists along the Arizona-Utah Border Is Producing a Caste of Severely Retarded and Deformed Children. *Phoenix New Times*. December 29.

FLDS 101. http://flds101.blogspot.com/

Goldstein, Melvyn C. 1987. When Brothers Share a Wife. *Natural History*. Vol. 96. No. 3, pp. 109–112.

Hollenhorst, John. 2011. Canadian Court Filing Alleges FLDS Child Bride Smuggling. *Deseret News*. February 21.

Jeffs, Brent. W. 2010. *Lost Boy: The True Story of One Man's Exile from a Polygamist Cult and His Brave Journey to Reclaim his Life*. Broadway.

Jessop, Carolyn, and Palmer, Laura. 2008. *Escape*. Broadway.

Krakauer, Jon. 2004. *Under the Banner of Heaven*. Anchor.

Moore-Emmett, Andrea. 2004. *God's Brothel: The Extortion of Sex for Salvation in Contemporary Mormon and Christian Fundamentalist Polygamy and the Stories of 18 Women Who Escaped*. Pince-Nez Press.

Palmer, Debbie, and Perrin, Dave. 2004. *Keep Sweet: Children of Polygamy*. Dave's Press, Ltd.

Perkins, Nancy, and Winslow, Ben. 2006. Fugitive Polygamist Leader Warren Jeffs Arrested near Las Vegas. *Deseret Morning News*. 2006.

Roberts, Michelle. 2008. Polygamist Sect Teen Gives Birth to Boy. *SF Gate*. April 30.

Singular, Stephen. 2009. *When Men Become Gods: Mormon Polygamist*

Warren Jeffs, His Cult of Fear and the Women Who Fought Back. St. Martin's Griffin.

Southern Poverty Law Center. 2005. The Prophet Speaks. *Intelligence Report.* Issue 117.

Taylor, John, et al. 2012. *The Complete Journal of Discourses.* Current Bush Press. LDS Reference eBook edition.

Chapter 2—The Not-So-Simple Life

ABC 20/20. 2004. Sexual Abuse in the Amish Community. December, 10.

About Amish. http://aboutamish.blogspot.com/

Amish America. Amishamerica.com

Amish Deception. http://amishdeception.com/

Byers, Bryan, Crider, Benjamin, and Biggers, Gregory. "A Study of Hate Crime and Offender Neutralization Techniques Used against the Amish." In *Crimes of Hate.* 2003. Gerstenfeld, Phyllis and Grant, Diana. Sage Publications.

Cross, Harold, and Crosby, Andrew. 2008. Amish Contributions to Medical Genetics. *Mennonite Quarterly Review.* Vol. 82, pp. 449–468.

Dinan, Stephen. 2011. Feds Sting Amish Farmer Selling Raw Milk Locally. *Washington Times.* April 28. http://www.washingtontimes.com/news/2011/apr/28/feds-sting-amish-farmer-selling-raw-milk-locally/

Fisher, Suzanne Wood. 2011. *Amish Values for Your Family: What We Can Learn from the Simple Life.* Revell.

Furlong, Saloma Miller. 2011. *Why I Left the Amish: A Memoir.* Michigan State University Press.

Gay, Malcolm. 2010. Sex-Assault Case Offers Glimpse of Amish Community. *New York Times.* September 2.

Global Anabaptist Mennonite Encyclopedia Online. http://gameo.org/

Hostetler, John A. 1980. *Amish Society*. Johns Hopkins University Press.

Johnson-Weiner, Karen. 2012. *New York Amish: Life in the Plain Communities of the Empire States*. Cornell University Press.

Kraybill, Donald. 2001. *The Riddle of Amish Culture*. Center Books in Anabaptist Studies. John Hopkins University Press.

Labi, Nadya. 2005. The Gentle People. *Legal Affairs*. January/February.

Mackall, Joe. 2008. *Plain Secrets: An Outsider among the Amish*. Beacon Press.

Murray, Brian. 2005. Puppy Farms under Fire. *Seattle Times*. November 27.

Ordnung for the Pinecraft Amish Church. 2012. Old Order Amish Church in Sarasota, Florida.

Sleeth, Nancy. 2012. *Almost Amish: One Woman's Quest for a Slower, Simpler, More Sustainable Life*. Tyndale House Publishers.

Chapter 3—Signs, Wonders, and Miracles

Asser, Seth. M., and Swan, Rita. 1998. Child Fatalities From Religion-Motivated Medical Neglect. *Pediatrics*. Vol. 101. No. 4, pp. 625–629.

Bentley, Todd. Fresh Fire USA. http://www.freshfireusa.com/

Burgess, Stanley, McGee, Gary, and Alexander, Patrick. 1988. *Dictionary of Pentecostal and Charismatic Movements*. Zondervan.

Burton, Thomas. 2004. *The Serpent and the Spirit: Glenn Summerford's Story*. University of Tennessee Press.

Butcher, Andy. 1999. Gold Dust Phenomenon Stirs Up Questions Among Charismatics. *Charisma*. September 8.

Carroll, Robert. 2003. *The Skeptic's Dictionary: A Collection of Strange Beliefs, Amusing Deceptions, and Dangerous Delusions*. Wiley.

Crann, Alice. 1997. Pastor Orchestrated First Revival. *Pensacola News Journal*. November, 19.

Goff, James. 1988. *Fields White Unto Harvest*. University of Arkansas Press.

Hanegraaff, Hank. 1997. *Counterfeit Revival*. Word.

Harrell, Jr., David Edwin. 1975. *All Things Are Possible: The Healing and Charismatic Revivals in Modern America*. Indiana University Press.

Hayford, Jack, and Moore, David. 2006. *The Charismatic Century: The Enduring Impact of the Azusa Street Revival*. Warner Faith.

Hinn, Benny. Benny Hinn Ministries. http://www.bennyhinn.org/

Hood, Ralph, W. and Williamson, W. Paul. 2008. *Them That Believe: The Power and Meaning of the Christian Serpent-Handling Tradition*. University of California Press.

Johnson, Tyler, G. 2011. *How to Raise the Dead*. CreateSpace Independent Publishing Platform.

Kernochan, Sarah, and Smith, Howard. 1972. *Marjoe*. Mauser Productions.

King, Patricia. http://www.patriciaking.com/

Larson, Bob. 1989. *Larson's New Book of Cults*. Tyndale House Publishers.

Mills, Joshua. New Wine International. http://www.joshuamills.com/Index.html

Nolen, William. 1974. *Healing: A Doctor in Search of a Miracle*. Random House.

Randi, James. 1987. *The Faith Healers*. Prometheus Books.

River Rock Christian Fellowship. David Herzog. http://www.rrcf.net/davidherzog.html

Stollznow, Karen. 2014. *Language Myths, Mysteries and Magic*. Palgrave Macmillan.

Trinity Foundation. Monitoring and Investigating Religious Fraud. http://trinityfi.org/

Winters, Amanda. 2010. Bethel's 'Signs and Wonders' Include Angel Feathers, Gold Dust and Diamonds. *Redding Record Searchlight*.

Chapter 4—Hoodoo, Voodoo, and Juju

ABC 7 News. 2009. Cursed Cow Tongue Found in Cornfield. August 24. Denver Channel.com http://www.thedenverchannel.com/news/cursed-cow-tongue-found-in-cornfield

Alvarado, Denise, and Doktor Snake. *The Voodoo Hoodoo Spellbook.* Weiser Books.

Ancient Magic Spells. www.ancientmagicspells.com

BBC News. 2006. Voodoo Head Found in Air Luggage. http://news.bbc.co.uk/2/hi/americas/4703328.stm

BBC News. 2011. Voodoo Ritual Sparks Fatal New York Apartment Fire. February 25. http://www.bbc.co.uk/news/world-us-canada-12585706

Bragg, Rick. 1995. New Orleans Conjures Old Spirits against Modern Woes. *New York Times.* August 18.

Brodin, Paul. 1996. *Medicine and Morality in Haiti: The Contest for Healing Power.* Cambridge University Press.

Charlotte, Kathleen, and Heaven, Ross. *Va-Va-Voodoo!: Find Love, Make Love & Keep Love.* Llewellyn Publications.

Courlander, Harold. 1960. *The Drum and the Hoe.* University of California Press.

Davis, Wade. 1985. *The Serpent and the Rainbow.* Harper Collins.

Debusmann, Bernd Jr. 2011. Grandmother Sentenced to Prison in Voodoo Burning Case. Reuters. April 6.

Fenton, Justin. 2012. Maryland Man Charged with Killing, Eating Man's Brain, Heart. *Baltimore Sun.* May 31.

Greenhouse, Linda. 1993. The Supreme Court: Animal Sacrifice; Court, Citing Religious Freedom, Voids a Ban on Animal Sacrifices. *New York Times.* June 12.

Lee, Henry, K. 2008. 'Psychic' Gets 2 Months in Bilking of $108,000. *San Francisco Chronicle.* December 10.

Lee, Henry, K. 2008. Psychic Jailed, Charged with Bilking Woman, 85. *San Francisco Chronicle*. December 20.

Littlewood, Roland, and Douyon, Chavannes. 1997. Clinical Findings in Three Cases of Zombification. *Lancet*. Volume 350. 1094–96.

Luscombe, Richard. 2012. Face-Eating Victim 'Will Recover' from Horrific Miami Attack. Guardian.co.uk. May 30.

Morrow Long, Carolyn. 2007. *A New Orleans Voudou Priestess: The Legend and Reality of Marie Laveau*. University Press of Florida.

O'Brien, David M. 2004. *Animal Sacrifice and Religious freedom: Church of the Lukumi Babalu Aye v. City of Hialeah*. University Press of Kansas.

Odierna, Judy. 2000. Disappearance Stalls Murder Case. Husband Sought for Questioning in 1996 Slayings. *Miami Herald*. April 30.

Planet Voodoo. www.planetvoodoo.com

Rigaud, Milo. 1969. *Secrets of Voodoo*. City Lights.

Yronwode, Catherine. 2011. Lucky Mojo. http://www.luckymojo.com/

Chapter 5—Full of the Devil

Americans Draw Theological Beliefs From Diverse Points of View. Barna Group. http://www.barna.org/barna-update/article/5-barna-update/82-americans-draw-theological-beliefs-from-diverse-points-of-view?q=demonic

Amorth, Gabriele. 1999. *An Exorcist Tells his Story*. Ignatius Press.

Associated Press. 1996. Woman Wounded by Crucifixes in Exorcism. *New York Times*. April 3. http://www.nytimes.com/1996/04/03/us/woman-wounded-by-crucifixes-in-exorcism.html

Brittle, Gerald. 1983. *The Devil in Connecticut*. Bantam Books.

Claridy, Robyn. 2011. Mother's Trial Begins in 2008 Rusk County Child Death Case. news-journal.com. Longview, Texas. April 5. http://www.news-journal.com/news/police/article_a5016e2e-cd67-5097-866f-a5ecd0c24102.html

Cuneo, Michael. 2001. *American Exorcism: Expelling Demons in the Land of Plenty*. Doubleday.

Day, Michael. 2012. Catholic Church Sets up an Exorcist Hotline to Deal with Demand. *Belfast Telegraph*. November 30.

Flock, Jeff. 2003. Autistic Boy's Death at Church Ruled Homicide. CNN.com. August 26. http://www.cnn.com/2003/LAW/08/25/autistic.boy.death/

Gold, Matea. 1997. Women Convicted of Killing Girl in Exorcism. *Los Angeles Times*. October 15. http://articles.latimes.com/1997/oct/15/local/me-42918

Hammond, Frank, and Hammond, Ida Mae. 1973. *Pigs in the Parlor: A Practical Guide to Deliverance*. Impact Christian Books, Inc.

Lee, Henry. K. 1995. 5 Women Accused of Murder in East Bay Exorcism Death. *San Francisco Chronicle*. March 17. http://www.sfgate.com/news/article/5-Women-Accused-of-Murder-In-East-Bay-Exorcism-3040337.php

Martin, Malachi. 1992. *Hostage to the Devil: The Possession and Exorcism of Five Contemporary Americans*. HarperOne.

Newport, Frank. 2007. Americans More Likely to Believe in God than the Devil, Heaven More than Hell. *Gallup News Service*. June 13. http://www.gallup.com/poll/27877/Americans-More-Likely-Believe-God-Than-Devil-Heaven-More-Than-Hell.aspx

Opsasnick, Mark. The Haunted Boy of Cottage City. The Cold Hard Facts behind the Story That Inspired "The Exorcist." *Strange Magazine*. 20.

Pastor Jack Radio. www.churchoftomjones.com

Randi, James. *An Encyclopedia of Claims, Frauds, and Hoaxes of the Occult and Supernatural*. St. Martin's Griffin.

Stollznow, Karen. 2012. Deliver Us From Bob Larson. Bad Language. *Skeptic* magazine. Vol. 17. No. 4.

Swarns, Rachel. 1997. A Family Divided by a Child's Death. *New York Times*. May 20. http://www.nytimes.com/1997/05/20/nyregion/a-family-divided-by-a-child-s-death.html

Chapter 6—Sympathy for the Devil

Aquino, Michael. 2002. *The Church of Satan*. Temple of Set.

Barber, Malcolm. 2006. *The Trial of the Templars*. Cambridge University Press.

Bernheim, Alain, Samii, A. William, and Serejski, Eric. 1996. (1897) The Confession of Leo Taxil. Reprinted from *Heredom. The Transacations of the Scottish Rite Research Society*. Vol. 5, pp. 137–168.

Carlo, Philip. 1996. *The Night Stalker*. Pinnacle.

Davis, Jr. Sammy. 1980. *Hollywood in a Suitcase*. Granada Publishing Ltd.

Duin, Julia. 2007. Yazidis Risk Persecution, Attacks to Follow Religion; Many Emigrate from Iraq for Fear of Being Targeted by Muslims. *Washington Times*. August 22.

ELO. http://www.ftmusic.com/biogs/elo/elo_biog.html

Gilmore, Peter H. 2007. *The Satanic Scriptures*. Scapegoat Publishing.

Hicks, Robert, D. 1991. *In Pursuit of Satan: The Police and the Occult*. Prometheus Books.

Huysmans, Joris-Karl. 2011. (1891) *Là-Bas*. Dover Publications.

Laycock, Donald, C., Kelley, Edward, Dee, John. *The Complete Enochian Dictionary: A Dictionary of the Language as Revealed to Dr. John Dee and Edward Kelley*. Weiser Books.

LaVey, Anton Szandor. 2000. *The Devil's Notebook*. Feral House.

LaVey, Anton Szandor. 1998. *Satan Speaks!* Feral House.

LaVey, Anton Szandor. 1976. *The Satanic Rituals: Companion to the Satanic Bible*. Avon.

LaVey, Anton Szandor. 1976. *The Satanic Bible*. Avon.

Loftus, E. and Ketcham, K. 1994. *The Myth of Repressed Memory*. St. Martin's Press.

Mann, May. 1974. *Jayne Mansfield*. Pocket Books.

Melech, Aubrey. 1986. *Missa Niger—La Messe Noir*. Sut Anubis.

Order of Nine Angles. *Codex Saerus. Black Book of Satan 1,2 & 3*. Lulu. com.

Ramsland, Katherine. The McMartin Daycare Case. Crime Library. http://www.trutv.com/library/crime/criminal_mind/psychology/ mcmartin_daycare/1.html

Satanism Central. Anton LaVey: Legend and Reality. http:// satanismcentral.com/aslv.html

Stollznow, Karen. 2011. Days of Our Lives. Past-Life Regression Therapy. http://www.csicop.org/specialarticles/show/days_of_our_lives/

Trott, J. 1991. *Satanic Panic*. Cornerstone.

The Church of Satan. www.churchofsatan.com/

What's the Harm? Satanic Ritual Abuse. http://whatstheharm.net/ satanicritualabuse.html

Chapter 7—It's All in Your Head

Asimov, Isaac. 1979. *In Memory yet Green: The Autobiography of Isaac Asimov, 1929–1954*. Doubleday.

Atack, Jon. 1990. *A Piece of Blue Sky: Scientology, Dianetics and L. Ron Hubbard Exposed*. Lyle Stuart/Carol Publishing Group.

Church of Scientology of California v. *Kaufman*. 1972. F.S.R. 591 per Goff J - in the Chancery Division of the High Court.

Fox, C. Davis, A., and Lebovits, A. 1960. "Experimental Investigation of Hubbard's Engram Hypothesis." *Psychological Abstracts*. No. 1475.

Hubbard, L. Ron. 1950. *Dianetics: The Modern Science of Mental Health*. American Saint Hill Organization.

Hubbard, L. Ron. 1955. "The Scientologist: A Manual on the Dissemination of Material." *Ability*. Major 1. Washington: The Hubbard Communications Office: 19.

Hubbard, L. R. 1988. The "Bring Back To Life" Assist. Hubbard Communications Office Bulletin. *The Technical Bulletins of Dianetics and Scientology* (1991 ed., Vol. XIII, pp. 323–324). Los Angeles: Bridge Publications, Inc.

Hubbard, L. Ron. 1988. *Scientology: The History of Man*. Bridge Publications, Inc.

Hubbard, L. Ron. 2001. *The Scientology Handbook*. New Era.

Hubbard, L. Ron. 2002. *Clear Body, Clear Mind*. Bridge Publications.

Hubbard, L. Ron. 2007. (1956). *Scientology: The Fundamentals of Thought*. Bridge Publications.

Hubbard, L. Ron. 2007. *The Creation of Human Ability: A Handbook for Scientologists*. Bridge Publications.

Lippard, Jim. 2011. The Decline and (Probable) Fall of the Scientology Empire! *Skeptic* magazine. Vol 17. No. 1.

Maisel, Albert. 1950. Dianetics—Science or Hoax? *Look* magazine. December 5.

Mark Bunker's Xenu TV. www.xenutv.com

Methvin, Eugene, H. 1980. Scientology: Anatomy of a Frightening Cult. *Reader's Digest*.

Operation Clambake. www.xenu.net

Penthouse. 1983. "Inside the Church of Scientology: An Exclusive Interview with L. Ron Hubbard, Jr." June issue.

Reiman, Janet. 2011. *Inside Scientology*. Houghton Mifflin.

Stollznow, Karen. 2013. The Scientology Handbook. Bad Language. Skeptic Magazine. Volume 18, Number 2

Urban, Hugh. 2011. *The Church of Scientology*. Princeton University Press.

What's the Harm? http://whatstheharm.net/scientology.html

Chapter 8—Something Old, Something New

Browne, Sylvia. 2005. *Phenomenon: Everything You Need to Know about the Paranormal*. HighBridge Company. p. 251.

Canfield, Jack. 1993. *Chicken Soup for the Soul: 101 Stories to Open the Heart and Rekindle the Spirit.* Health Communications, Inc.

Chopra, Deepak. 2008. *Life After Death: The Burden of Proof.* Harmony.

Lluch, Alex. 2009. *Enjoy Life and Be Happy in 30 Seconds: Daily Steps to Enrich Your Life.* WS Publishing.

Magnetic Qi Gong. http://www.roaringlionpublishing.com/

Chopra, Deepak. 2007. *The Seven Spiritual Laws of Success: A Pocketbook Guide to Fulfilling Your Dreams (One Hour of Wisdom).* Amber-Allen Publishing.

Dyer, Wayne. 2009. *Excuses Begone!: How to Change Lifelong, Self-Defeating Thinking Habits.* Hay House.

Fee, Natalie. 2009. Energise Yourself. *The Green Parent.* August/September, p. 20.

Haidt, Jonathan. 2007. *The Happiness Hypothesis: Finding Modern Truth in Ancient* Wisdom. Basic Books.

Isaacson, Walter. 2011. *Steve Jobs.* Simon & Schuster.

Kirkwood, Annie. 1992. *Mary's Message to the World.* Blue Dolphin Publishing.

Kubin, Jacquie. 2013. Cleveland Miracle: Amanda Berry, Gina DeJesus, Michelle Knight rescued. *Washington Times.* May 6. http://communities.washingtontimes.com/neighborhood/political-potpourri/2013/may/6/cleveland-miracle-amanda-berry-gina-dejesus-michel/

Malkmus, George, Shockey, Peter and, Shockey, Stowe. 2006. *The Hallelujah Diet: Experience the Optimal Health You Were Meant to Have.* Destiny Image Publishers.

McDowell, Al. 2009. *Uncommon Knowledge: New Science of Gravity, Light, the Origin of Life, and the Mind of Man.* Author House.

Okawa, Ryuho. 2009. *The Science of Happiness: 10 Principles for Manifesting Your Divine Nature.* Destiny Books.

Randi, James. 1997. An *Encyclopedia of Claims, Frauds, and Hoaxes of the Occult and Supernatural*. St. Martin's Griffin.

Stollznow, Karen. 2010. The Belief with No Name. The Good Word. Committee for Skeptical Inquiry. December 21. http://www.csicop. org/specialarticles/show/the_belief_with_no_name/

Stollznow, Karen. 2010. Skepticism and the Paranormal: A Rose By Any Other Name. In Bonett, W. (Ed.) *The Australian Book of Atheism*. Scribe Publications.

Stollznow, Karen. 2011. Braco the Gazer. The Good Word. Committee for Skeptical Inquiry. April 25. http://www.csicop.org/specialarticles/ show/braco_the_gazer/

Stop Sylvia Browne. www.stopsylvia.com

Trudeau, Kevin. 2005. *Natural Cures "They" Don't Want You to Know About*. Alliance Publishing.

Wattles, Wallace. 2007. *The Science of Getting Rich: Find the Secret to the Law of Attraction*. Wilder Publications.

Wattles, Wallace. 2007. *The Science of Success: The Secret to Getting What You Want*. Sterling.

Whitecliff, Angelika. 2009. *21 Days with Braco*. Awakening Within.

Willis, Paul. 1997. Jasmuheen. The Correx Archive. http://www.abc.net. au/science/correx/archives/jasmuheen.htm

Yahoo News. 1999. Fresh Air Dietician Fails TV Show's Challenge. October 5. http://www.rickross.com/reference/breat/breat13.html

Zehme, Bill. 2001. *Lost in the Funhouse: The Life and Mind of Andy Kaufman*. Delta Books.

Chapter 9—Friends in High Places

Bacon, Margaret Hope. 2000. *The Quiet Rebels: The Story of the Quakers in America*. Pendle Hill Publications.

Bill, Brent, J. 2005. *Holy Silence: The Gift of Quaker Spirituality*. Paraclete Press.

Boulton, David, ed. 2006. *Godless for God's Sake: Nontheism in Contemporary Quakerism.* Dales Historical Monographs.

Cooper, Wilmer. 1999. *Growing Up Plain among Conservative Wilburite Quakers: The Journey of a Public Friend.* Friends United Press.

Dandelion, Pink. 2007. *An Introduction to Quakerism.* Cambridge University Press.

Durham, Geoffrey. 2011. *Being a Quaker: A Guide for Newcomers.* Britain Yearly Meeting.

Fox, George. 1975. (1831). *The Works of George Fox, Volume 1.* AMS Press.

Hamm, Thomas. 2003. *The Quakers in America.* Columbia University Press.

Jones, Rufus M., ed. *George Fox: An Autobiography.*

Meggitt, Justin. 2011. Naked Quakers. Apocalyptic Obsessions and Public Nudity—The World of the Early Quakers. *Fortean Times.* http://www.forteantimes.com/features/articles/5023/naked_quakers.html

Merril, Eliphalet, and Merril, Phinehas. 1817. Quakers in New Hampshire. *The Gazetteer of the State of New Hampshire.* C. Norris & Co.

Nathan, Otto, and Heinz Norden. 1975. *Einstein on Peace.* Pro Quo Books.

Nontheist Friends. http://www.nontheistfriends.org/

Index

About the Author

Karen Stollznow, PhD, is a linguist with a background in history and anthropology. She is a columnist, podcaster, and the author of *Haunting America*, *Language Myths, Mysteries and Magic*, and *Red, White and (True) Blue*. Karen was a researcher at the University of California, Berkeley, and has spent many years writing about a diverse array of topics, including language, culture, religion, and anomalous claims. Karen was born in Sydney, Australia, and has a PhD in linguistics from the University of New England, Australia. She currently lives in Denver, Colorado.